2005:
BLOGGED

2005: BLOGGED

DISPATCHES FROM THE BLOGOSPHERE

FRIDAY
BOOKS

EDITED BY
TIM WORSTALL

2005: Blogged is a collection of blog posts, by various authors, previously published on the Internet. All posts have been republished with the permission of the original authors, who retain copyright in their work. Wherever possible, posts have been published unedited, in their original form. All opinions expressed are the authors' own and do not necessarily reflect the opinions of either the editor or publishers of *2005: Blogged*.

First published in Great Britain in 2005 by Friday Books
An imprint of The Friday Project Limited
83 Victoria Street, London SW1H 0HW

www.thefridayproject.co.uk
www.fridaybooks.co.uk

British Library Cataloguing in Publication Data.

A catalogue record for this book is available from the British Library.

ISBN 0 9548318 3 7

Design by Staziker Jones
www.stazikerjones.co.uk

Printed and bound by Bath Press.

The Publisher's policy is to use paper manufactured from sustainable forests.

CONTENTS

Welcome to **Blogged:2005**   1

November 2004   5

December 2004   27

January 2005   45

February 2005   63

March 2005   81

April 2005   103

May 2005   121

June 2005   147

July 2005   167

August 2005   197

September 2005   223

October 2005   251

General index   262

Blog index   264

WELCOME TO BLOGGED: 2005

INTRODUCTION

In September of this year an advertising agency commissioned a survey to discover how popular certain newly coined words were amongst ordinary members of the British public. The shocking news was that although half of these ordinary citizens – apparently made up entirely of taxi drivers, hairdressers and pub landlords – knew what a chav was, a staggering 70% had no idea what a blog was. Which, considering that there are now somewhere in the region of 19 million blogs worldwide and 300,000 in the UK alone, is a little surprising. Ordinary people eh? What are they thinking? However, just in case you're one of them, we should probably give you a quick explanation of what a blog actually is. A 'blog' is a 'weblog', or, if you prefer, an 'online journal'. There. Now you know.

Happily there is a lot more to blogs than a nifty contraction. Essentially, blogs have given rise to a revolution in personal communication. Blogs enable their practitioners – or 'bloggers' – to pass opinion on absolutely any subject under the sun, and then share that opinion with anyone with a modem. The overwhelming proliferation of blogs over the past five years therefore should come as no surprise. Blogging appeals to people's innate desire to communicate, to 'have their say'. However, it differs from every other form of communication thus far – everything from cave paintings to text messaging – in as much as there are absolutely no limits to the amount of people to whom bloggers can peddle their opinions.

Suddenly, geography is no barrier to widespread communication. Where once, in order to speak your mind you'd need a garden fence, a box in Speakers' Corner or at the very least a pub table, now all you need is a computer and an internet connection. Once you're set up and in front of your keyboard, you are free to create a global virtual community of people who share your interests and hang on your every word. If you're any good, of course.

On the one hand, this opportunity for unhampered vox populi is a breakthrough, a triumph for freedom of speech which has been hailed in some quarters as nothing short of revolutionary, signaling the rise of the citizen journalist and absolute freedom from the power structures that usually restrict or twist information. On the other hand, it also makes one very well aware of the value of a good editor. Which is where this book comes in.

I ploughed through some 5,000 UK blogs myself and over the last year several hundred other bloggers have directed me to particularly fine pieces I may otherwise have missed. They themselves were directed by others, so while we obviously haven't been able to cover all 300,000 UK blogs, we have undergone a filtering process of several thousand people to bring you what we think is some of the very best British blogging. Pieces on politics, books, Morris Dancing (and why not?), elections, disasters, parents, children, love, sex, and so very much more. Hopefully what you'll take from this book is some idea of the range of topics discussed in British blogs, as well as the variety of styles used. Most of all however, we hope you'll get some idea of just how much fun this whole blogging thing is, from the point of view of both the blogger and the bloggee.

There's fine writing in this anthology, as well as a few words from me. My thanks to all my fellow bloggers who provided the good stuff and made compiling this book such a joy.

Tim Worstall
November 2005

NOVEMBER 2004

✎ 2 November

‹ED› A CONSISTENT THEME, FROM BOTH RIGHT AND LEFT, IS THE WAY IN WHICH THE BBC IS BIASED. USUALLY, IT HAS TO BE SAID, AWAY FROM WHATEVER CHERISHED BELIEFS HELD BY THE SPEAKER A STATION OR CHANNEL HAS BEEN DISCUSSING. DUMB JON TAKES THIS ONLY AS HIS STARTING POINT: ‹/ED›

Civilisation's oldest enemy returns

The thing about living in a bubble is that there are no normal people around to point out even the most absurd contradictions in your position. Take the Beeb's efforts last Wednesday – on the same channel, on the same night, the Beeb ran both 'The Power of Nightmares' and a supposed expose of the evils of the booze industry. So the people flying airliners into buildings aren't a threat, but the brewers are going to kill us all.

The programme itself, 'The Booze Business: Consuming Spirits', was a masterpiece of the Beeb's po-faced, finger-wagging moralising. The programme tracked a group of young ladies out on the town. Now take a wild shot in the dark which town it was filmed in? Yep – Newcastle. Let no man say the Beeb is obsessed with stereotypes. The actual report was a perfect example of the 'gorillas in the mist' style Beeb reporters adopt every time they pass the Watford Gap, combined with the aforementioned sermonising, and no little humbuggery. The voice-over informed us that the ladies had spent over £100 on booze – no, actually they'd spent £20 on booze and £80 on tax. Hearing a whiny Liberal complain that people are spending too much on booze when it's people like him who have driven prices up in the first place is like hearing the guy who killed his parents lay claim to the sympathy of the court because he's an orphan.

Still, the Beeb was proving, once again, to be a perfect exemplar of the prejudices of lemon-sucking, Metropolitan Liberals. There's no two ways about it: foul stench, reports of unusual activity in the sewers... yep, the prohibitionists are back, and with them one of the defining battles of human civilisation.

Alcohol has been one of the common factors in the development of modern life. As far back as archaeologists go, they find evidence of hooch. Hell, man may even be a Johnny Come Lately here. Not only will several higher mammals make special efforts to drink booze when it's available, but even in the wild several primates will go out of their way to obtain those types of fruits which are prone to fermentation. What we do know for certain is that booze has been our loyal companion through the long march of human civilisation [if only there was a large group of people who didn't drink, we could see if their civilisation really was as rich and civilised as the prohibs say it must be].

Booze has been with us from the dawn of history, and quite possibly so have the pinch-mouthed battalions of lemon-sucking freaks pushing prohibition. They say booze isn't healthy, yet what of those studies claiming that consuming certain forms of alcohol can improve health? Shouldn't these freaks be out encouraging teetotallers to sink a few? Maybe it isn't health per se that motivates them. They say people spend too much on booze, but they happily rake off the proceeds of punitive taxation. They claim booze is linked to violence amongst young people, so how come our schools are so violent? As I recall, most comprehensives only serve lager, so maybe youth violence is down to the actual youths, rather than the sinister brewing collectives.

No, you want to know what really motivates these twisted human leeches? Check out this 'ere poster [*a Soviet anti-drinking one... Ed*]. That's how they see it – drunks refusing to play their part in society, refusing to accept their responsibilities to be worker bees in the sociological hive. I doubt that one prohib in a thousand would question the fact that the poster is from the USSR, that the drunk is being criticised for not allowing himself to be a willing slave in the service of evil. To fellow drunks, this bloke isn't a waster, he's a hero, an almost Randian figure refusing to allow his mind to be enslaved by a Satanic regime. But don't expect the prohibs to see that. The prohib, almost by definition, is a collectivist – who else would rant and rave about someone else drinking?

The prohib may have a laundry list of complaints against vitamin XXX, but it all boils down to one thing, a peevish, schoolmarmy rant that people aren't taking the right things seriously. This seems like a simple thing, yet it lies at the heart of the great divide between drunks and the pasty-faced creeps who wish to persecute us.

To the prohib, all life is a grim struggle, all individuality is the enemy. Think of a prohib and you think of some screechy, red-faced hag. Think of a drunk and you think of Dean Martin. The prohib trades on the supposed horrors awaiting the drunk. The drunk has no need of such fear mongering, he simply points out that life is good, and it can be even better with vodka.

Prohibs claim that drunks are irresponsible losers and deadbeats, that all the successful people are maniacal teetotallers: after all, how can a mind rotted by alcohol possibly match the spotless mind of the teetotaller? I believe we tested this hypothesis some years ago, when we compared the performance of two Chief Executives, one sober [*Chamberlain*] and one drunk [*Churchill*].

That's really what it's all about: who your role model is. Whether you think life is just great as is, or whether you want to ascend to the glory of your inner something and claim your eternal something else and then... Who cares? If you really can't stand booze then we, unlike YOU, are not forcing our lifestyle on anyone. Leave us alone, shut it and just sit in the corner and enjoy an Evian or something.

House of Dumb
http://houseofdumb.blogspot.com

✎ 4 November

‹ED› THE US ELECTION SAW GEORGE BUSH BACK IN THE WHITE HOUSE. IN GENERAL REACTION WAS AS YOU MIGHT THINK, THOSE ON THE LEFT WANTING KERRY, THOSE ON THE RIGHT, BUSH. HARRY'S PLACE SHOWED A LITTLE MORE NUANCE, OR, IF YOU PREFER, USED IT AS A CLUB TO BEAT THEIR ANTI-WAR LEFT OPPONENTS OVER THE HEAD WITH: ‹/ED›

Votenfreude?

I've been trying not to chuckle at some of the stuff I've overheard in the past few days because, after all, I didn't want Bush to win the election and I was disappointed Kerry failed.

I really liked the idea of the US and UK both being governed by centre-left leaders committed to defeating Islamist terrorism and winning the struggle for democracy in Iraq. I was happy to save my *schadenfreude* for when the anti-war crowd and the European illusionists slowly woke up to the fact that their new friend in the White House really meant what he said about Iraq and about fighting Islamist terrorism and wasn't just trying to steal a few Republican votes. Or at least I hoped that was going to be the outcome.

So when one Stopper, whom I have the misfortune to have to listen to on most days, had an emotional How Could It Happen? moment on Wednesday, I just kept out of it. No votenfreude from me.

But they are pushing it.

I mean it is hard to read this without at least having to supress a slight smile or a chuckle:

> We went to bed daring to hope and awoke to the crushing news. And ever since we've been swapping emails and texts about how miserable we feel. Emma Brockes on how George Bush's victory catapulted liberal Britain into Collective depression. *[The Guardian... Ed]*

I woke up on Wednesday morning (not having stayed up late) and found out that America still had a right-wing president (as it usually does). Not the result I wanted but hardly a surprise and certainly not a depression-provoking shock.

Let's be honest, how many of those 'liberals' in collective depression in the UK really give two hoots about the minimum wage, union rights, gay marriage or any other domestic issue in the States? The main reason they are so depressed is that they wanted to feel vindicated in their opposition to the removal of Saddam – they wanted to feel that even the bloody Yanks agreed with them about Iraq. Well, I ain't going to join them in their discomfort over that one.

If we take the candidates at their word then 99 percent of American voters chose candidates who backed the liberation of Iraq and who are committed to finishing the job and to defeating Islamist terrorism in Iraq and elsewhere.

The only candidate whose views on international issues were close to the collective depression of liberal Britain was Ralph Nader and his vote was sub-Respect.

The fact that Kerry did not run on an 'anti-war' ticket in the first place was the real defeat for the Stoppers. They lost long before the vote, which is good but really doesn't matter because they always lose.

What matters for the American left are the kind of points that Gene has been making here over the past few days. As someone who has never visited the States, I'll leave it to those like him to analyse the defeat.

The Stoppers over here and their echoes in the media will no doubt turn their frustration even more on Blair now. They couldn't get their mitts on the evil one so they will try even harder to abuse his 'poodle'.

The very sad, weepy *Guardian* piece [...] above hints at this already:

> 'I am deeply ashamed to call myself American,' wrote another, while,
> 'I'm ashamed to be English,' countered a third, in a competitive orgy of
> shame. Lots of people talked about powerlessness. 'And that,' said one,
> ominously, 'won't lift until we get our own general election.'

They never learn do they?

Four. More. Years.

Now *that* will be votenfreude.

Harry's Place
http://hurryupharry.bloghouse.net

✎ 5 November

‹ED› THERE WAS ANOTHER ELECTION AS WELL,
THE REFERENDUM ON THE NORTH EAST
ASSEMBLY. THE NO CAMPAIGN WAS A GRASS
ROOTS ONE, LARGELY RUN BY NEIL HERRON
(OF METRIC MARTYRS FAME). GIVEN THE RESULT
THEY RATHER HAD A RIGHT TO CROW: ‹/ED›

The people speak

'A decisive defeat.' That was the verdict of the BBC at just gone one in the morning,
with 78 percent of the votes cast recording a 'no' to elected regional assemblies
against a pitiful 22 percent 'yes', with 893,829 votes cast, a 'turnout' of 47.71 percent.

Not a single one of the 22 electoral areas voted for the proposition, with Newcastle
(the area thought to be most in favour) recording 75 percent against, Sunderland,
80 percent, Tony Blair's Sedgefield 72 percent and Alnwick 81 percent.

Earlier that evening the BBC showed how out of touch it was, from its coverage of
the NE referendum. Just after eleven, BBC News 24 interviewed political analyst Tony
Travers from the LSE [London School of Economics] who spoke of the result being
'very close', with the possibility even of a very narrow 'yes' margin. All that was on
the basis of a prediction from John Prescott, that totally objective observer of events.

By then, I had already received unofficial reports from the count indicating massive support for the 'no' campaign, with some areas voting 5:1 against Prescott's folly. Minutes later on BBC News 24, we had reporter Richard Moss confirming an unofficial 'no' victory, without giving any indication of the scale, against a higher than predicted 'turnout' approaching 50 percent.

But to show quite how out of touch he was, he then lined up representatives from the 'three main parties' for a discussion: Joyce Quinn for Labour, Martin Callanan for the Tories and Ed Davey speaking for the Lib-Dems.

There is the BBC framework: it cannot see outside the 'bubble' of the established political orthodoxy, yet, if there was anything that characterised the campaign, it was the leading role of the 'peoples' no campaign, carried outside the cloying grip of the parties.

After the result, Prof. John Tomany, leader of the 'yes' campaign, at least showed some understanding of the situation. Speaking on the result, he said that the verdict reflected peoples' growing rejection of political institutions. Concluded Tony Travers, Prescott's ambitions for regionalisation in England were 'as dead as a doornail'.

Needless to say, the BBC did not interview Neil Herron. But, whatever the claims from the johnny-come-latelys, we know who really did the work. And now for the big one.

Neil Herron
http://neilherron.blogspot.com

✎ 5 November, From Michael Knowles, Chairman of the Campaign for an English Parliament:

‹ED› THE ANTI-REGIONALISM WAS ALSO EVIDENT AT THE CAMPAIGN FOR AN ENGLISH PARLIAMENT, THEIR PREFERRED SOLUTION BEING REASONABLY CLEAR FROM THEIR NAME: ‹/ED›

The North East of England votes no to a regional assembly

The Campaign welcomes the overwhelming vote of the people of the North East of England to reject a Regional Assembly. The early hours of 5 November 2004, Guy Fawkes Day, is a historic moment in the history of the English people. The people of the historic northern English counties of Northumberland and Durham and of Tyneside, Wearside and Teeside have spoken for all of England in repudiating the Govenment's plan to partition their country into competing regions. The vote of over three to one, of 700,000 to 200,000, is massive. In no way can Mr Prescott, the minister who has been campaigning for the balkanisation of England, now defend his proposals. No rejection of them could be more decisive. No spin can explain this huge vote away. A referendum was held, the outcome was decisive. The vote of the people must be respected in all its implications. The North East has seen through the government's regional assemblies for what they are: an attempt to partition England into competing regions, into what the economist Will Hutton well described as 'a veritable witches' nest of internecine rivaliries'; and it has rejected them.

The government did not partition Scotland and Wales into regions when it gave them devolution. Instead it gave devolution to both Scotland and Wales as nations. Scottish and Welsh devolution was a firm and clear recognition that Scotland and Wales were unified and distinct nations within the United Kingdom. Scotland got one parliament for the whole nation, Wales one assembly for all the Welsh people. England should be treated equally within the Union, as one nation. Its nationhood and its unity should be recognised just like Scotland and Wales.

The rejection of a regional assembly by the people of the North East of England, an unambiguous and overwhelming rejection, puts an end once and for all to the government's plan to divide England up into regions in the name of devolution. But England must have devolution within the UK just like Scotland where devolution has been real and genuine. There must now be equal treatment by the UK government of each of the three historic nations of the island of Britain. England as a nation must now have its own Parliament with the same powers and responsibilities as the Scottish Parliament. So should Wales. No other form of devolution is genuine and effective and no other form is fair. Each of the three nations of the island of Britain must stand in the same relationship to the UK government.

Likewise, the people of England must now receive per person the same amount of expenditure as is given to Scotland and Wales. It is absolutely wrong and immoral and undemocratic that the people of Scotland and Wales recieve per head £1100 more than the people of England for expenditure on health, education and social services. Likewise, the people of England must be able to decide for themselves, just like the people of Scotland and Wales, if they want foundation hospitals or student tution fees or free personal care for the old or free prescriptions for their citizens aged between 18 and 25.

Only an English parliament can bring this about.

The Government held a referendum in the North East of England thinking it was one part of England where they could successfully start the partitioning of England. The Government has been proved totally wrong. England is one nation. The Campaign for an English Parliament welcomes the outcome of the referendum and invites the Government to begin to treat England fairly and equally, in the way it treated Scotland and Wales. It invites the government to prepare plans for genuine devolution for England in the form of an English Parliament.

If there is to be devolution for England, as there must, there is now no alternative.

Campaign for an English Parliament
http://thecep.org.uk

✎ 12 November

‹ED› THE MEDIA DISCOVERED THE CHAVS, AND JOHANN HARI IN THE INDEPENDENT WAS UNHAPPY AT THE WAY THEY WERE BEING PORTRAYED. SQUANDER TWO PUT HIM RIGHT: ‹/ED›

Johann Hari is wrong

The angry young man's latest diatribe. It's about as insightful as gravel.

Mr Hari's argument can be summed up thus:
- All poor white people are chavs.
- All chavs are poor and white.
- It is wrong to hate people for being poor.

Therefore, anyone who criticises chavs is a hateful elitist classist bastard.

Assuming the *Independent* pay by the word, they should hire me instead.Now, I don't call them 'chavs'. I lived in Glasgow from '96 to '03, and Scots call them 'neds'. In fact, when I first moved to Scotland, the Scots had the word 'ned' while the English simply didn't have a word to describe them at all. I don't know why they eventually chose 'chav', but I prefer 'ned'. I'm now in Northern Ireland, where they're called 'steeks' and 'spides'. 'Spide' is pretty good: it just sounds inherently derogatory.

I'm not poor, but I'm not that well-off, either. I can't afford a ned car, or ned clothes, or the amount of alcohol and cigarettes neds get through every day, not to mention the harder drugs. I can't afford to take the amount of time off work that neds seem to enjoy. Contrary to what Hari seems to think, fast food isn't that cheap – certainly not compared to cooking at home. I like the occasional burger or fish supper, but, unlike your average ned, I can't afford to go out for one every day. However, I can (just) afford a mortgage on a three-bedroom house in a fairly expensive area.

During my time in Glasgow, my building was set alight by neds three times, once seriously endangering my life. The reason for this was so that ned kids could try and jump onto the back of the fire engine when it left. Windows in the common stairwell were smashed by neds a couple of times, just for fun, like. The communal front door was kicked in by neds. Before we finally managed to get the communal stairs secured, they were a popular location for neds to come and drink, smoke dope, scrawl their names, smoke heroin, inject heroin, occasionally spit at my friends, and – on one memorable occasion – have a crap.

My then girlfriend and I once walked out of the front door to be greeted by the wonderful sight of a ned standing on the stairs with his trousers round his knees, injecting heroin into his penis. The ned living in the ground floor flat threatened my life a couple of times, but he wasn't there long: his landlord got rid of the bastard and replaced him with an extremely nice, friendly, reasonable, poor single mother who was definitely not a ned and didn't want her sons to become neds.

Eric's got the right idea, as has Harry, despite feeling he needs to descend into Marxist terminology to describe the problem. It took a heroic effort to read past the word 'lumpenproletariat', I can tell you. Please.

Anyway, here's the thing. Everyone hates neds, but the people who hate them by far the most are poor people. Everyone has to put up with the little bastards' vandalism and violence and abuse and theft and bad clothing choices, but poor people also have to put up with being associated with it by class-obsessed idiots like Hari.

Squander Two
www.squandertwo.net/blog

✎ 13 November

‹ED› THE DECADES-LONG SLOW MOTION TRAIN WRECK THAT WAS ROVER FINALLY CAME TO A SHUDDERING HALT THIS YEAR. THE YORKSHIRE RANTER WAS PROVIDING DETAILED ANALYSIS 6 MONTHS BEFORE THE FINAL END: ‹/ED›

MG Rover – How John Towers made my all-time shit list

Back in early 2000, if you had barged into Tommy's Bar at Royal Holloway, University of London, and demanded of me who had most impressed me in the last six months, I would have unhesitatingly told you that John Towers, the former production director of Rover Group who had just saved the Rover plant from closure, deserved all our congratulations. The previous owners, BMW, had wanted to shut down the car plant and flog the land. That didn't stop them wanting to hang on to the profitable bits – the Mini production line, the Rover 75 line and the Midland Powertrain gearbox plant – of course. But the core business and thousands of jobs would go. Nobody, at first, looked like doing much. Although the tabloids worked themselves into an anti-German froth, they didn't feel at all certain in arguing for government intervention. After all, that was exactly what they opposed, no? The Trade and Industry Secretary, Stephen Byers, seemed at first to agree. A small, boutique, New Labourish sports car business might – might – survive. But nothing more.

As the complicated negotiations went on, though, it became clear that something might yet be saved. There were doubts about the numbers. There was a growing critical mass of anger in the Labour Party and, most of all, the trade unions. And then – there was action. A group of former Rover executives were backed by an odd coalition of interest to put together their own bid. Much of the cash came from rich franchise dealerships, with more from companies involved in supplying the plant, and quite a bit from the unions and their members. On the way, some of BMW's claims about Rover inefficiency turned sour – after all, if BMW's management were so great, surely they would have been able to know how many unsold cars they had in stock? But the potential buyers found themselves forced to buy satellite photos from Russia to discover how much inventory was parked on the two and a half mile runway of Bruntingthorpe airfield, depreciating peacefully in the wet winter. Armed with a figure for the car mountain, they finally raised the rest of the funding from a provincial US bank. There was a gap in the plan of around £10 million, but in the end the state coughed up.

Under the final agreement, the New Mini tooling would be handed over to BMW's ex-Rover plant at Cowley, the Rover 75 tooling going the other way. The car pile would be handed over to the North Carolinan bankers in return for working capital. BMW would lend some £425 million to the new firm at a zero interest rate. Many people thought it would never work, but the first few sets of figures were encouraging. An arbitration resulted in the Powertrain plant also being handed to Rover, which gave them the capability to build whole cars. There was talk of joint ventures with other car makers to develop a new range. You'd have doubted that Towers would ever have got on my shit list back then. But, so far, none of the foreign deals have worked. The new cars have not happened, but something else has.

That something else recently got Towers called by a name which has iconic status in British language – the unacceptable face of capitalism. The phrase was first used by Prime Minister Edward Heath, speaking of Lonrho mining boss Tiny Rowland. The next man to be the unacceptable face was Robert Maxwell, not long before his death. It is a serious thing to say, even if the man to say it was the head of BMW in Britain, who might not be entirely neutral. Towers and the four others who became the new firm's directors have gripped the headlines by organising a trust fund for their benefit that receives substantial sums of money from the firm. But it's not only that. They also gave the firm a new and bizarre corporate structure. Their own holding company (Techtronic), the final owner of the whole firm, owns the various business units. So far, so straightforward. They include the group's property assets, its brand, a luxurious country-house conference centre, the profitable Midlands Powertrain and parts units, and a financial unit that owns the portfolio of loans offered to customers who bought on credit. They also, though, include a shell company that owns their controlling stake in MG-Rover Group, the actual car manufacturer.

They don't own the whole of MG Rover Group though. Remember the employees who bought shares back at the time of the firm's rescue? They own the remaining minority. But they don't have Techtronic shares, and hence no interests in the totality of the group. Their shares are in MG Rover Group – that is, Rover less its more profitable assets. Another interesting fact is that BMW loan. The loan was made, free of interest, to Techtronic. Techtronic disburses it as required to MG Rover. But Techtronic charges MG Rover interest on it, interest that presumably benefits only the Techtronic shareholders. The comedian Tony Hancock, according to my dad, once portrayed a con-man who started a company with his straight-man. He explains to the mark that there are two classes of shares, A and B. The dupe opts for the A's and Hancock's character gleefully accepts the B's. The sting? The A shares entitle you to put money into the company, but only the B's let you take it out.

The Yorkshire Ranter
http://yorkshire-ranter.blogspot.com

✎ 22 November

‹ED› THE RIGHTS AND WRONGS OF THE IRAQ WAR HAVE BEEN HUGELY CONTROVERSIAL EVERYWHERE THIS YEAR AS IN THAT BEFORE IT. IN THE BLOGOSPHERE THE BITTEREST ARGUMENTS HAVE BEEN BETWEEN THE PRO- AND ANTI-WAR LEFT. NORMAN GERAS HAS BEEN ONE OF THE STALWARTS OF THE PRO-WAR LEFT. HERE HE TAKES ISSUE WITH THE WAY A GUARDIAN PIECE ASSIGNS MORAL RESPONSIBILITY: ‹/ED›

The war has two sides

In Friday's *Guardian* Ian Brown, who has worked for various NGOs, says about the murder of Margaret Hassan that 'the failure to close the Care office in Baghdad has had appalling consequences'. On the question of why Care didn't suspend operations in Iraq, he believes the answer lies in the trend among international aid organisations and NGOs to be increasingly dependent on government funding:

> In many countries, close links to the US government go unnoticed. Not so in Iraq. And there are clear indications that Care's operations in Iraq were compromised by links to the US and UK administrations.

In addition to the funding situation, he goes on to observe that Care didn't come out in opposition to the Iraq war. They joined the protest march on 15 February last year only 'to raise awareness of the potential humanitarian consequences of war in Iraq'.

Potential humanitarian consequences? After the devastation of Afghanistan, there could be no doubt that the invasion of Iraq by the world's most powerful army would trigger a humanitarian disaster. Were Care and many other aid organisations... more concerned about a cut in funding than the consequences for the Iraqi population?

Brown concludes:

> Margaret Hassan, as the director of Care in Iraq, was caught in the compromise NGOs make when they rely on western governments for their funding. No matter her vociferous condemnation of the invasion, no matter her genuine dedication to helping those in need, Iraq is simply too dangerous a place for aid workers.
>
> She may have been abducted by gangsters in a plot to extort money which went tragically wrong. The more likely scenario, I believe, is that she was killed because she was considered to be collaborating with the enemy. Indeed, elements within the Iraqi resistance have long since called for all foreigners, except journalists, to leave the country.

Note first, here, what Brown, concerned for the independence of humanitarian NGOs from government, understands by independence: not just that they shouldn't rely on government funding, but that on a major and very divisive political issue they should not be *neutral*. He criticizes Care for not opposing the Iraq war. But surely their independence of government entails their freedom to come to an independent judgement? This would presumably allow a choice between opposing the war, supporting it, and doing neither. But apparently not; independence of government, and on an issue where there was a deep division of opinion about the morality and the likely consequences of the war, was to think just what Ian Brown thought. Nor does he offer a single word in defence of the view that humanitarian organizations, which according to him should be drawing their funding from general public support, will increase that support by becoming overtly politicized. I think his view is wrong, but I've posted about it before, so I'll move on.

The main thing I want to draw attention to is this. In all the criticisms Brown levels or implies – against the governments and political leaders who took the US and Britain to war in Iraq, against Care International and other NGOs for their reliance on government funding, and against Care again for not suspending operations in Iraq – notice who gets a free pass. Those who have actually been taking hostages and killing them in Iraq are treated by Brown as if they were merely part of the natural background and not (what they in fact are) the people to blame for these murders. In an attempt, probably vain, to forestall some predictable objections, let me make it plain what I am not saying. I am not saying that Ian Brown approves of either the killings or their perpetrators. I'm confident he doesn't. What I *am* saying is that the lack of balance in the way he respectively assigns and doesn't assign criticism and condemnation puts him in the position of simply accepting the terms in which the conflict is viewed by the hostage-takers and their ilk.

He may not intend this, but it happens willy-nilly. Thus: NGOs are 'compromised' by taking funding from western governments; Margaret Hassan was 'considered to be collaborating with the enemy'; 'elements within the Iraqi resistance have long since called for all foreigners... to leave the country.' So, that's just how it is, is it? They get to set the terms? No matter that these are people in breach of some of the most fundamental of humanitarian norms and of rules of conflict that are encoded in international conventions; people who have attacked Red Cross personnel, and attacked UN personnel, and kidnapped civilians, and decapitated them, and all the rest of the sorry and now familiar litany. We have to shape our norms and our conduct according to *their* lights. Where does this end? Brown criticizes Care for relying on government funding and not pulling out of Iraq. But why does he stop there? By the same logic, he could have said that Margaret Hassan was herself compromised by working for a compromised organization – and was therefore guilty for her own death.

Well, no to that, and no also to what leads to it. Because they, the murderers, don't get to set the terms, our terms. They're on the other side. We have different, and better, norms. Brown's article wouldn't have been worth this much commentary, but for the fact that it typifies so much anti-war criticism. The responsibilities of the other side are just put in brackets and everything that happens has to be the fault of someone on our side. But that's not the way it is or has ever been. Like any other, the war has two sides.

Normblog
http://normblog.typepad.com/normblog

‹ED› NOT EVERYTHING IN BLOGGING IS ABOUT POLITICS OR ECONOMICS, MUCH OF IT IS ABOUT THE REALLY IMPORTANT THINGS IN LIFE AS JONNY BILLERICAY POINTS OUT: ‹/ED›

Monday, 22 November 2004

Thursday evening. Next door

'Well I don't believe a word of it,' I snorted, as I weighed up whether to be satisfied with conquering the continent of Australia or whether to mount a sneaky additional raid on Madagascar. 'I have never heard of this 'Virgin Vie' party thing.'

Big A rolled the dice and annihilated my armies. We agreed it was highly unlikely that the girls' evening really involved demonstrations of cosmetics and face creams. I poured another large glass of wine.

'Let's face it. It's an Ann Summers party, isn't it?' I observed.

We nodded angrily, the undoubted truth dawning on us. We are unaccustomed to being lied to by our spouses. Short Tony attempted to sweep his armies into Europe via Iceland, but was repulsed.

'Well I just hope it doesn't go on too late,' I stated. 'I have a Very Important Meeting tomorrow, and the last thing I need is the LTLP crashing home in the early hours carrying all sorts of probe implements and demanding to be pleasured.'

'It's disgusting,' agreed Short Tony.

Big A handed in a set of cards, and proceeded to destroy my African presence. Despite some canny dice rolling my interest there was at an end. We reflected on their sad evening, as we enjoyed our board game.

'Even now, she is probably parading round your living room in a rubber basque.' I shook my head in annoyance. 'Like a common whore.'

We were now extremely annoyed by their behaviour. I made an abortive raid on China. We poured some more wine.

Tuesday, 23 November 2004

Friday, early hours. Next door

Big A has fallen asleep on the sofa. There is no sign of the girls. Short Tony and I are tired of waiting up for them.

We decide to fetch them home and fall out into the dark night. The hundred yard journey to Big A's house in stretched to a couple of miles in our particular zig zag fashion.

The house is quiet, the curtains drawn. We are still cross about being fed this ridiculous 'cosmetics party' spiel.

As we walk up the front drive I have an idea.

'Let's see if we can find a gap in the curtains,' I suggest. 'We might be able to catch them red-handed in their lewd outfits of shame.'

We tumble into the front garden and up to the large bay window. We are extremely quiet as only drunk people can be, with lots of whispering, giggling and hisses of 'sshhh!!!' There is no gap in the curtains, but a noise from within suggests that our plan has been rumbled.

'Quick!' cries Short Tony. 'Into the bushes!'

We leap into the bushes.

The front door opens and a couple of people emerge. Phrases such as 'I could have sworn I heard something' are bandied. The door closes again.

'Wouldn't it be funny,' observes Short Tony, 'if we rang the doorbell and then hid again?'

I consider this. I have an encyclopaedic knowledge of British comedy from the late seventies onwards including the UK stand-up scene, coupled with a single appearance at the Edinburgh Festival dressed in a tutu. However, ringing the doorbell and then hiding would clearly surpass anything that anybody had ever done in the name of being funny, ever in the world, ever.

Short Tony creeps out, tiptoes to the door, pushes the bell and then dives back into the bushes.

Again the door opens and there are confused noises, before the ladies retreat back inside.

We are beside ourselves with glee. The girls seem unable to work out what is happening. I reflect that they are clearly embarrassingly drunk, as I crouch sniggering in the rosemary bush with another grown man.

This is probably what Kevin Spacey was really up to.

'Right,' whispers Short Tony. 'Your turn.'

I scuttle towards the front door.

(Five turns later)
'You know what?' I ask Short Tony, as once more the girls retreat inside in confusion. 'We could do this all night and it wouldn't become boring.'

(Three turns later)
They are scouring the front garden with a torch. But they are rubbish at finding us. We are like two Norfolk Andy McNabs, using our resourceful survival skills to remain hidden in the rosemary bush.

(Two turns later)
Blows from a large rubber torch rein down on my arms and upper body, as I struggle to protect my head. 'You bastards, you bastards!' Mrs Big A keeps repeating. 'We were really worried!' Our attempts at apologies intermingle with nervous laughter and howls of pain.

I hadn't realised that they sold torches at Ann Summers parties. It is probably a Vag-lite.

The LTLP stands back from the scene with her arms folded, looking cross.

'You were a bit late,' I explain. 'I came to fetch you home.'

JonnyB's private secret diary
http://jonnybillericay.blogspot.com

✎ 26 November

‹ED› PERHAPS THE ONE ISSUE THAT UNITED BLOGGERS OVER THE YEAR WAS THE ASSAULT ON CIVIL LIBERTIES: ID CARDS, THE RELIGIOUS HATRED BILL AND, HERE, THE CIVIL CONTINGENCIES ACT. FROM THE EDGE OF ENGLAND'S SWORD, THIS IS QUITE MILD BY THE STANDARDS OF OTHER COMMENTATORS. ONE WRITER AT THE SAME BLOG, IN OCTOBER, COMPARED IT DIRECTLY TO THE NAZI'S ENABLING ACT OF 1933: ‹/ED›

Uncivil contingencies

A lot of comments were generated by my post on Hunting the other day, and a number of topics came out of it for further debate. The first of these that I want to cover is the Civil Contingencies Act (yes, it went through). A number of commenters suggested that Blair might suspend elections (one of the powers covered in the Act), but others made the point that Mr Blair wins elections, and therefore has no reason to suspend them. Another point being made was that politicians are in politics to do what they think is good, and talk about dictatorships was unreasonable. I think both of these arguments have merit... to a point.

If we step back from the detail of the CCA for a moment and examine it at a high level we can consider the question 'what is it for?' The answer to that question is actually fairly easy. The CCA is an attempt to encode in British law concepts such as martial law and state of emergency, which have not hitherto existed. The detail of what this entails seems to be the product of a brainstorming session of what powers agents of the state might need in the event of a serious emergency (i.e. an Iranian nuke going off in London after it mysteriously found its way into the hands of terrorists).

Viewed in the light of this, the draconian powers included in the Act actually make some sense (apart from those concerning elections which the Executive should never have the power to suspend – in fact I don't think anyone should have that power).

Where things have gone wrong in the drafting of the law, is that in any brainstorming session you have to throw away a load of the ideas that come out as you tie things together into a coherent set of thoughts. This has not been done. I don't believe that the stuff in the law about any government whip being able to invoke it is there to enable factional coups. I think it is there because someone was worried about dotting every 'i' and crossing every 't' in case the entire government gets wiped out. For the same reason, because we don't know every possible attack that might be used on us the law has been written vaguely to allow for it to be invoked for just about any reason. I don't think that is deliberate, I think it is a catastrophic mistake the consequences of which have not been thought through.

The whole excercise smacks of the new political class. They fill the government benches (and a vast amount of the opposition ones too). They are people who have never held a real job, but have always worked in government or activism. And they think in terms of what they know – the rigidity of the state permeates their ideas. Worse, they are increasingly out of touch with our political heritage. The key marker here is that the Commons overturned a Lords amendment that ensured the CCA did not contain the power to suspend the Magna Carta. There is precious little that is actually enforceable in that document – 8 centuries of laws have superceded it, so this is pure symbolism, but the symbology is important. Can you imagine Harold Wilson doing such a thing?

People like that now constitute the establishment. And no matter how good and decent they are they have created a monoculture at the heart of the state. And because of this, the technocratic mindset holds sway over things as never before. Thus it is no surprise that they seek to standardise and plan in detail for the unplannable.

What they miss, with their lack of regard for the past and its institutions is that societies like ours can adapt to chaos and self-organise. They do not need government oversight 24/7.

The other problem with encoding emergency procedures in law is that it makes them easier to invoke. Very rarely is a law placed on the statute book and never used. Previously most of these emergency powers either existed in some vague form (e.g. Orders in Council) or did not exist but would be used in a real emergency anyway and damn the niceties. This state of affairs necessarily created a high bar to using them. By replacing this with a simple procedure the CCA makes these powers much more available. And having done this, in spite of fine words to the contrary, it is a certainty that one day these laws will be used for something that is not really an emergency. It won't be to suspend elections, it will be one of the lesser powers, but it will happen. (Remember this government tried essentially to steal Railtrack when it discovered that a little-known clause in the privatisation legislation enabled them to do so.) And each time the CCA is used, using it again will become easier.

So, by creating these powers – even in good faith – the government has put in place a mechanism that could end our democracy. The political class is becoming more and more out of touch with the electorate and going the way of the continent in ruling more and more things off limits for debate, at the same time as weakening or redefining the invisible threads that tie the country together. Unfortunately they don't even realise what they are doing. First Past the Post protects the status quo for now, but it can't hold things together indefinitely. Just because Tony Blair isn't going to suspend elections, doesn't mean someone else won't.

The Edge of England's Sword
http://www.iainmurray.org/MT

DECEMBER 2004

✎ 7 December

‹ED› EU REFERENDUM HAS BECOME THE LEADING
BLOGOSPHERIC LIGHT OF THE EUROSCEPTIC
COMMUNITY. RICHARD NORTH AND HELEN
SZAMUELY HAVE KEPT UP A STEADY STREAM
OF PIECES LIKE THIS, ALL IN PREPARATION FOR
THE (ASSUMED TO BE) COMING REFERENDUM
ON THE NEW CONSTITUTION: ‹/ED›

Give him a kicking

As expected, Jack Straw today delivered his speech on the EU constitution at the
Centre of European Reform, London, hosted by Charles Grant, director of the
Centre and one time biographer of Jacques Delors.

Surrounded by Europhiles and thus utterly at home with an uncritical audience,
Straw was there 'to set out today the case for the new EU Constitution'. And his
basic theme was:

> If we approve this Constitution, we will be making it our kind of Europe,
> a Europe in which Britain is strong. If we reject it, we will end up with a weak
> and marginalised Britain in a worse kind of European Union.

There is nothing new there, particularly – the usual dismal lack of confidence
of the political élites, that would have Great Britain a snivelling, weak, isolated
wretch if we dare so much as to think of not going all the way with whatever
the 'colleagues' throw our way.

There is a subtle variation here, through. Whereas we would usually be 'weak and
isolated' if we left the EU, we are now to become similarly 'weak and isolated' if
we don't ratify the constitution. Whatever the situations, therefore, in the Straw
book, we are 'weak and isolated'.

Before getting to that point, however, Straw has plenty of time to throw around the
usual quota of ad hominem epithets, no doubt to the delight of his Europhile friends.
In fact, we had the full vocabulary. Dissenters were called 'Europhobes', 'sceptics',
'anti-Europeans', as well as 'queasy anti-Europeans' and 'anti-European zealots'.

One really does wonder if Straw understands that these are voters he is talking about, the people whom he wants to vote for the constitution. Is it arrogance, stupidity or simply recklessness, that he feels entitled so freely to insult what is in fact the majority of the nation?

Anyhow, he starts off with a 'paradox' (which is not a medic with a red beret, just in case you were wondering), suggesting that it was the contention amongst the opponents of the constitution 'that Europe has pulled the wool over British eyes'.

'We thought we were joining a free trade area,' the argument goes according to Straw, 'but we were in fact joining a far more supra-national and integrated organisation than we wanted. The advocates of that view hanker after a return to the state of nature – to the European Community as we joined it in the early 1970s.'

Jack Straw is so aptly named, for here we see his propensity to live up to his name, building up 'straw dogs' so that he can knock them down. 'Europe' as he puts it, was at the time of our joining the EEC, relatively open about its ambitions for political integration. It was not 'Europe' who pulled the wool over British eyes, but British politicians, and Straw is continuing in that cynical tradition.

Asserts Straw, 'even supposing it were possible to get our 24 partners to agree to that kind of Europe', it would not be better than today. It would still have most of the features to which the 'anti-Europeans' most object: primacy of EU law, the ECJ [European Court of Justice], and so on.

And, in any case, 'it is misleading to claim that the British people didn't know what we were going into, for those issues featured strongly in the debate on Europe at the time of our referendum in 1975.' So there.

Straw obviously feels it is important to get that point in, but what is he trying to prove? In fact, who cares? History says otherwise and, if he disputes it, perhaps he should read the account of the 1975 Referendum by David Butler and Uwe Kitzinger – Europhiles both – who readily attest that ideas of political union were deliberately suppressed.

Passing that by, Straw tells us that the shape of the Europe of the 1970s would today suit us much less well than what we have now:

> Europe circa 1973 means an EU without the Single Market; barriers everywhere to British businesses; energy, transport and telecoms run by isolated national monopolies; the Common Agricultural Policy entirely untouched by the reforms to it which we have since secured, and secured

I might add through majority voting. There would be no mechanisms for working together against illegal immigration, drug trafficking and international organised crime; and only the most rudimentary ones for using our collective influence on the world stage.

Notwithstanding that the electricity supply to No. 10 Downing Street is provided by a French firm, that the CAP is still a mess, despite numerous reforms, Straw wheels out the canard about the lack of mechanisms for working together on illegal immigration, etc.

Yet, on 29 September 2003, there came into force the United Nations Convention against Transnational Organised Crime, which provides precisely the international framework that Straw claims would be absent without the EU. And he should know. The UK signed it on 14 December 2000.

It is not so much, therefore, that people like Straw tell lies – which they do – but what they leave out. Everything is 'spun', distorted, not real, mendacious in spirit if not actually in fact.

For instance, he tells us that the Single Market 'secured huge advantages for British firms' and 'access to markets on equal terms across the whole of Europe'. What he doesn't say is that the Single Market brought with it an explosion of red-tape that drove thousands of firms to the wall, and the 'access to markets' meant that EU member states also had access to ours, creating a massive accumulated trade deficit with the EU.

Now, the new Treaty will make the EU even more efficient and more effective. Furthermore, 'It is clear from every word of the new Constitution that the EU is an organisation of sovereign nations, which can act only where its members have decided to do so in common. It has only those powers which the nations confer on it.'

Oh, p-leese... I can't even be bothered to deconstruct that one. I will just make one comment. The 'nations' in this context are not the people, you moron, they're bloody governments. They have conferred the powers on the EU, and without our consent: we the people – remember us? That is why we are having a referendum, and the answer is NO!

And on we drone. The Treaty limits the powers of the EU. Yeah, yeah. The Universe has limits, but it's still bloody big, Jack Straw. And the EU's powers are too bloody big. One would be too much.

You can't actually engage with this sort of argument. You just get mad. You can't easily dissect it. The result is inevitably more boring that the original. In a less civilised world, you would just shoot people like Straw, but we can't – not yet. But he who would so freely insult us – we can give him a 'kicking'... by voting No!

EU Referendum
http://eureferendum.blogspot.com

✎ 7 December

‹ED› IT SHOULDN'T BE SURPRISING THAT THOSE WHO LOVE BOTH BOOKS AND WRITING HAVE MADE A CORNER OF THE BLOGOSPHERE DEDICATED TO THOSE ARTS. THE NEXT ENTRY IS A REVIEW OF A BOOK BY NATALIE BENNETT AT PHILOBIBLON. NOTE THAT THE BOOK WAS PURCHASED FROM A SALE OF THOSE SENT TO A NEWSPAPER BUT NOT REVIEWED BY IT – BLOGS DO ALLOW THE SMALLER AND MORE SPECIALIST VOICES TO BE CONSIDERED. ‹/ED›

Luckily, most of the sales of review copies of books held in newspaper offices (which raise money for charity) are held at lunchtime, when I'm not there, otherwise I'd have already had to move out of home to make space for the bookshelves

But I was reminded of what I'm missing by a rare sale I managed to get to, where I bought (along with lots of other books), *Birth of the Chess Queen: A History*, by Marilyn Yalow, 2004, Pandora.

It explains that when chess was invented in India, then transplanted into the Muslim world (where non-figurative pieces were used because of Islamic iconoclasm), and finally arrived in Europe with the Moors, the piece that stood beside the King was the vizier.

The first chess queen recorded appears in a manuscript written in the late 990s in the Einsiedeln Monastery in Switzerland. The monk who wrote it was German-speaking, although of course he was working in Latin. He makes no particular remark about her presence, so the piece was obviously well established. (p. 17)

A pawn, as today, could become a queen by getting to the other end of the board, but only if the original queen had been taken (p. 18).

> an attempt to preserve the uniqueness of the king's wife, his only permissible conjugal mate, according to Christian doctrine... The idea of multiple queens on the chessboard proved so anxiety-making for Europeans that it remained a subject of contention for centuries to come.

The author seeks to find a unique model for the chess queen, proposing either Adelaide of Germany, queen to Otto I, 'a second Charlemagne', or her daughter-in-law, Theosophano, the Byzantine princess, queen to Otto II and mother and regent to Otto III.

This I'd suggest is problematic – perhaps one sycophantic courtier might have had the idea of commissioning a set featuring a single powerful queen, but the idea would sure have not caught on broadly, with chess seen as a model for courtly life, unless queens in general were significant 'players' in politics and war.

Yalow indeed makes this point, saying (p. 26.):

> for a brief period in the 980s, the rule of queen's regent was dominant in Western Europe. Not only were Adelaide and Theophano regents for Otto III, but Adelaide's daughter Emma was regent for the French King Louis V, the duchess Beatrice of Lorraine ruled for her minor son, and the youthful Aethelred II in England was under his mother's tutelage.

It is surely no accident that about this time the chess piece appeared.

It's 'funny' how little focus gets put on such periods of history.

P.S. This is an interesting read, but irritating when the academic writer makes patronising attempts to cater to an 'ordinary' audience. Reaching them surely does not require the profuse use of exclamation marks!

Philobiblon
http://philobiblion.blogspot.com

✎ 9 December

‹ED/› THE POLICEMAN'S BLOG HAS, OVER THE YEAR, BECOME ONE OF THE TOP UK BLOGS. WRITTEN BY A SERVING POLICE OFFICER IT PROVIDES A WINDOW INTO POLICE PROCEDURE AND AT TIMES, MUSES ON THE STATE OF THE LAW ITSELF. HERE'S HIS REACTION TO THE MURDER OF JOHN MONCKTON IN A HOME INVASION BURGLARY: ‹/ED›

Hot burglaries

The wife and children of Mr Monckton will doubtless be relieved to know that the burglary rate in England is declining significantly. They will also be pleased with official reassurances that the risk of being confronted in one's own home by a burglar is astonishingly rare. Not as astonishingly rare as it is in the US, where the right to defend one's family has not been taken away from the individual and given to the state.

Whenever I go to a burglary, I reach for the modern English policeman's weapon of choice: the photocopier (double sided, black and white, 40 copies per minute). I have to print out leaflets to put into letterboxes asking if people saw anything at about the time of the burglary. I usually do about five houses either side of the attacked property and ten on the opposite side of the street and any other properties that may be significant (shops, garages, etc). I also take a detailed statement about what has been taken, the layout of the house and any damage caused, and I give the crime number to the injured party. SOCO will arrive (if they can finish before 9.00 pm) and often recover footprints and glove marks. Finally, I leave a leaflet offering the services of Victim Support and advise the homeowners to take better security precautions in the future. The victim's faith in the police restored, I leave to return to the police station to write a detailed report of my actions.

The English middle classes are at their best when they are burgled: the stiff upper lip, the offer of tea, the uncomfortable draught caused by the smashed window in the kitchen ('don't worry officer, we've not touched anything'). They display a resignation which I used to find touching, but now makes me rather frustrated.

The proposed bill to make cosmetic changes to the idea of reasonable force might be the start of a sea change, but it probably won't. Either way, it has produced interesting comment from the government who have concluded that most burglars are high on drugs and won't take any notice of a change in the law because they don't know what they are doing anyway. I get this a lot from victims: 'I suppose it's just kids looking for drug money to feed their habit office.' For too long victims have been told that crime is a consequence of drugs, which in turn [is a problem] caused by family breakdown and social injustice; the only option is to turn their homes into fortresses and if all else fails, go for counselling.

Most burglars I meet are extremely rational people: they are aware of things like fingerprints and DNA and they know what to say in police interviews. They choose homes with single glazed rear windows and try to be quiet when they break in. Burglars make a calculation before they go into a house; they take into account all the factors. Will someone be in? If they are in will they hurt me? Are there valuables in the house? Are the police about? What about neighbours?

When victims take steps to protect themselves, they can have a dramatic effect. For example, in the US, 13% of burglaries are 'hot' (occur when occupants are inside the property) whereas in England and Wales the rate is 50%. What accounts for this difference? The fact that the occupants might be armed and the burglar might get killed.

This shifts the odds dramatically in the homeowner's favour and changes the calculation that the burglar has to make: Is it worth dying for the jewellery that might be upstairs? In England, burglars don't have to make that calculation.

It's time they did.

The Policeman's Blog
http://coppersblog.blogspot.com

✎ 12 December

<ED> JUST BEFORE THE US ELECTION, THE
GUARDIAN RAN SOMETHING CALLED 'OPERATION
CLARK COUNTY'. IN ESSENCE, WRITE TO THE
VOTERS OF THAT COUNTY AND REMIND THEM
THAT ALL OF US NICE EUROPEANS DIDN'T
LIKE GEORGE BUSH (ALTHOUGH THE ACTUAL
INSTRUCTIONS WERE FRAMED A LITTLE
DIFFERENTLY). THE RESULTS WERE A TAD
DIFFERENT FROM THOSE PREDICTED
(OR DESIRED): </ED>

Was it the *Guardian* wot won it for Bush?

I just had a discussion about Operation Clark County, that fatuous attempt by the London-based Socialist-leaning *Guardian* newspaper, to persuade Ohio voters to back John Kerry in the November 2 election. The question being considered was: did the *Guardian* (nicknamed the *Grauniad* for its frequent typographical errors and its leftist obsessions) win the presidential election (accidentally) for George Bush? In 1992, the *Sun* newspaper proclaimed on its front page after the fourth consecutive defeat for the British Labour Party that 'It Was the Sun Wot Won It'. Did the *Guardian*'s patronizing meddling produce a similar, if unintended effect?

The set-up was as follows. The *Guardian* calculated (correctly) that Ohio would be a key state in the presidential election. Ian Katz and Oliver Burkeman, the 'geniuses' behind the campaign selected Clark County on the basis that Al Gore had supposedly won that county by a mere 324 votes or 1%. The *Guardian* also claimed that George W. Bush had won Ohio by 4%, but that polls were showing a tight race with a virtual dead heat expected.

The truth was slightly different. Clark County did go for Gore, but only by 0.56%, and Bush won Ohio by 3.51% in 2000. So the background information was slightly wrong to begin with.

Robin Grant of *perfect.co.uk* went one better, not only claiming to have set up the campaign but actually collecting local press coverage, including expressions of outrage from Clark County residents. Grant's smug chuckles at the right-wing bloggers look funny now, but not the way that he had intended.

The result of thousands of *Guardian* readers sending letters to independent voters in Clark County was nothing less than dramatic. The campaign, despite being a 'roaring success' was cancelled as soon as letters began to arrive in Ohio.

A typical report of the time reads:

> The *Springfield News-Sun* also received about a dozen e-mails, starting early in the day, about the *Guardian* campaign, from places as diverse as New York, New Jersey, Georgia, Alaska and Switzerland, almost all of which expressed some degree of outrage.

The local paper ran a story with the headline 'Butt out Brits, voters say'. *USA Today*, describing the *Guardian* as a 'left-leaning newspaper', poured scorn on the campaign, portraying it as at best a publicity stunt.

Both local Republican and Democrat campaigns described the move as self-defeating. The scorecard shows the cost of Operation Clark County to John Kerry's hopes of winning Ohio.

Clark County	2004		2000	
	votes	%	votes	%
Republican	34,938	5.78	27,660	48.06
Democrat	34,534	48.74	27,984	48.62
Others	331	n/a	1,915	n/a

Ohio	2004		2000	
	votes	%	votes	%
Republican	2,858,727	50.82	2,351,209	49.98
Democrat	2,739,952	48.70	2,186,190	46.47
Others	26,952	n/a	167,058	n/a

Republican majority or deficit (%)			
	2004	2000	swing
Ohio	+2.12	+0.56	0.7% to Democrat
Clark County	+0.56	-2.04	1.3% to Republican

So the *Guardian* swing was 2.0% from the Democrats to Bush. Clark County was the only Ohio county to switch from a Democrat majority in 2000 to a Republican one in 2004. In fact such a swing only occurred in 5% of the whole country's 3,113 counties according to USA Today. If we imagine what effect Operation Clark County might have had if the Guardian had run it across the whole of the USA we get some startling results.

Kerry would have failed to win the only State to switch his way from 2000, New Hampshire with 4 electoral college votes. Worse still, Michigan (17 votes), Minnesota (10), Oregon (7), Pennsylvania (21) and Wisconsin (10) would all have fallen to the Republican onslaught if the *Guardian* effect had been felt in those states. The final outcome would have been a 355 to 183 electoral college massacre for Senator Kerry.

It gets worse.

The *Guardian* ended up giving out contact details for 14,000 voters out of the 56,000 originally planned for. If these had been sent and they had achieved the same scale of effect then the swing would have been **eight per cent** more to Bush. So a nationwide *Guardian* campaign could have given a further eight states totalling 130 electoral college votes for Bush. At 485 to 53, the Democratic Party can only pray that next time round no progressive billionaire pays for such an operation.

The short answer to the original question is 'No', Operation Clark County cannot be credited with finding the 118,775 votes for George Bush that got him re-elected. In the event, the entire voting population of Clark County going for John Kerry would not have been enough. But the margin of victory, which encouraged Senator Kerry to concede gracefully on November 3, might not have been there without the efforts of *Guardian* readers. I understand that the local Republican campaign office wrote a letter of thanks to the *Guardian*.

One final question. Did the *Guardian* pay for the copy of the electoral roll, or do the taxpayers of Clark County have to find an extra $25? I hope Mr Katz pays up. It's the least he can do for the 'impoverished' masses of Ohio.

Antoine Clarke's election watch
http://antoineclarke.blogspot.com

✎ 20 December

‹ED› SHUGGY NOTES THAT CHARLES CLARK SPEECH IN THE COMMONS ON THE ID CARD BILL: ‹/ED›

The reassurance of Newspeak

I've been a tad worried about the state of British liberty of late – prompted, I thought, by recent departures by this government from established legal liberal principles such as the right to trial by jury, freedom from arbitrary arrest and detention, and now the proposed introduction of ID cards. I needn't have worried: freedom is slavery and those who advocate 'woolly liberal thinking' are the real enemy, as Melanie Phillips and Charles Clarke have helpfully explained. Take this, for example, from today's *Times**:

> I claim that the ID Cards Bill that I am introducing today is a profoundly civil libertarian measure because it promotes the most fundamental civil liberty in our society, which is the right to live free from crime and fear. Both in practice and in principle ID cards are right. I hope that they will gain wide support throughout our society, and the sooner the better.

So giving citizens the obligation to pay to be monitored by the state is 'civil libertarian'? What a relief; had I known this, I would have supported them earlier. But I was still worried by the detention of terrorist suspects in Belmarsh Prison where, I understand, they have been detained without charge, trial or access to legal representation. Given this mindset, I was inclined to agree with the Law Lords who ruled 8 to 1 that these detentions violated all known principles of human rights. Fortunately, Melanie Phillips is on hand to explain that liberal societies, when under threat are entitled to cease to be liberal, thus preserving freedom – and it's anyone who disagrees with this erudite reasoning that is the real enemy**:

> The human rights culture is actually a mortal enemy of life, liberty and democracy. The Law Lords' judgment is but the latest example.

Phew, these meddling judges really are a menace! Hitherto, I'd imagined that it was countries such as ours with a 'human rights culture' that enjoyed the most liberty. Now I've seen the light: freedom has been most advanced in countries unburdened with this insidious legal sophistry. Only I'm still a bit confused

* www.timesonline.co.uk/article/0,,1072-1409799,00.html
** www.melaniephillips.com/diary/archives/000947.html

because one historical example would be the Soviet Union, where the state was protected from its enemies in much the same way – but, inexplicably, Ms Phillips doesn't like the comparison. Can't think why...

Shuggy's blog
http://modies.blogspot.com

✎ 21 December

‹ED› THE ID CARDS BILL PASSED (AND THEN FAILED AT THE ELECTION TO BE BROUGHT BACK) AND PERRY DE HAVILLAND AT SAMIZDATA ANNOUNCED THAT THIS WAS THE STRAW THAT BROKE THE CAMEL'S BACK: ‹/ED›

For me, Britain died today

Although I knew this day was coming, it is profoundly depressing nevertheless. It is now the law that ID cards will be imposed by force in Britain, with the support of the Leaders of the Conservative Party *and* the Labour Party. They have won and as far as I am concerned, the guttering flame of the culture of liberty in Britain just blew out.

I do not expect a truly repressive state to be implemented for many years yet (hopefully), but the infrastructure of tyranny is now well and truly in place, all of which came to pass with a soundtrack of a faint bleating sound of an indifferent public in the background. You might as well flip a coin to figure out which party will usher it in but a authoritarian panoptic state *is* coming. If this is what the majority of British people want, then may they get exactly what they deserve, but I am out of here. For those of you who will be happy to see me go, trust me, the feeling is mutual.

I realise most people will just shrug their ovine shoulders and find my worries inexplicable, crazy even, as it is not like Blair and Howard are setting up Gulags, right? No, of course not. Who needs those when there is a camera on every corner and your every purchase and phone call will eventually be logged on a central government database? As far as I am concerned, the war is over and my side lost.

I have to try and speed up my business ventures and get out as soon as I can afford to do so. I shall try to be out of Britain and have my primary residence in the USA by 2007 at the latest to avoid being forced to submit to this intolerable imposition... and I shall be taking my wealth-generating assets with me. I cannot say I am looking forward to winters in New Hampshire but I do not really see that I have much choice anymore. I do not see the United States as a paragon of civil liberties (to put it mildly), but at least it is a place in which the battle can be fought within the last bastion of the Anglosphere's culture of liberty.

Damn it.

Samizdata.net
www.samizdata.net/blog

✎ 28 December

‹ED› BLITHERING BUNNY IS AN AUSTRALIAN WHO'S LIVED HERE FOR YEARS. THERE ARE STILL SOME THINGS ABOUT THE COUNTRY HE DOESN'T QUITE GET: ‹/ED›

When I first heard Pink Floyd's song 'Welcome to the Machine', I was puzzled about the lines

> You dreamed of a big star, he played a mean guitar, *He always ate in the Steak Bar*. He loved to drive in his Jaguar.

The Jag – fine. But what was so big shot about eating in a steak bar, I wondered? Eating in a steak bar in Australia was no big deal – was Britain really so poor? Should we be sending them food packages?

A decade or so later on, I arrived in Britain and realized that eating a steak was still a big deal – they cost a fortune (and still do). I'm still not exactly sure why – Britain did turn out to be (relatively) rich after all – but I bet it's something to do with the Common Agricultural Policy.

As a result, someone who was happy enough to eat pub 'counter meals' for the rest of his life suddenly found himself having to start going to posh restaurants just to get a half-decent steak. An Australian academic friend of who came over last year was appalled to see that a good 'counter meal' man had gone all Fancy in the Nancy Isles. I had to explain, with a hint of desperation in my voice, that this was the only way you get get a decent meal here.

The only thing was that you had to learn not to calculate what the bill came to in Australian dollars. Otherwise you started gasping for air. A £50 bill – modest by posh Pommy restaurant standards – multiplied by 2.5 equals 125 bucks, about 5 times what the same quality of meal would cost you in Australia.

Spending a couple of weeks in America brought back memories of what it's like to be able to go into almost any food joint and get a decent – and usually excellent and filling – meal. It doesn't matter how down-to-Earth the place, most likely you'll get a huge hamburger with fries, a large glass of Coke they keep filling up for free, or masses of ribs, giant milkshakes, etc.

This, of course, was a constant reminder of how bad British take-away food is. It really is dog shit. When do you ever come across a British take-away shop staffed by jolly people who really enjoy working with food, and who just love to fill up their customers stomachs with simple but good food? For years I lived on take-away food in Australia. Mrs Bunny just couldn't believe this could be healthy. Now she does. (Sort of – I'm not saying it's as healthy as good home-cooked food, but it's closer than you'd think if you only judged by British standards).

But – clutching at straws – there's one advantage to the British system. There's simply no challenge to getting a good meal in the US or Oz. But in Britain – now there's an operation for you to rise to. Weeks must be spent scouring Good Pub Guides. Reviews must sought out from all manner of obscure publications. Tales from friends must be solicited, and taken into account. Then the booking a week ahead, and finally the 50-minute drive to an isolated country town. The incredible acceleration of the Scorpio on winding country roads, and the subtle roar of the mighty Cosworth engine. Can this little village really be where a top chef works? The holding your breath as you walk in – does it look decent and welcoming, or are there just a few sour locals giving you dirty looks? The 40% failure rate. The happiness when you can take friends there the next time to celebrate the success of the last mission. The shame of realizing how boringly middle-class you've become. Is this really how you get your kicks these days? Drinking extra pints and eating the whole bowl of pork scratchings and feeling like you're 20 again.

Yes, food can be so bad in Britain that one can take a perverse pleasure in just finding a decent place to eat: a pleasure denied us in the Colonies.

Blithering Bunny
www.blitheringbunny.com

‹ED› EVERYONE JUST LOVES CHRISTMAS DON'T THEY? IT'S SO WONDERFUL TO HAVE THE CHILDREN BACK AT HOME, FILLING UP THAT EMPTY NEST. BUT HAVE YOU CONSIDERED WHAT THEY THINK OF THE MATTER? ‹/ED›

Cold turkey

23rd December

9.30pm – Arrive at parents' house. Admire nativity scene in window overlooking front garden, placed there by my mother because 'the Sun says the government is banning them'.

10pm – Admire 'Santa Please Stop Here' sign on the lawn, special holly patterned paper doilies and plastic robin hanging from the window that chirps Jingle Bells when you clap at it. Retire to bed with headache.

24th December

7.30am – Parents let dog into bedroom to wake me up with 'kisses'.

8.15am – Pick all the 'Strawberry Delights' from the Quality Street for breakfast.

12.30am – Walk to shop for paper. Write 'bum' in the frost on every car on the way there.

5pm – Go for walk around village with parents in the bitter cold to admire neighbour's ten-foot light-up Santa and sleigh.

6–9pm – Dodge requests for pictures of me by the tree.

11pm – Lose twenty quid and a box of chocolate liqueurs to my father at poker.

25th December

6.30am – Am woken by father outside my door singing 'Frosty The Snowman'. Swear and go back to sleep.

6.45am – Am woken by father outside my door singing 'When Santa Got Stuck Up The Chimney'. Place pillow over head and go back to sleep.

7am – Am woken by father outside my door singing 'When Grandma Got Run Over By A Reindeer'.

7.01am – Get up. Greeted in living room by my mother in 'Mrs Claus' outfit and flashing red nose. Drink three glasses of my father's 'special punch'.

7.15am – Open presents. Where do you even *buy* a handmade reindeer garter belt?

7.30am – Retire to bedroom to watch Radiohead DVDs bought for self.

10am – Start feeling a bit unhinged. Come out to ask if it's time for dinner yet. It isn't.

12.00 noon – Father rolls in drunk on cherry brandy from the Dymchurch British Legion Christmas lunchtime quiz. Now it is.

4pm – Realise have been inadvertently wearing plastic moustache from cracker at dinner for four hours.

5pm – Begin Star Trek film-watching marathon.

11.30pm – Conclude Star Trek film-watching marathon when Spock starts to look quite attractive.

26th December

10–12 midnight – Eat cheese footballs.

27th December

7am – Am woken up in order to 'beat the crowds at the sales'.

8am – Arrive at sales. Nowhere yet open.

10am – Spend gift vouchers on gin and pornography.

4pm – Arrive back in London. Kiss the ground.

greenfairydotcom
www.greenfairy.com

JANUARY 2005

✎ 5 January

<ED> BLOGS ARE OFTEN USED BY
PROFESSIONALS IN THE MEDIA TO POP OUT
LITTLE ITEMS THAT ARE TOO TRIVIAL FOR
THEIR PAID JOBS AT THE MAJOR OUTLETS AND
SOMETIMES, AS IN THIS CASE, FOR ITEMS THAT
IT WOULD NOT BE POLITIC TO MENTION: </ED>

Do you believe in astrology?

Reviewing the papers on the wireless the other night, I was looking forward to
getting stuck into the day's horoscope specials – especially Jonathan Cainer's
in the *Daily Mail*, where (to much TV ad trumpeting) he was claiming that the
discovery of another planet in our solar system last year means our lives will
change from here on in.

That claim summed up the utter fuckwittery of horoscopes. It implied that either
(1) all horoscopes prior to that were totally wrong because they knew nothing of
the planet, which seems a remarkably damning thing for a horoscope writer to say
about his industry, and life's work, or (2) that Cainer was, by divining our destiny,
also dictating it, because the planet could not exert any influence on our lives
without him first being aware of its existance.

But then trying to apply logic to horoscopes is a bit like scientifically testing a
medieval poultice: the whole thing's going to fall apart pretty quickly, and it's
hardly a newsflash when it does. If we're going to insist on sub-dividing all
humanity into one of a handy few personality types, each with an easily recalled
character and destiny, count me in for Jung/Myers-Briggs ahead of Russell Grant.

Anyway – insomniac London never got its sleep disorders cured by my witty,
detailed and irrefutable dismantling of the superstitious twaddle, mainly because
there were better things to talk about (like – er – real news in south east Asia) and
the fact the guest on before me was... an astrologer, doing phone-in predictions
for lucky listeners' years ahead. I kept quiet. Know your audience, and all that.

So, it's a great joy to see Lucy Mangan doing a substantially better job of dismantling
it in today's paper, and with proper sweary words too, for added effect.*

* www.guardian.co.uk/g2/story/0,3604,1383330,00.html

Mangan's (ex) friend: 'I'm a typical Pisces and my mum's a typical Leo.'

> Mangan: You're a fatuous insult to the species. You should be stripped
> and burned at the stake of commonsense. I will stoke the fires with Jonathan
> Cainer horoscopes ripped untimely from the Daily Mail, and as the flames
> lick ever higher, I will suck the smell of grilled moron greedily down into
> my lungs.

Wonderful stuff. No smiley.

Complete Tosh
www.completetosh.com

✎ 6 January

‹ED› JERRY SPRINGER, THE OPERA: THE
COMPLAINTS OVER ITS AIRING ON THE BEEB
AND THE ACTIONS OF CHRISTIAN VOICE (THEY
INSPIRED A GOOGLEBOMB; A SEARCH FOR
'IGNORANT BIGOTS' WOULD TAKE YOU TO
THEIR SITE) ALL POPPED UP IN JANUARY.
INSERT JOKE HERE PICKED UP ON PART OF
THE MEDIA COVERAGE: ‹/ED›

Reality nicks my punchline

Well, there you go – they're beyond parody.

This was going to be a short post – a link and a joke. The link was to be Tim's*
excellent post on the Sun's latest deranged effort that takes the BBC to task for
showing Jerry Springer: The Opera, which they claimed features 3,168 instances of
the word 'fuck', and 297 'cunts'. The joke, such as it was, was that perhaps – given
the pretty much indefensible claim of 8,000 swearwords in a two hour show – our
stalwart moral guardians were using the following logic: it's a musical, there's a
50-strong chorus, and every time that chorus swears in a song, BAM! 50 counts
right there. Five instances of that and you're well on the way to the figure of 297.

Well fuck me a bus, but that's only what they've gone and done – completely
undercutting my lame-ass gag in the process, the rotten gits. In the comments at

*http://www.bloggerheads.com/archives/2005/01/jerry_springer.asp

Bloggerheads, Justin quotes the *Daily Mail* (and reading the full article, I swear there's a slight air of embarrassment in those final few lines, as though – surely not! – they'd committed to the 8,000 figure without checking it and are now feeling slightly daft as they tack such a weak explanation on the end):

> The total number of obscenities is calculated by multiplying the number of swear-words by the number of people singing them.

No, seriously. What planet are we on again? I swear it's a little game Murdoch and his ilk like to play called 'Make the Lefties' Heads Pop' – winner is the one who can get the most liberal bloggers to link to a completely outrageous article with cries of '*Can you fucking believe this??*'

Insert Joke Here
http://insertjokehere.blogspot.com

✎ 7 January

‹ED› BLOGNOR REGIS ON HOW DIFFICULT IT CAN BE TO RELATE TO TRAGEDIES SUCH AS THE TSUNAMI: ‹/ED›

Human face on tragedy

I'd read through the *Harry's Place* discussion on dreadful sitcoms earlier this evening which couldn't have helped, but still, I was more than a little shocked when the headline 'Sally Gleeson police find body' popped up in my XML reader.

A hurried click and a read later, I discover that it's a different Sally Gleeson. However, now I'm overcome with guilt that I was only really interested in this unfortunate woman's fate because she shared her name with an actress who was in a sitcom thirty years back.

I felt similarly dirty when I first heard about the Dunblane shootings. I was a passenger with three others in a car heading down the M5 all chatting away when it came on the Radio One news. The sound level was a bit low but I heard something about '14 people having been killed' and in my mind I dismissed it as being in Yugoslavia or Israel, you know, where these sort of things happen, a bit sad but, hey, life goes on, shrug. Then I heard it was in Scotland. Scotland? 'Oi, turn that up quick.'

Why should 14 children being killed in Scotland be of greater significance than their equivalents in other lands? Why act differently depending on who the victims are? I've discussed this with others before now and they've come to the same conclusion; it shouldn't but it does, it's human nature.

Which brings us to ones response to the tsunami.

Assistant Blog puts the intellectual argument very well in this post:*

> Like everyone else, I've watched so much news in the last few weeks that I'm finding it difficult to keep watching. But I had to give up on regional news a day or two in, it's instance on parochial angles, 'human interest' stories near-nauseating. Part of me realises that if there are 200 Brits in danger that makes 400 horrified parents, countless children, friends and colleagues who need to know more, and I appreciate that that will always be the case. But it is sickening to see that headline, whenever it appears – 'massive earthquake in India, 4 British feared dead'.

Likewise Brian Micklethwait puts the case for emotion:**

> Call me shallow and Dianaficated – and knowing our commentariat I am sure several will – but this catastrophe only really impinged upon my feelings, as opposed to my numbed and astonished brain, when I learned that Lord Attenborough had lost his fourteen year old grand-daughter.

The list of British confirmed killed in the disaster and this report of two dead from a village up the road a way brings, to me anyway, a recognisable human face to a disaster suffered on such an unimaginable scale.

Although it pains me greatly to say it, Stalin was correct (*one death is a tragedy, a million is a statistic*) and perhaps we have a need to understand the experiences of a few individuals before we are able to scale upwards and take in the full magnitude of the overall catastrophe. I'm not sure it's possible to do it the other way. In such cases you have to look at the trees to be able to see the wood.

Blognor Regis
http://blognorregis.blogspot.com

✎ 8 January

‹ED› THE LAW WEST OF EALING BROADWAY IS WRITTEN BY A MAGISTRATE IN, UMM, WEST LONDON. HE IS NOT OVERLY ENAMOURED OF THE ADMINISTRATION OF THE COURTS: ‹/ED›

Pissups and breweries

Once upon a time, every town of any size had a magistrates' court. They had a Clerk to the Justices who has been described as a cross between a butler and a family solicitor. Local people dealt with local malefactors.

Then efficiency beckoned. Courts were amalgamated, so that in rural areas users might have to drive 40 miles each way to court. So did police and lawyers and Council Social Workers, and all the rest of them, so the costs saved by amalgamating courts were passed to other agencies and to the public.

London was expensively reorganised under the Greater London Magistrates' Courts Authority (snappy, eh?). The GLMCA planned to close and flog off some courthouses, and use the cash to build whizzy new ones. Every single closure was vetoed by one means or another leaving the grand plan wrecked. It didn't matter though, because a couple of years into the GLMCA's life it was decided to set up Her Majesty's Court Service (well, at least they didn't call it Consignia) and the GLMCA will die unlamented on 31 March 2005.

Nearly all of the people in the system expect the new setup to be at least as useless as the GLMCA. But by the time this becomes apparent, the perpetrators will have collected their gongs and their pensions and retired.

The boss of HMCS is a former male nurse.

The Law West of Ealing Broadway
http://thelawwestofealingbroadway.blogspot.com

✎ 13 January

‹ED› PRINCE HARRY GOES TO A PARTY DRESSED IN A NAZI UNIFORM AND ONE WOULD ALMOST THINK THE WORLD HAD ENDED. PD BERGER, AN ENGLISHMAN IN NEW YORK, RATHER CALMS THINGS DOWN: ‹/ED›

Harry the nazi

So there I was, minding my own business over breakfast, when I hear on the BBC World Service that Prince Harry is being lambasted for going to a fancy dress party dressed as a Nazi. And I thought, surely people can't be so offended. I mean isn't Mel Brooks' comedy *The Producers* based on making fun of the Nazis? And aren't there people in the world like Le Pen and idiots who deface Jewish gravestones that we ought to be far more critical of?

I still remember the swastika daubed on the outer wall of the prayer house in the Jewish section of Harehills cemetery in Leeds, where my grandparents are buried. I remember looking at it as we walked inside to pray. I also remember the group of teenage thugs who stood a few hundred feet away, watching the funeral, and I remember thinking that it was probably one of them who defaced the prayer house. I remember all I was taught in school and synagogue about the Holocaust, all the documentaries, films and books. Most vividly though, I remember meeting the survivors and their children (and their children's children) and thinking what terrible consequences it wrought.

But Prince Harry dressing up as a Nazi did not bother me at all. And I wondered how many other people really cared. Those who are speaking out – the leaders of the Jewish community, the Jewish leader of the Opposition (that's the Tory party and Michael Howard for the millions of Brits who still don't know) and the countless non-Jewish great and the good – have no choice but to firmly condemn him, of course. And yes, there will be some who will be offended. After all, thousands were offended by the screening of *Jerry Springer, The Opera* on the BBC. But really, truly. When the world seems such a hideous and cruel place as it does right now, does it matter what a 20-year-old prince wears to a fancy dress party? Or is the hysteria just being played out because British newspapers have nothing better to do than launch a new witch hunt every couple of weeks (Blunket, Brown v Blair, Harry) while the rest of us worry about Asia, Iraq, Darfur, Africa, and Aids?

Englishman in New York
http://pdberger.com

<ED> YOU CAN TAKE THE BRITON OUT OF BRITAIN BUT IT APPEARS TO BE RATHER MORE DIFFICULT TO TAKE THE BRITAIN OUT OF THE BRITON. BLOGGING IN FROM NEW ZEALAND, NICE MONGOOSE TELLS US: </ED>

My baby boy Benjamin has just had his 3 month old birthday, which is nice. It's an important stepping stone for a baby, it means that lots of bad things that might happen to you if you are not a perfect baby are unlikely to happen now. Kinda like saying he's clear of the woods.

I did realise though that there is something wrong with him. Something that no matter what I do I cannot cure. He's a Kiwi, not English. He'll miss out on so many things in his life.

Things like being obstinate, having a real proper Queen (not one forced on you – it's not the same). He'll never truly appreciate tea, or decent beer, he'll drink pissy flavourless lager. All Australasian beer is rubbish – it's fizzy water with a dash of raw spirit and some E numbers (I'm not bitter (snigger)). He'll never wear a hankie on his head on a rocky beach in the cold. He'll never find war museums interesting or build airfix kits. He won't get Wallace & Gromit. He'll never have a school dinner (or though, gauging from that J. Oliver show, the kids eat shit now not mince & onions and cabbage). He won't experience the pure joy of waking up on Xmas day with the knowledge that it's too fucking cold outside to do anything other than sit in front of the telly drinking and eating and doing nothing (Xmas is demanding in the sun, you have to go to beaches or around to people's decks, etc).

He'll speak a decibel too loud, he'll sound like he's asking questions the whole time. He'll be far too interested in muscly men chasing a stuffed pig arse to cheek around a field 'for my liking'. He'll have even less choice in politics. He'll play outside in the fresh air when he should be inside playstationing and getting asthma. He'll eat real food – meat raised in fields on grass. Vegetables with flavour. He'll have the right number of digits on each hand and perfect little toes – no nuclear power here. He'll learn to swim in the sea – with no turd in it. He'll not have the pallid english complexion (though he'll have to take out shares in sun cream to avoid cancer). When he goes to scouts he won't be getting badges for picking up shitty litter and hypodermics from his local rat-infested park, he'll be learning to sail.

Poor little bastard is going to be a Kiwi. Well there is one saving grace.

At least he won't be Australian.

Nicemongoose
http://www.livejournal.com/users/nicemongoose

✎ 20 January

‹ED› SHOULD WE HAVE 24-HOUR DRINKING? APPARENTLY THE RESTRICTIONS THEMSELVES WERE THE ERROR: ‹/ED›

Bishop opposes restrictions on drinking

I know that I have been having a pop at religion over the past few days but even I have to admit that sometimes religious leaders say some sensible things.

In today's *Guardian*, David McKie quotes the 19th century Bishop Magee of Peterborough, opposing the impending legislation to restrict drinking:

| Better England free than England sober.

Now there's a man after my own heart. I reckon he would support the return to 24-hour drinking.

Pub Philosopher
http://pubphilosopher.blogs.com

✎ 22 January

‹ED› BLACK TRIANGLE ON THE LATEST MEDICAL MIRACLE FROM NORTH KOREA: ‹/ED›

Korean radioactive quack cures

Deep in the bowels of an extinct volcano, the glorious father of the Korean nation Kim Jong Il sits watching a selection of his world famous collection of Daffy Duck cartoons. Surrounded by his elite female '*pleasure squad*' unit, he sips his Hennessy V.S.O.P, wondering whether he should order a fluffy white cat to stroke, and muses if Castro has returned his copy of *The Godfather*.

His magnificent thoughts are interrupted by a goosestepping officer entering the room, and a sharp click of heels on the marble floor.

'Glorious leader, we have a problem.'

'What?' Kim Jong Il mentally notes down the name of the officer for execution, problems in North Korea? As if.

'We have a surplus of radioactive materials, which we need to dispose of. It is only low-grade and of no use to our weapons programme, but it is becoming a storage problem.'

Only the other day Kim Jong Il had heard of a large consignment of gloss paint produced by a forced labour camp near the Chinese border. For months the camp had produced revolutionary red, only to find it was not of the exact shade required by the state. Kim Jong Il was inspired.

'Put the waste in the surplus paint we have.'

'Yes glorious leader. Only a leader of high intellect and courage could formulate such a wonderful idea. What shall we do with this mixture then?'

'It will be the latest in medical treatments, I dictate it to be so. We shall paint this on our sick, in our hospitals and bathing houses. We will lead the world in high-tech radioactive medicine. Now leave me to my revolutionary work.'

A click of the heels later, the officer turns and leaves. The theme tune of Looney Tunes fills the room as he leaves.

Or so it seems...*

Long-Wave Infrared Ray Radiation Paint Developed

Pyongyang, January 7 (KCNA) – The Building-materials Institute under the Paektusan Architectural Center of the Democratic People's Republic of Korea has succeeded in developing long-wave infrared ray radiation paint efficacious for the treatment of diseases. In an interview with KCNA, director of the institute Ri Tok Ho said the clinical test proves that the paint, made of natural mineral powder and various nontoxic substances abundant in the country, gives no harmful effect to the human body.

It is good for the recovery from fatigue, treatment of diseases and saving of heat energy. It can be coated on concrete wall, wood, iron sheets and stone

*www.kcna.co.jp/item/2005/200501/news01/08.htm

materials including interior walls of steam bathhouse, physical treatment room and drying room and the floor for heating.

The serviceable life of the painting is five years at minimum. The wave band of long-wave infrared ray radiated by the painting is 8–12 micrometers and its radiation rate is 93–95 percent.

The long-wave infrared rays help the sauna bathers perspire without feeling heart suffocation and breathing trouble even under the temperature above 100 degrees centigrade. It, therefore, is potent for the cure of heart diseases, neuralgia, skin disorders, circulatory sicknesses, women's troubles such as postpartum diseases, sterility and disorders of menstruation, waist pains, bone fracture and other diseases.

Its production cost is very low as it is simple to make.

The West has had its own unfortunate attempts at using Radium as a quack cure, but nice to see that North Korea has finally caught up with 1920s America...*

Byers was the founder of the A.M. Byers Company, one of the world's largest steel companies. In 1928, the Pittsburgh industrialist and one-time U.S. amateur golf champion (1906) injured himself on a party train following a Harvard-Yale football game. At the recommendation of his doctor, he began drinking Radithor, and he continued to do so long after the injury healed – he averaged three bottles a day for two years. Byers stopped consuming Radithor in 1930 when his teeth started falling out and holes appeared in his skull. Perhaps more than anything else, his death in 1932 alerted the public, and much of the medical profession, of the harmful effects of 'mild' radium therapy.

Black triangle
http://www.blacktriangle.org

---

*www.orau.org/ptp/collection/quackcures/radith.htm

✎ 24 January

‹ED. YEAR ON YEAR THE PRIZE SEASON COMES
ROUND AND SOME, IN THIS CASE CONCERNING
THE MAN BOOKER PRIZE, ARE NOT CONVINCED
IT IS ALL A GOOD IDEA. GRUMPY OLD BOOKMAN
EXPLAINS: ‹/ED›

The Booker Prize and absolute nonsense

Companies that sponsor prizes do so chiefly, I suspect, to obtain cheap publicity. And in that regard the Man Booker company, sponsors of the (Man) Booker Prize for fiction, do better than most.

Last week, for instance, there were masses of stories […] just about the choice of a chairman for the judges, and whether the judges will actually read the whole of each book or not.

But that is not what I want to witter on about today. No, what I thought I would do is draw your attention to the merciless winner-take-all mechanism which accompanies this annual jamboree.

When you and I are faced with a book, and asked to say whether it is a masterpiece or an overblown piece of self-indulgent nonsense, there is no universally recognised scale against which we can measure the book and come to a clear conclusion. Judging a book is a matter of taste and sensibility, and you are likely to maintain that your taste and sensibility are superior to mine. (You are probably right, since my taste is notoriously vulgar.)

As far as the Booker Prize is concerned, it is safe to say that the choice of the 'best' book of the year is inevitably a matter of opinion rather than fact. And not even unanimous opinion. In almost every year there are press reports of disagreements among the judges, and in some years we hear of 'compromise choices' or the chairman's casting vote. We also know that, in one particular case, the eventual winner was unusually 'fortunate'.

In 2002 the winner of the Booker Prize was *Life of Pi* by Yann Martel. Many newspaper reports at the time told us that this book had been rejected by Faber, the firm which had published Martel's earlier work; the book had also been turned down by at least five other major publishers. So if Canongate had not taken the book, it is likely that the manuscript would have remained in the author's filing cabinet. Furthermore, if the book had been accepted by one of the bigger firms, it would not even have been entered for the Booker Prize in the first place, because the big firms (only allowed two nominations) have to enter their most famous authors; if they don't, the famous authors are likely to go elsewhere.

The *Life of Pi* saga provides a beautifully clear demonstration of the random nature of decision-making in publishing. Here we have a book which was turned down for publication by numerous 'good judges'. It was entered for the Booker Prize by a small firm which had no stronger candidates. And it so happened that the particular set of judges who were reading in 2002 happened to like it best. Or a majority of them did.

All rational observers will agree that *Life of Pi*, or any other Booker winner, cannot sensibly be described as the best book of the year in any absolute sense. *The Life of Pi* episode shows us, undeniably, that there might have been other books that year which were either not published at all or were published by big firms which were not able to submit them – books which could, quite possibly, have found favour with the judges if they had been submitted. The most that can be said of the book which wins the Booker Prize is that it is the one which (of those presented for consideration) the judges liked the best.

But observe, please, what happens when the winner of the Booker Prize is announced (in any year). What happens is that the media, the critics, and the public, all behave as if there *is* some *absolute* sense in which the winner is the best book of the year. They act as if the book has been held up against a ruler, a universally agreed scale, and has been found, indisputably, and scientifically, to be 'better' than any other.

A couple of weeks ago, for instance, I was given a copy of the *New York Review of Books*, in which there was a lengthy review of the most recent Booker winner; the article runs to 108 column inches. Similar things no doubt happen every year. And this 'star treatment' will be repeated in newspapers and magazines throughout the English-speaking world.

It is the winning novel, please note, which is treated in this way – not the runners-up; and certainly not the good books which were not submitted by their publishers; and definitely not the books which didn't even make it into print. It is the winning author who will be interviewed on television, invited to writers' conferences, and made the subject, in due course, of earnest PhD theses by bespectacled young people who can think of nothing better to do with their time than waste it by deconstructing a novelist's prose. This is the winner-take-all mechanism in its most unforgiving form.

The runners-up, the non-shortlisted books, and the unpublished books, all those are losers who disappear from our sight, never to be heard of again. And yet we know, beyond doubt, that but for the workings of randomness, which favoured the winner and disfavoured the others, there might be one, ten, or a hundred other books which could, in different circumstances, have proved to be more enticing to the judges than did the eventual winner.

The winner-take-all mechanism in the book world is thus shown to be brutal, vicious, and deadly.

There is no point in complaining about it: it is just the way things happen; the world in general, and the book trade in particular, is unfair, unjust, and patently absurd in its workings. But all those who work in the book trade, in particular those who write and sell novels, need to be aware of this situation. And they need to ask themselves whether a business in which randomness is so powerful a factor in the distribution of rewards is a business which sensible people should allow themselves to be involved in.

Grumpy Old Bookman
http://grumpyoldbookman.blogspot.com

✎ 27 January

‹ED› HOLOCAUST MEMORIAL DAY AND ONE OF THE PARTICIPANTS AT THE CEREMONIES IN LONDON IS THE WRITER OF NAKED BLOG: ‹/ED›

Arbeit macht frei

And so it passes, time passes, the hour passes, and sixty years also pass. It was good the old people turned up, here in London, to mark the holocaust liberation. Lord Winston the Jew with his fertility treatments put to one side. Stephen Fry the half-Jew we never knew but with that name we maybe should have guessed. The 'hommosexual' as the gay half-Jew said the word. The gypsy violinist showing us once again what that great instrument can do, not always for the Germans, but for the folk people too. The other Queen, the real Queen, still smarting from her grandson's greatest error of his life – past, present and future. But her grandfather never did learn how to speak English, das glaub Ich und das weiss Ich. The black man in the wheelchair – telling us how he wouldn't have been let to live. And the Prime Minister acting tears in his voice so desperate for re-election.

The Queen, the queen, the politician and the doctor. The guilt is in all of us, as the other great Jew of my life, Yehudi Menuhin, said when he played the violin in Berlin after the war. Who among us can hold his hand on his heart and say that he would never do the same? Ever, no matter what the circumstance?

Mary in the pub tonight said that even people ten years younger than her (she's in her sixties), couldn't fully grasp the enormity or understand. I think she meant me. Becky the barmaid of eighteen said *Schindler's List* told people all about it. I told her Spielberg is a Jew making a fortune from his own people's horror. She looked surprised.

A few days ago I talked about DVDs in an HMV store. What I didn't mention then is a French film called *Nuit et Brouillard* ('Night and fog'), which I haven't set eyes on for thirty years. Made twenty years before that, in 1955, it's the bleakest and most searing depiction of the horror, made whilst still so fresh in the film maker's mind.

You should never watch this film, for if you do you'll see yourself in a whole new light. Because the horror is in all of us – in you, not just in 'them' – waiting to choose its moment, its charismatic leader and its identifiable victims.

In the eighties my own people suffered a second holocaust – a viral pandemic. Many perished. **But** all were put at risk of the gas ovens, courtesy of the British press, with the people baying again for our poisoned blood. Semper vigilans. We are deeply flawed.

Naked Blog
www.nakedblog.com

✎ 29 January

⟨ED⟩ CHARLES CLARKE DECIDED TO ABOLISH
ONE OF THE BASIC FREEDOMS THAT WE HAD
HITHERTO ENJOYED, NOT BEING LOCKED UP
WITHOUT BEING CHARGED WITH SOMETHING IN
FRONT OF A JUDGE. STUMBLING AND MUMBLING
HAD SOMETHING TO SAY ABOUT IT: ⟨/ED⟩

Destroying freedom

I don't normally like 'me too' blogging, but proposals to impose control orders on potential terrorists are so contemptible that I should add my puny voice to those of Simon Jenkins, Civitas, Samizdata, Blimpish and Laban Tall.

Here are my observations.

1. Don't think these proposals will only apply to a handful of people. Laban Tall draws attention to this chilling claim, in the *Scotsman:**

    > Speaking after the Home Secretary, Charles Clarke, announced new laws to control the movements of terrorist suspects, Mr Clarke's adviser, Stephen McCabe, told The Scotsman he saw this extending to other groups suspected of using violence to further their ends. The Labour MP said: 'We can envisage this applying to animal rights extremists and the far-Right, for example.'

    For example?

2. Charles Clarke says potential terrorists can't always be prosecuted because 'it isn't always possible to bring charges given the need to protect highly sensitive sources and techniques.' But what exactly is the danger here? MI5 agents can give evidence in court in secret. And surely, in gathering evidence in the first place they are putting themselves in danger. Or am I missing something? Could it be that health and safety culture is infecting the security services?

3. Mr Clarke says: 'There are serious people and serious organizations trying to destroy our soceity. We are in a state of emergency.' What? Against the BNP or animal rights activists? And just how great is the threat from Al Qaeda? Is it really greater than that posed during the cold war or by the IRA during the 1970s, neither of which justified suspending habeas corpus? I'll grant that Al

*http://news.scotsman.com/index.cfm?id=98972005

Qaeda want to kill thousands of us. But this does not amount to destroying our society. Al Qaeda cannot do that. Only we can.

4. Could it be that what the government is truly scared of here isn't just the threat of a terrorist outrage, but the chaos that surrounds it? Part of New Labour's managerialist ideology is a terror of disorder, of not being in control. Could it be this that makes it so more sensitive to the danger of Islamic terrorists than previous governments were to IRA terrorists or the Soviet Union?

5. Even if we accept that there's a need to intern people, why should it be the Home Secretary that has these powers? Why not judges?

6. Charles Clarke asks us to trust the government to use these powers sensitively and sparingly. But if we could trust each other, we wouldn't need government in the first place. And surely, there is no proposition for which there is more historical evidence than that we shouldn't trust governments. And should we really believe that these people are to be trusted to make sensitive and delicate decisions about the balance between 'national security' and civil liberties?

Yes. There is a small group of vicious men who are trying to destroy our most valued western traditions – it's called the government.

Stumbling and Mumbling
http://stumblingandmumbling.typepad.com

✎ 31 January

‹ED› BILL O'REILLY, AN AMERICAN TV SHOW HOST, WAS FOUND TO HAVE BEEN DISCUSSING MATTERS SEXUAL, HIS DESIRES AND THE LIKE, INVOLVING THE STRATEGIC PLACEMENT OF A LOOFAH IT IS BELIEVED, WITH ONE OF HIS FEMALE CO-WORKERS. HARRY HUTTON ENLIGHTENED US ON THE BASIC PROBLEM: ‹/ED›

Non-kinky sex is a waste of time

They are still laughing at poor old 'Falafel' Bill O'Reilly. I would like to record the fact that my opinion of Bill O'Reilly has gone up since this scandal, on the grounds that non-kinky sex is a waste of time. Anyway, what is so 'scandalous' about a newsreader forcing a vibrator up his foxhole? It is just another way of spending one's afternoon off. (There are no atheists in foxholes.)

The only civilized reaction to this type of thing is a patient shrug. Every adult must at some point have paused during some slapstick piece of debauchery and thought, 'Christ, this is *ridiculous*'. Having testicles is like being chained to the village idiot; sad, but there it is. And when we have solved every racial, political and economic problem, we will still be stuck with that one.

Chase me, ladies, I'm in the cavalry
http://chasemeladies.blogspot.com

FEBRUARY 2005

✎ 6 February

‹ED› THE US SUPER BOWL PROVIDES BLOGJAM WITH AN OPPORTUNITY FOR SOME PRIME SNARK: ‹/ED›

Extremely super

I love the Super Bowl. This time last year I was reporting live on Janet Jackson's breast expose, and this year's show has started in equally priceless fashion – Alicia Keys dueting with dead genius/junkie/philanderer Ray Charles, with backing vocals provided by several dozen special needs children, the camera lingering awkwardly on their hopeful, bewildered, innocent faces. The song? 'America The Beautiful'. Given US television's obsession with physical perfection, it's a freakishly brave move by the network – mawkish, cloying televisual slop at its very finest. Add to the mix New England quarterback Tom Brady, whose grandmother died at a nursing home superbowl party this week, and we could be heading for the most schmaltz-ridden sporting event in history. And just think, Paul McCartney is still to come at half-time...

Blogjam
www.blogjam.com

✎ 10 February

‹ED› THE ROYAL WEDDING, THE EVENT, SO FAR, OF THE YEAR. PERHAPS, AS MUGGED BY REALITY TELLS US: ‹/ED›

Embarrassing, irrelevant, inbred, half-witted Greco-Germanic anachronism to wed hideous, overprivileged, idle-rich moose

The first consciously political gesture I ever made was in 1977 when, shortly after buying a copy of God Save the Queen by the Sex Pistols, I proceeded to slap the SWP's [Social Worker's Party] *Stuff the Jubilee* stickers all over my school – an act which prompted an angry morning assembly concerning 'the tiny handful of misguided fanatics' who wanted to spoil the nation's celebrations.

In 1981, on the day that Charles and Diana married, a friend of mine threw a huge house party so that we would have somewhere to escape to. I can clearly recall helping to man-handle the TV into the loft so that no one would be tempted to switch the damn thing on and pollute the waters of our little oasis of royalty free sanity.

When Diana was wrapped around a pillar in a Parisian tunnel in August 1997 I had just come to the end of a month of working double shifts, seven days a week at Royal Mail in Sheffield and actually slept through most of the ensuing pantomime.

On the eve of the Queen Mother's funeral in April 2002 I was drunk and watching the evening news, vainly waiting to see if anything else had happened that day. On came an interview with some forelock-tugging simpleton who, in order to beat the crowds and get a good view of the funeral procession, had camped en route with only a sleeping bag and a framed portrait of the brown toothed old witch to keep out the chill. The temptation to jump in my car, drive down to London and kick the pathetic fucker unconscious was almost too much to resist.

Later that year I would find myself glued to the TV, mouth agape with disgusted incredulity, as Ben Elton, a once respected figurehead of the revolution, bowed and scraped his way through hosting the Golden Jubilee concert at Buckingham Palace.

As the title of this blog probably suggests, my radical leftist ardour has long since cooled. However, there is one arena in which the fire still burns as fiercely as it ever did, one arena in which I believe the Bolsheviks got it *exactly* right.

And that is where it concerns how to deal with royal parasites [*with a link to a picture of the execution of the last Tsar... Ed*]*

Mugged by Reality
http://mugged-by-reality.blogspot.com

---

* http://www.click2history.com/stories/death_tsar/images/scene.jpg

✎ 14 February

‹ED› IN THE CASE OF THE TERRORIST SUSPECTS HELD IN BELMARSH, THE LAW LORDS DECIDED THAT NO, IT WAS NOT OK FOR PEOPLE TO BE HELD INDEFINITELY WITHOUT TRIAL AND SPECIFICALLY THAT AS THAT COULD NOT BE DONE TO UK CITIZENS IT COULD NOT BE DONE TO NON-UK CITIZENS WITHIN OUR SHORES. AS WE KNOW, CHARLES CLARKE WENT ON TO SUGGEST THAT THE SOLUTION WOULD BE THE ABOLITION OF HABEAS CORPUS, ALLOWING ALL AND EVERYONE TO BE HELD INDEFINITELY WITHOUT TRIAL... IN DIRECT CONTRAVENTION OF THE ADVICE FROM TONY HATFIELD: ‹/ED›

Advice to Charles

While Charles Clarke is deciding how to respond to the law lords' ruling, can I suggest he digs out Robert Bolt's play *A Man for All Seasons*? Specifically the scene in which Sir Thomas More finds out that Richard Rich, his protégé, is going to betray him. More's daughter, Margaret Roper, and son in law urge him to have Rich arrested.

> 'Father,' says Margaret, 'that man is bad.'

> 'There is no law against that', More replies. And continues: 'The law, Roper, the law. I know what's legal, not what's right. And I'll stick to what's legal.' Meanwhile, Richard Rich has scarpered. 'And go he should,' says More 'if he was the devil himself until he broke the law'. But Roper protests. 'He would cut a great road through the law to get after the Devil.'

> More replies. 'And when the last law was down, and the Devil turned round on you – where would you hide, Roper, the laws all being flat? This country's planted thick with laws from coast to coast, and if you cut them down do you really think you could stand upright in the winds that would blow then?'

Tony Hatfield's retired ramblings
http://tonyhatfield.blogspot.com

<ED> ONE OF THE ADDITIONS TO THE ELECTION CAMPAIGN – IT HAD NOT STARTED FORMALLY AT THIS POINT BUT EVERYONE KNEW IT WAS COMING – WAS BACKING BLAIR. THE NAME IS IRONIC, OF COURSE, FOR THEIR AIM WAS ANYONE BUT BLAIR. THEY LAID OUT THEIR REASONS THUSLY: </ED>

The Tories are terrorists!

We would first like to refer you to our Frequently Asked Questions list which begins as follows:

What exactly is it that you want from me?

We want you to register to vote. Then, when the election comes around, we want people who live in 'safe' Labour seats or marginal ones to vote for the candidate most likely to beat the Labour candidate. Not the anti-war-person, or the seems-like-a-nice-person, but the candidate most likely to beat the Labour candidate.

You'll note the Tories aren't mentioned in the core aim, but the negative charge most often levelled against this site is that we're all about getting people to vote Tory. In fact, there are a few people out there who are well and truly freaked out about that:

To paraphrase Marcellus Wallace; 'That's fear f*cking with you. F*ck fear. Fear only hurts, it never helps.'

We'll try to come up with a better quote later in the piece. In the meantime, we'd like to point out that there are a number of parallels between the Tories and terrorists, in that Blair has been using our fear of both to stay in power and get away with all kinds of things the public would never tolerate without the presence of a serious bogey-man. Or two.

Remember September 11th = Remember Margaret Thatcher

Dark times. Spectacularly dark times for many. But you can't let it blind you to the reality of the actual current threat, which in both cases is not as pronounced or as immediate as Blair would have you believe.

Blair: back me or the terrorists win = Blair: back me or the Tories win

Blair has used both arguments to convince the electorate and members of his own party to back and/or tolerate all sorts of things that actually work towards the aims of both. In the case of terrorists, Blair has the whole country running scared over phantom threats. Our logistical and political support for the US has actually sparked terrorist activity in Iraq (where previously there was none). The terrorists hardly need lift a finger. In the case of the Tories, Blair is adopting/hijacking all sorts of Tory policies in order to edge them out of the game. The Tories also hardly need lift a finger.

You're supporting the terrorists! = You're supporting the Tories!

This ends all sorts of debates. Just trying to get folks to consider the motivation(s) of terrorists brings you dangerously close to the use of empathy (*gasp*). For some people, empathy and sympathy are the same thing, especially when fear and outrage are involved. This is where the parallels are not exact, but the linear pattern in very similar. In the case of the Tories, we have asked people who live in 'safe' Labour seats or marginal ones to vote for the candidate most likely to beat the Labour candidate. For some people this involves voting Lib-Dem, SNP, Plaid Cymru, etc. – but for others this involves voting Tory. Fear and outrage turns the focus on this one single aspect and turns our strategic (and quite reluctant) use of some Tory candidates into outright support for the Tory party.

But what if terrorists attack? = But what if the Tories win?

And what are you willing to give up to stop this happening? Do you want to be unable to get permission to fart without an ID card? Are you willing to risk detention without trial? Lord Hoffmann said it best; 'The real threat to the life of the nation… comes not from terrorism but from laws such as these.'

Refuse to stand up to Blair and we sleepwalk into a police state. Refuse to stand up to Blair and we continue with a de-facto Tory government.

And in both cases many cannot see the threat Blair poses because of the overwhelming fear of terrorism and/or a return to Tory rule.

We repeat: we will not be cowed and we will not be diverted.

The policy stands.

In 'safe' Labour seats and marginal seats we want you to vote for the candidate most likely to beat the Labour candidate. Sometimes this will involve voting Tory.

Some of our supporters may only support us partially in that they will never ('Never! Do you hear me? Never!') vote Tory, and may instead opt for another party – perhaps even Respect or the Greens. Fair enough. Your call.

But we want all Labour MPs to know that there are many people who would fully support them were it not for Blair... and that we're so unhappy about Blair's leadership that we would not only consider voting Tory as a protest vote, but also voice this intention publicly.

1. Well, here we are, Tony. We're this angry. We'd like to ask you to pull your head in, but we've seen what you're capable of, and we have no intention of trusting you again. You can soften your position on detention without trial or downplay the possibility of a pre-emptive strike against Iran, but we know that the moment your survive the election you'll be back at it again.

2. Well, here we are, Labour MPs. We're this angry. Get rid of Blair and get Labour back on track. Don't make us do anything you might personally live to regret.

3. Perhaps we'd best make it clear that many of us directly involved with the campaign think that the Tories are complete and utter bastards. Except for Boris Johnson. Boris rules.

Backing Blair is not about voting for the Conservatives, but voting *against* Tony Blair. In the most effective way possible. In many cases this *will* mean voting for the second-place candidate who may well be a Tory. Now that's a tough call, but it's something you're going to have to get over, and something those of us behind Backing Blair have already had to face.

Because as long as Tony Blair is leader, voting for Labour is effectively voting for a Tory government anyway.

Who made the bigger commitment to private investment in public services? That's right, under Tony Blair, Labour has given more support to PFI [Private Finance Initiative] than the preceding Conservative government, support to a policy that mortgages the future of improved public services in order to give 'apparent' short-term benefits.

Who committed British military forces to 9 war zones in 8 years? Right again, Tony Blair.

Who is attempting to pass laws suspending habeas corpus and seriously eroding civil liberties? Bingo, Tony Blair.

So come polling day, we want you to get out there and vote. Strategically. Without compromise. Vote for the person most likely to take the seat from Labour.

In many constituencies their lead is so large that the chances of unseating Labour is virtually zero. But still vote against. Our protest needs to be visible, ruthless, and visibly ruthless.

Now, onto that slightly better quote we were promising you...

'The only thing we have to fear is fear itself – nameless, unreasoning, unjustified terror which paralyzes needed efforts to convert retreat into advance.' – *Franklin Delano Roosevelt, First Inaugural Address, March 4, 1933.*

We would do well to remember this quote in today's context. Because Tony Blair wants you to be afraid, to live in fear of terrorists and Tories.

Yesterday, Blair likened his relationship with the electorate to a troubled marriage. He's asking for one more chance.

We couldn't think of a more appropriate comparison. In fact, we would ask you to stare in the mirror and consider your fresh and faded bruises. Are you really so reliant on Blair that you're afraid to walk out the door? Are you really so blind to his abuse of your trust that you're willing to believe he can change?

Backing Blair
http://www.backingblair.co.uk

‹ED› (YES, THREE FROM THIS DAY. THERE MIGHT BE A LESSON ABOUT BLOGGERS AND DATES IN THERE SOMEWHERE.) THE HUNTING BAN COMES INTO EFFECT IN A FEW DAYS. IN THE ENTIRE, YEARS LONG, ANGUISHED DEBATE, IT'S BEEN RARE TO SEE THE ISSUE SUMMED UP QUITE AS NEATLY AS THIS FROM THIRD AVENUE: ‹/ED›

Explaining the irrational

Everyone who lives abroad has to end up at some point trying to explain some curious facet of life in their own country which amuses or bemuses the population of their adopted home.

So is it with me and the banning of fox hunting.

How do I explain that a country that allows factory farming is now preparing to criminalise the killing of a small number of vermin?

Personally, I can't, because to me it makes no sense.

Of course, what the anti-hunting lobby really object to is not the death of the fox, but the fact that people experience pleasure in achieving it. And legislating to control thoughts rather than actions should have no place in a liberal society.

Third Avenue
http://thirdavenue.typepad.com

✎ 15 February

‹ED› NOT ALL BLOGGERS IGNORE VALENTINE'S DAY, OF COURSE. ACERBIA SEEMS TO HAVE HAD A PARTICULARLY INTERESTING ONE: ‹/ED›

My fucking freaky valentines

Back in the dusty archives of my site I put forward a request for a full-time stalker. Somebody who would really boil the bunny and rock the cradle, pick the ice and single the white female. I wanted Glen Close, Rebecca DeMornay, Sharon Stone and Jennifer Jason Leigh bundled together into a four-disc special edition stalker that would infiltrate my life and make things interesting. My life needed spicing, my salad needed tossing, my puppy needed defenestrating, and my knives needed sharpening.

And I got one.

She started off by just sending cards with innocuous little messages like *You don't know it but I think of you all the time and I know when you smile*. These were usually followed up by a text message asking *Am I doing it right?* to which I would reply *Who is this? How did you get this number? Stop texting me*.

From there we progressed quickly onto phone calls. I'd change number about once a week, to the point of exasperating and alienating all my friends and family. She'd call up and breathe huskily at me down the line. I'd hang up. She'd redial and breathe some more. I'd hang up. She'd send a text saying *Stop playing hard to get* before calling again and doing her best Darth Vader impression. I'd break down into tears and head for the nearest mobile phone provider.

Then things started getting creepy. My mother would call my girlfriend, distraught at the news that I had been in a car accident, only to be set straight that I hadn't and it was just somebody playing a practical joke. Similarly my girlfriend was arrested for shoplifting, but released after the video evidence was discredited as a misidentification. The penguin I had adopted at London Zoo was viciously mauled one night, and a week later, as he recovered, fed rat poison by a veterinary nurse nobody recognised. Then the gifts started arriving.

Teddy bears with their eyes dangling from threads that would crackle from the Xerox copies of pictures of me, taken with a telephoto lens, stuffed inside. New phones with Deep Heat smeared on the earpiece. Boxes of chocolates laced with laxatives. But last night was the final straw.

Climbing the stairs to my landing I saw a white cardboard cube, tied up with black ribbon. When I picked it up, there was a metallic tinkle, like spare change in a pocket and a wet flopping sound. The base of the box seemed solid and yet the cardboard itself was damp. I took it inside and left it on the countertop in the kitchen until my girlfriend arrived.

'Are you going to open it?'

'I don't know, it could be Gwyneth Paltrow's head inside,' I replied.

'The gift that keeps on giving! Open it! Open it!'

I undid the ribbon and lifted the lid. The stench of raw meat and cold blood suppurated forth, permeating the air in the kitchen. Inside the box was a square of inch-thick plywood with a heart, pierced by nine-inch nails and wrapped in barbed wire. The bottom of the box was drenched with a thin pool of blood and a pink card cut into the shape of a heart had been stapled onto the heart with the words 'My love' scrawled in red crayon.

'My God!' my girlfriend recoiled with a hand over her mouth 'that's disgusting!'

'You would say that; you're a vegetarian.'

'What are you going to do with it?'

'Well, I was thinking some garlic and fried onions and a side of cheesy mash...'

Acerbia
www.acerbia.com

✎ 19 February

‹ED› BYSTANDER, OF THE LAW WEST OF EALING BROADWAY, HAS VIEWS ON A COMMON, ALTHOUGH UNDEFINED, OFFENCE: ‹/ED›

Over here, officer

The idea of 'cool' is an irritating reality of 21st century England. It allows the young and even the dispossessed to adopt the languid attitude of an eighteenth-century fop. To show an interest in practically anything violates the canons of coolness. 'Whatever' is the teenager's airy dismissal of anything requiring the slightest intellectual or emotional effort. The only exception to the iron rule is that anything to do with football and drunkenness may be enthused about.

Coolness requires young men to spurn the seat belt in their vehicle; presumably maxillo-facial trauma will enhance street credibility. Now failing to wear a seat belt is a non-endorseable offence that is usually dealt with by the issue of a £30 fixed penalty ticket. What it does do though, is to cause police patrols to stop and speak to the driver. This prompts the usual enquiries as to the state of the vehicle, its insurance and licence, whether the driver has subjected himself to the rigours of a driving test, whether he is drunk, whether he has drugs about his person, whether the car contains goods that were until recently the property of an innocent householder, and whether the driver himself might be wanted on an arrest warrant. In a high proportion of seat-belt stops one or more of these factors is present, and the man (it's always a man) ends up in front of the court.

I have no wish to be baked in a tabloid pie, but it would be very satisfying to be able to say: 'Look, you stupid little git, if you had been wearing the belt the police would have left you alone. There is no specific offence of acting like a prat, but if there were you would be guilty of it.' Perhaps the week before I retire...

The Law West of Ealing Broadway
http://thelawwestofealingbroadway.blogspot.com

✎ 20 February

<ED> BRITISH POLITICAL BLOGGING IS RADICALLY DIFFERENT FROM THAT IN THE US. MARTIN STABE POINTS OUT WHY. IT'S WORTH NOTING THAT THIS ANALYSIS HAD BECOME MAINSTREAM, APPEARING IN THE GUARDIAN, FOR EXAMPLE, WITHIN A FEW MONTHS: </ED>

British blogs: A waste of time?

A recent *Times* article* has given the British political blogosphere some much-needed attention – including some from some rather unsavoury sources.**

While Iain Duncan Smith fantasises about blogs saving the Tories,*** Nosemonkey of *Europhobia* thinks the British blogosphere is a largely pointless waste of time.****

I fear Nosemonkey may be right. Although Iain Duncan Smith doesn't seem to grasp this, it's impossible to understand the success of political blogging in the United States without taking account of the particular political context in which it operates.

First, blogging has filled a niche that the particular structure American journalism has left open: partisan reporting. The ideology of journalism that has emerged in the United States since the 19th century is professional 'objectivity'. A widely-held norm of objectivity lends itself to criticism based on charges of partisan bias.

American journalism's notion of objectivity has an economic basis. American print journalism is based on a system of regional monopolies that attempt to be slavishly centrist in order to attract the widest possible audience. Broadcasting is still dominated by the networks which operate in a similar way, although the recent advent of cable and satellite channels is challenging that.

British mainstream journalism, by contrast, is relatively more diverse. The big media are national in scope and compete in a highly competitive market for eyeballs that they must segment along partisan lines to survive. Brits understand

*http://business.timesonline.co.uk/article/0,,9075-1485305,00.html
**http://yorkshire-ranter.blogspot.com/2005/02/do-they-got-intuhweb-in-europistan.html
***http://www.guardian.co.uk/comment/story/0,3604,1417983,00.html
****http://europhobia.blogspot.com/2005/02/uk-blogging-officially-pointless-waste.html

this instinctively. They know that their journalism is biased. People who read the *Daily Mail* or the *Guardian* understand that they are getting a particular point of view. Brits are accustomed to a partisan media, and know how to decode the news accordingly. A blog screaming about the manifold biases of the *Sun* isn't telling us anything we don't already know.

For the same reason, there is less need in Britain for additional partisan view points – the British 'MSM' [Mainstream Media] is organised in a way that provides them. There's not much room for a blogger to rant about the views of the *Guardian* when *Telegraph* columnists already do it far more effectively for a huge audience.

The media scalp-hunting that has characterised American bloggers' most celebrated successes occurs all the time in Britain – within the mainstream media. The Andrew Gillian and Piers Morgan stories might have been conservative blogger scalps if their errors of fact-checking had occurred in the United States. The tabloids also provide the political pseudo-scandals that might have emerged on blogs in the United States: think Chris Bryant.

A second weakness of the British blogosphere is that electoral politics in Britain are far less media-dependent than in the United States. In contrast to America's lengthy, national, extensive and media-driven electoral campaigns fought over geographically huge constituencies, Britain's short general election campaigns are still fought largely at the level of relatively small parliamentary constituencies. Retail politics – leaflets in letterboxes and doorstep canvassing – dominate campaigns.

Rather than months of media mudslinging providing grist for the blogger mill, British general elections trigger strict impartiality rules in broadcasting.

The lack of expensive broadcast campaigning also means that campaign finance is also less of a battleground than it is in the United States. A blog-driven grassroots fundraising effort like the celebrated efforts of Howard Dean or Ben Chandler is therefore unlikely to occur here.

Finally, there are sheer numbers. Britain has a similar (but still slightly lower) level of Internet penetration to the United States'. But relative numbers are meaningless: in blogging, it's absolute numbers that matter. The blogosphere network works by having a large number of nodes (i.e. readers) who can contribute to the distributed information-gathering structure that makes blogs effective.

The big American political blogs are predominantly national in scope. An effective national sub-blogosphere may therefore require a critical mass that Britain alone may not be big enough to deliver. With a popuation of 60 million, Britain is only about the size of the *three* biggest American states combined.

To attract a potential internet-user population of the same order of magnitude, a sub-blogosphere would have to emerge at the pan-European level. But language differences alone make that unlikely.

MartinStabe.com
http://martinstabe.com/blog

‹ED› THE ARTICLE BY IAIN DUNCAN SMITH ALSO SPARKED THESE THOUGHTS FROM HARRY AT HARRY'S PLACE: ‹/ED›

IDS and Woody on the blogosphere

Former Conservative Party leader Iain Duncan Smith has an article in the *Guardian* on the blogosphere titled: Bloggers will rescue the right – Beat the metropolitan elite with the tactics of US conservatives.*

> But the blogosphere will become a force in Britain, and it could ignite many new forces of conservatism. The internet's automatic level playing field gives conservatives opportunities that mainstream media have often denied them.

Well blogs open up opportunities for all sorts of people. I am convinced that blogging in Britain will continue to grow in size and influence but I'm yet to be convinced it will take the same shape and charachter as the US blogosphere.

As I've said before, in political terms, the interesting thing about the way the British scene has developed is that it has given a space to political views that don't get much representation in the mainstream media. On the left, many of the most popular sites come from the pro-liberation left which has been largely ignored by the liberal media, while on the right it is radical free-market libertarians such as *Samizdata* who get the serious traffic as such views are hard to find in the conservative press.

But there is nothing to say that will always be the case and it is going to be fascinating to see how things develop.

****

* http://www.guardian.co.uk/comment/story/0,3604,1417983,00.html

Blogs aren't all about politics of course and last night I attended the East Lancashire Bloggers Summit – well, I went out for a few pints with my mate The Tinbasher.

Tinbasher is a blog about a pretty obscure topic – the sheet metal industry and about one small business in particular. The site creator Paul Woodhouse, who lives just three minutes walk from my parents, has managed to make the site the talk of the blogging business world, getting nominated for awards, attending conferences in the States and generally being treated as a pioneer of a small business blog that works.

And by all accounts it is working pretty spectacularly for Paul and the firm Butler Sheetmetal. The interest created through his blog has brought in business from well outside the company's core area in East Lancs and generated plenty of publicity as well as orders.

We discussed a lot of blogging related matters but we couldn't avoid a little self-satisfied chuckle at the fact that one of the world's most noted small business blogs and one of the UK's leading political blogs are both produced by people from the same town in Lancashire.

Perhaps that is one element of the blogging revolution that has been overlooked. The media is so London-centric, written by people living in the capital and too often for people living in the capital yet with blogs you can get an article published or promote your business from anywhere. You don't need contacts in the London media or PR world – you can just crack on and do it.

If you can type that is.

   <note> The Tinbasher blog is featured on 4 August. </note>

Harry's Place
http://hurryupharry.bloghouse.net

✎ 24 February

‹ED› JOHN B AT SHOT BY BOTH SIDES MAKES ANOTHER OF HIS PITHY OBSERVATIONS: ‹/ED›

End this food smuggling menace

The Contaminants in Food (England) Regulations 2004 is a harsh law indeed.

> Any person who fails to comply with any of the requirements specified in a notice served under paragraph (1) shall be guilty of an offence and liable on summary execution to a fine...

It's disturbing enough that we've reintroduced the death penalty for people who import inappropriate food into the UK – but fining people after they've been executed seems particularly harsh.

Shot by both sides
http://www.stalinism.com/shot-by-both-sides

✎ 25 February

‹ED› THIRD AVENUE, AN ENGLISHMAN OBSERVING OUR GOINGS ON FROM THE BIG APPLE, NOTES THIS: ‹/ED›

The decline of Britain

Today's *New York Times* informs me that schools all over Britain have had to be closed over the past few days because of the 'frigid period' the country is experiencing.

Frigid? No wonder the country needs immigration...

Third Avenue
http://thirdavenue.typepad.com/third_avenue/

✎ 28 February

Gonzo consulting

I'm in London at the building at 'fifty nine & a half' for my 'turn', the presentation
and Q&A session I regularly give on the current project. It's to a group of
significant stakeholders, and will cost someone £400 for the pleasure. That's if I
don't have dinner on the train home.

But my mind wasn't on it at all. The thing I like about Government Offices,
or offices with even a tangential connection with government, is the art they
have access to. Like Ministers, the chief executives of many of these organisations
can borrow from the national art collections to decorate their premises.

I am not sure the chief executives actually do the choosing themselves, but
someone obviously does, because often the art is quite coherent. The other strange
thing is that it is nearly always 'modern' – maybe the old masters are not available
under the scheme – and there are some real surprises to be had. In the foyer of the
Government office for the East Midlands for example is a John Piper print, signed
and numbered, and probably with a value more than the salary of the team behind
the reception desk. In an office in Queen Anne's Gate the coffee machine was
overlooked by an Elizabeth Blackadder original watercolour, of inestimable value.
The incumbents had no idea what it was, or the insurance risk it created.

So as I walked into the foyer today, I wasn't surprised to see the paintings,
and took them in my stride. But that was before I spotted The Frost. It was on
a back-facing wall, out of sight of the casual visitor, and I dropped my case in
surprise and walked over to check my instinctive identification. Good grief!
A 1965 Terry Frost collage, an original, about 20 by 36 inches. It was in a naff frame.
But it was an important piece – Frost's sixties work is *Important*.

Now I know Terry Frost only died recently, and news of his knighthood may not
have reached that department yet, but surely somone there knows what it's
worth? Don't they? Surely? The receptionist sure didn't know what she was
guarding – I checked. No sign of an alarm system. No camera.

Lets put it this way; 'liberate' that painting, and assuming you can sell it, you can buy a new Porsche – the expensive one, and retire on the change. However old you are now.

So London 20sixers, get a white van, and some overalls, and toolbox, and run up a work order for taking the picture for restoration or somesuch, and in ten minutes your financial problems are solved. Oh, that's when you get the address... I need a head start!

The Beachhutman Blog
www.20six.co.uk/beachhutman

MARCH 2005

✎ 3 March

‹ED› THE BLACKBOARD JUNGLE IS ANOTHER OF THE BLOGS THAT PROVIDES AN INSIGHT INTO THE EVERYDAY DETAILS OF ANOTHER WORLD – IN THIS CASE, AS THE NAME WOULD LEAD YOU TO EXPECT, TEACHING IN AN INNER CITY SCHOOL: ‹/ED›

It was a surprise to see Aliye, snorting a damp fag heavily as she mooched alongside her bad-girl friends, anywhere near the school.

A permanent fixture in the school's mock mini 'prison' area, she'd been told never to come back around six months ago. Been enrolled – against her better judgement – on a vocational course at the local trades college. Lasted four weeks before they also threw her out.

I have a soft spot for Aliye, since she was fourteen and used to wander into my form class to pointlessly scream abuse at me twice daily. Not the abuse, however – that's merely lessened, switched to different perpetrators now – but the regularity of her visits, the clear indication that she felt she had nowhere else she felt like she needed to go.

When she was placed into my exam class at fifteen, I feared the worst. Yet, actually, as long as I allowed her to wander off rather than beat some provocative boy to a bloodied pulp, we coexisted happily. Her sendings out were always a perfunctory affair – a sad, wistful, 'okay Aliye, I think we've reached our limit now' was enough to have her mooch to the girls' toilets and smoke for the rest of the lesson. The difference between her behaviour and that of other troubled students, I think, was that where they just wanted attention, and saw confrontation as a means to that end, she felt genuine disaffection. Aliye wasn't really concerned if you shouted at her or not. She wasn't really concerned if you noticed she was in the room or not.

I might have let her slip beneath the radar, and left it at that, if I hadn't taught her brother, Haydar. He'd been a difficult person to place in the right tier of examinations, and his incredibly bolshy mother had given me hell for underestimating him.

Her sole contribution to lessons was an occasional 'will you shut up, Miss, you been talking for thirty minutes now, and it's jarring me.' Like all teachers, I hear the sound of my own voice a little too warmly, and – unexpectedly – I found I appreciated the honesty. Her written work was competent, sometimes verging on good. Anything else was non-existent.

His mother'd been exactly right: Haydar secured himself an A. I learnt my lesson – teach to their potential, not to their performance.

So Aliye's disaffected grumpy slouch confused me. I didn't push the issue, but quietly, continually made it clear I thought her capable of the top grades.

Until she disappeared.

Nowadays, Aliye mooches around sitting on walls and smoking, getting up in the afternoons and waiting for her friends to finish school to mooch some more. She's sixteen and has no hope of gaining any qualifications at all.

Chatting to her in the street tonight, I pointed out that an appeal from her father to the DfES or to the local council would probably gain her access to the school just to take her examinations. Why didn't she appeal? There was still time.

For that matter, why hadn't her mum said anything? Mum would have raised merry hell if Haydar had been treated like this.

But Aliye is Turkish. And a girl. Culturally unimportant. Aliye's mum is not at home any more, and nor is her brother. Aliye's dad isn't confident with authorities. 'He gets confused,' she says. 'He doesn't know what to say or who to ask.'

Social engineering. I can see it's behind the brilliant results reached by this year's crop of sixteen year olds, but it hurts when you see the kids it leaves behind. If Aliye were middle class, she'd be getting A grades right now, not skulking around council estates counting the days till she's pregnant.

I made her promise to ghost-write a letter to the local borough of education. Get her dad to sign it. Conscripted her friends to make sure she got reminded. Promised to take up her case with the head.

But with a heavy heart. Kids like Aliye don't fall into the 'matters' bracket. Whatever we do now, we've told her that very, very clearly. And that's the sort of lesson it's especially hard to unlearn.

The Blackboard Jungle
http://blackboardjungle.blogspot.com

‹ED› IT ISN'T ALWAYS THE BLOGGER THAT PROVIDES THE ENTERTAINMENT. THE ABILITY OF THE READERS TO ADD COMMENTS MEANS THAT THE AUDIENCE IS EXPLICITLY CONTRIBUTING TO THE CONVERSATION. AFTER A POST DERIDING THE MORE DEEP-GREEN MEMBERS OF THE ECO-WARRIOR WORLD AT THE DAILY ABLUTION, A PERFECT DESCRIPTION OF THE DESIRED FUTURE WORLD WAS PROVIDED BY WINDOWLICKER: ‹/ED›

Imagine a Birkenstock stamping on a human face – forever.

The Daily Ablution
http://dailyablution.blogs.com

✎ 5 March

‹ED› TALES FROM THE CHALK-FACE IS ANOTHER OF THE EDUBLOGS (AS THE RATHER UNLOVELY AMERICAN DESCRIPTION HAS IT) AND HERE DEVELOPS THE POINT MADE BY THE BLACKBOARD JUNGLE ABOVE: ‹/ED›

Cans of beans

To really appreciate what working in an inner-city comprehensive school in England entails, I suggest you read Lectrice at The Blackboard Jungle. In her two recent posts she encapsulates the nature of the job perfectly. Her posts for Wednesday, 2 March 2005 and Thursday, 3 March 2005, resonated with me particularly.

In one post she outlines the frustration you feel from the ones who 'get away'; bright students who, for many reasons, do not, or are not allowed to, fulfil their potential. This blog is usually a moan about the (mis)management and nonsense you face every single day when you are at the bottom of the school hierarchy. But believe me, the sense of frustration you feel when a bright student, from a poor background misses the golden opportunity educational advancement can offer makes the initiative and target-led crap you receive daily pale into insignificance.

I cannot remain objective here, I am one of those who 'got away'. I see myself in those students who arse around all lesson and 'fail'.

This week I have looked at a number of students in my Year 11 class (15- and 16-year-olds) and thought: what could have been? As we head towards the final furlong of their GCSE course, I know most will 'fail'. Indeed, the majority of pupils in the class could have easily been the cast-offs from Jim Henson's last, unrealised project.

However, one girl and two boys in particular relate to poems and novels sensitively and keep the class going, through their enthusiasm and insight. They are the sort of pupils who cannot be bullshitted either – they have fantastic 'shit radars'. The poems, plays, novels they think are 'gay' I, too, do not rate highly either. Although the joy of hearing a bottom-set group of pupils getting enjoyment out of reading a text is ultimately an unsettling experience. Firstly, you wonder: are they taking the piss? Secondly, you think you are Robin Williams in 'Dead Poets Society' and have to stop yourself from exclaiming: 'Right! All on the desks now!' Finally, it leaves you with a melancholy feeling of, is this all too little too late? Why weren't these kids engaged with study at an earlier age?

As I said earlier this week, this job is much more than teaching. We are human and that means we are complex animals: contrary, unpredictable and flawed. Sometimes we fail our students and sometimes they fail themselves. Sometimes their parents fail them, sometimes fate fails them. Our society (in the guise of government) fails them, too, by treating them like commodities, by trying to impose uniformity; by not allowing for difference. Government targets and statistics do not recognise the human element of this complex interaction at the chalk-face. Every can of beans must contain 400 grams – every child must reach a certain attainment level at a certain age.

Yeah, right.

Tales From the Chalk-face
http://talesfromthechalkface.blogspot.com

✎ 8 March

‹ED› ROBERT FISK OF THE INDEPENDENT IS
A FAVOURITE TARGET FOR BLOGGERS ALL
OVER THE ANGLOSPHERE. HIS SOMEWHAT,
UMM, IMPASSIONED REPORTING IS THE SUBJECT
OF ENDLESS PARODIES. INDEED, HIS NAME
PROVIDES ONE OF THE NEW VERBS OF THE
MEDIUM: 'TO FISK'. THAT IS, TO TAKE A PIECE
OF JOURNALISM AND PROVIDE A LINE-BY-LINE
REFUTATION OF THE FACTS, OPINIONS AND
CONCLUSIONS, IN THE END SHOWING THAT
THE REPORTER BEING TARGETED IS A
KNOW-NOTHING LOON. HERE POOTERGEEK
TAKES THE PARODY ROUTE: ‹/ED›

The last outpost of traditional rule

The ever-temperate front page of the *Independent* screams, 'IS LEBANON WALKING
INTO ANOTHER NIGHTMARE?' Without a copy to hand, I think you can imagine the
name and the roseate visage that make up the byline beneath the headline.
Because the Indie charges for access to the online version of its output I can only
quote the opening paragraph of the article that follows:*

> Lebanon confronts a nightmare today. As the Syrian army begins its
> withdrawal from the country this morning, after mounting pressure from
> President George Bush – whose anger at the Syrians has been provoked by
> the insurgency against American troops in Iraq – there are growing signs
> that the Syrian retreat is reopening the sectarian divisions of the 1975–1990
> Lebanese civil war.

This is illustrated with a picture of young, beige, male protesters screaming at
the camera. One has a bare chest, a studded leather strap around his wrist. He is
acting up with a knife. Its implication: these people are Savages, who will be lost
to Chaos without the Firm Hand of their uniformed Ba'athist overseers.

---

* The *Independent's* website is at www.independent.co.uk

I might not be able to share with you Robert's latest, but I can, by the magic of PooterGeek's Future News feature, bring you the entire text of a yet-to-be-published masterpiece from the prizewinning journalist:

> McDonald's and Wal-Mart now stretch from Gulf to Mediterranean. The American Empire smothers the history and pride of an entire region under a film of 'democracy'. One country, however, still holds firm. There is no Starbucks in Fiskistan. Only the UN staff flown in to counsel victims at special rape crisis centres own 4x4s – and those centres would not be needed if a decade of American-sponsored sanctions had not driven the men of Fiskistan to sexually assault the largely Kurdish servant population. Here the cinemas show no Jerry Bruckheimer 'actioners'; only the plaintive traditional sound of the Fiskistani nose whistle echoes out across night vistas of the rocky desert.

> Fiskistan is the forgotten front in the so-called War on Terror. For a few months in the 1950s, members of the First Ambridge Battalion of the Queen's Infantry seized this tiny country – then divided into a patchwork of statelets dominated by rival warlords – in order to secure a supply line during the Suez campaign. For that short time guerrilla fighters led by Muarbad Fiski made life for the reluctant colonial rulers hell, as they were forced to butcher young Englishmen fresh from the Home Counties to protect their nomadic existence from foreign interference.

> Yesterday, American troops, closely followed (as we have come to expect) by British forces, showed that they have learned little since that folly, as they marched back into the country whence they were driven just over half a century ago. The assault by the so-called Coalition on the borders of this minuscule territory raged for over seventeen minutes before Lt Col Ronald Fothersgill made his historic mobile phone call to Queen Elizabeth herself, informing her that Upper Fiskia was once again under British military control.

> Deeper in Fiskistan than even the most advanced of the 'Coalition' soldiers, I spend the day at The Re-Education Facility of the Glorious Leader where guards and guarded shudder at the thought of the invasion. Outside the barbed wire fence set up to protect the site from the advancing US Marines, smiling Fiskistani children play. The human skull they are kicking around in a makeshift football game keeps getting lodged in the craters left by American depleted uranium cluster bomblets, their already-deadly payload laced with MMR vaccine and Sudan-1.

Asif is one of the administrators. He lives in constant dread of the arrival of the Americans. I ask him about his fears. His reply speaks for many. He pauses in his work and stubs out his cigarette on the forehead of one of the residents of the camp, seated in a rather substantial chair beside him. He politely wipes his hands clean on a beautiful traditionally embroidered Fiskistani handkerchief before shaking my hand and addressing me:

'My father was a jailer. His father was a jailer. These electrodes were handed down to me through the generations, just like our presidency. (May His Glorious Countenance Shine Upon The Fatherland Until Eternity.) They were first used by my grandfather on the balls of the last openly elected leader of the opposition. I hold history in my hands. When these Yankee dogs come here with their human pyramids, and their pointy black hoods, and their digital cameras, all of this heritage will be wiped out – just as the Jews have wiped out Palestine. They know nothing of our ways. Who will keep order when there are twenty different brands of toothbrush on the shelves? Who will pull the teeth that they brush? Eh? I spit in their decaf latte!'

His sadness is palpable. Whatever happens next it will be the end of an ~~ear~~ era.

As I leave the facility, a group of uniformed staff approach along the path to the main gate, almost ready to begin their shift. I greet them with a friendly nod. They respond with a shouted question: 'English?!'

I tell them that I am a journalist for the *Independent*. In a moment they are upon me. One pulls a pistol out of his holster and beats me about the head with its butt: 'Unfunny bastard Miles Kington! Robbie Williams! Kilroy! Celine Dion! Die pigdog!'

The others are kicking me with their boots, punching me with their bare hands, only pausing to roll up the khaki sleeves of their fatigues. I know I am paying for all of our crimes, for every step in our crusade to bring 'freedom' to peoples of whom we know little more than the sorry tales of our previous doomed expeditions to plunder their lands. I welcome the blows. I want them to beat me with their swarthy, manly, Arab forearms until my blood washes away the crimes of the Bushes and the Blairs. Spank me, Ahmed! Spank me for my sins! I want to feel your brown cosh…

[At this point, unfortunately, Nurse Wilson had to remove Robert's hands from his laptop.]

PooterGeek
www.pootergeek.com

✎ 9 March

‹ED› CRITICISM OF THE BLAIRITE MANNER OF RUNNING THINGS FROM THE LEFT, BY CHICKEN YOGHURT: ‹/ED›

Your intelligence: not just insulted but given a good kicking as well

Jesus Christ. Is it me or is there nary a day goes by when we don't have another half-baked, ill-thought out and invariably populist piece of shite announced by New Labour in its frantic attempt to curry favour before the election?

They're like panicky Alan Partridge feverishly pitching evermore ludicrous ideas (Monkey Tennis, Arm Wrestling with Chaz and Dave, Intercity Sumo) in a desperate attempt to save his career.

Imagine Alan Milburn sitting at a typewriter in a basement somewhere. He hasn't slept or eaten for days and is surrounded by ashtray after ashtray of fag-ends. He stinks of sweat. He hammers away at the keys, periodically ripping the paper out of the machine, thrusting it into the hands of whichever cabinet minister has drawn the short straw, and gasping, 'here, give them this.' Like a little boy who's left his homework until five minutes before it's due to be handed in, any old shit will do.

So today we have Health Secretary John Reid announcing that 'new community matrons' will help children 'draw up personal health plans to improve their quality of life'. The accompanying bumpf is called 'Delivering Choosing Health' – a title whose construction says it all, i.e. What the fuck?

Now, it doesn't take Jamie Oliver to tell you that children could not give a flying fuck about healthy eating. They love eating shite. I almost expect the news that Turkey Twizzlers are being banned from school dinners to be met with an exponential increase in ASBOs.

And the private companies who supply school dinners care even less. My own daughter attends a school supplied by Scholarest. Needless to say, she takes a packed lunch. I look forward to seeing John Reid telling these outside contractors to stop serving warmed, over mechanically recovered chicken's doings and start slashing their profit margins so they can serve decent food. I don't really expect parents to be told it's their fault.

Ruth Kelly can cry crocodile tears and promise higher standards in school dinners but there'll be no more cash to add to the 37p a head that currently pays the bill.

According to the 'Delivering Choosing Health' (PDF, 600k) glossy, '3 out of 10 boys and 4 out of 10 girls are not doing the recommended one hour per day of physical activity.' If New Labour want to tear kids away from their PlayStations, Hollyoaks and masturbation, why the hell did they give the ok to the sell off of school playing fields?

Instead, we get some infuriatingly empty, transparent, here today and, dare I say it, gone tomorrow piece of guff about children being in charge of their own health. What a load of old (or, rather, New) bollocks.

You can prove it yourself. Set up a Google News Alert for 'Delivering Choosing Health'. Google will send you an e-mail every time the initiative is mentioned in the news. Don't expect to be inundated.

UPDATE: Here's what the Number 10 website has to say about the initiative:*

> ## Healthy kids equals healthy nation, says Reid
>
> Teaching children to eat well and encouraging them to exercise is vital if Britain is to become a fitter country, according to a new Government report.
>
> The Government has published 'Delivering Choosing Health', a plan which sets out practical benefits for local communities.
>
> There will be a range of actions to help children make healthier choices, Health Secretary John Reid said.
>
> Youngsters, with support from their parents, will draw up personal health plans for life setting out how they will eat the right kind of food and how often they should exercise.
>
> Community matrons will play a key role in supporting kids to help them lead healthier lifestyles.
>
> Schools will also begin piloting the use of pedometers to encourage their pupils to think about the amount of exercise they take.
>
> John Reid said:
>
> 'We know how important it is to make sure healthy habits start young. That's why we are taking a range of actions to get kids involved in making healthier choices about the food they eat and how much exercise they take.'

* http://www.number-10.gov.uk/output/Page7286.asp

I know I'm going on about it but this kind of horseshit is why I'm so sick to the back teeth of this shower. Instead of proper school meals and physical education it's an onus on parents and pedometers. Pedometers! I wonder if they're special New Labour ones that double-count your footsteps? Parents are going to help children draw up their health plans. What of the sows and their porcine broods I saw entering McDonald's in Brighton on Saturday? They quite *clearly* have their children's best interests at heart.

It's this bogus idea of putting power into the hands of the people. As if New Labour were ever in the business of divesting real power to anybody. It plays well in the media, giving a nebulous notion that people have control over their lives. But the majority, with their soaps and lottery and Turkey Twizzlers, are too lazy, ill-educated or lulled to the point of cultural narcolepsy to give a toss.

If people really cared about their health and the health of their children there'd be organic greengrocers on every high street instead of fast-food outlets. But they don't and there aren't. No amount of gentle, half-arsed prodding by the Government is going to change that. Which is why 'Delivering Choosing Health' is utterly redundant except as a big butterfly net to catch naive floating voters.

But Reid's plan sounds so rosy, so very New Labour. A cunning splicing of tradition and modernity, grown in a vat in a febrile laboratory. Matrons. It's a lovely word that conjures a lovely image. I wonder if they'll be warm, buxom and well, matronly? Pedometers. A fitter, healthier generation, marching in step into the future, groomed for their optimum positions in the economy, little computers counting their steps to greatness.

Chicken Yoghurt
http://chickyog.blogspot.com

‹ED› SOMETIMES WE JUST GET ASKED THOSE IMPOSSIBLE QUESTIONS, DON'T WE? ‹/ED›

On lumps

When a baby is tiny, its fingers don't have the surface area to be able to accurately make judgements about objects. Hence putting everything in their mouth – the biggest concentration of nerve endings in their body at that time.

Given this, why is it that thirteen-month-old Daisy now feels the need to take any remotely solid bits in her food out of her mouth and feel them with her fingers?

Blatant Optimism
www.sparklefluff.com/blatantoptimism

✎ 11 March

‹ED› ONE OF THE THINGS THAT MAKES BLOGGING SO DIFFERENT FROM OTHER METHODS OF COMMUNICATION, BE THEY PHONES, NEWSPAPERS OR JUST PLAIN WEBSITES, IS THE WAY IN WHICH THEY ARE DELIBERATELY SET UP TO SPREAD THE CONVERSATION. SOMEONE NOTES SOMETHING, MAKES A COMMENT, THAT IS THEN THERE FOR MILLIONS (ALTHOUGH, TO BE MORE ACCURATE, PROBABLY THE FEW HUNDRED WHO WILL SEE IT) TO QUOTE AND MAKE THEIR OWN COMMENTS ON. AN EXAMPLE OF THIS IS SOMETHING SEEN BY SLUGGER O'TOOLE, THE MAJOR NORTHERN IRELAND NEWS BLOG: ‹/ED›

Double standards and the democratic deficit...

UNBELIEVABLE! Westminster's 'Father of the House' Tam Dalyell has apologised to the people of Northern Ireland after 44 Labour MPs voted in support of tuition fees for students here. A year ago, they all voted against the introduction of these fees in England. Thanks guys. We know you care, honest.

The News Letter reports:*

> Veteran parliamentarian Tam Dalyell apologised to the people of Northern Ireland yesterday after a controversial vote supporting the implementation of university fees in the Province.
>
> The Scots MP was one of 44 Labour voters branded hypocrites by Conservative David Lidington after it emerged that they had all voted more than a year ago against the introduction of similar charges in England.

* http://www.newsletter.co.uk/story/18829

The Northern Ireland Higher Education Order was voted through by 250 to 116 on Tuesday night, moving it on to the next stage but not yet bringing it into law.

However, several MPs including Clare Short and Glenda Jackson admitted to the News Letter that they were unaware exactly what they were voting for.

Slugger O'Toole
www.sluggerotoole.com

‹ED› THIS IS THEN PICKED UP BY THE GREEN RIBBON (BY TOM GRIFFIN, AN IRISH JOURNALIST IN LONDON): ‹/ED›

Belfast Gonzo at *Slugger O'Toole* points us to a very interesting story in the Belfast *News Letter*.

So this is how the British constitution works:

Members of the Scottish Parliament vote against tuition fees for Scotland.

English MPs vote against tuition fees but England gets them anyway, because of the votes of Scottish MPs.

Northern Ireland MPs vote against tuition fees for England, but Northern Ireland gets tuition fees because of the votes of English MPs.

It's hard to resist the conclusion that Scotland's got the best of the deal here. Northern Ireland at least has the option of devolution, something which does not as yet seem to be on offer for England.

The Green Ribbon
http://tomgriffin.typepad.com/the_green_ribbon

✎ 12 March

‹ED› NANNY KNOWS BEST IS DEDICATED TO EXPOSING THE INCREASING ENCROACHMENT OF THE NANNY STATE. THIS IS ONE BLOG THAT IS UNLIKELY TO EVER RUN OUT OF MATERIAL: ‹/ED›

The dangers of allotments

Nanny clearly has too much time on her hands these days, as she seeks to poke her nose into the minutiae of her charges' lives.

It is reported that Nanny's chums from a 'council allotment working party' sent Andrew Pittman a 3-page 'risk assessment', outlining the risks of his allotment.

The document gave him a list of recommendations, including:

• Putting a lid on his water butt to avoid drowning

• Covering the end of bean canes to prevent eye injuries

• Moving tools off footpaths to avoid tripping

• Replacing glass frost covers with plastic ones

Needless to say Mr Pittman is unimpressed, as indeed am I.

You may wonder how it is that Nanny has the time, and the resources, to waste on such nonsense.

Well the answer is simple, nearly 7 million people now work for Nanny; many holding non-productive jobs such as admin. These people have time on their hands, and as such have to justify their own existence; hence the creation of 'risk assessments'.

As to the cost, Nanny doesn't give a stuff about that; the costs are covered by our taxes.

Nanny Knows Best
http://nannyknowsbest.blogspot.com

✎ 19 March

‹ED› MUCH OF THE YEAR SEEMS TO HAVE
BEEN TAKEN UP WITH A LOW-LEVEL DEBATE
ON WHAT IT MEANS TO 'BE BRITISH'. WE'VE HAD
SUGGESTED CHANGES TO THE EDUCATION
SYSTEM, CITIZENSHIP CEREMONIES AND AFTER
THE LONDON BOMBINGS THIS HAS INTENSIFIED
WITH LEARNED (AND BORING) PONTIFICATIONS
ON WHAT IT ALL MEANS. THIS IS SOMETHING
OF A SURPRISE TO THOSE OF US WHO HAVE
READ DAVID HADLEY AT STUFF AND NONSENSE,
FOR HE PERFECTLY CAPTURES JUST WHAT
IT IS TO BE BRITISH: ‹/ED›

British and proud of it

A couple of days ago I read an article on the (UK) *Prospect* website where various folk (including Kenan Malik, Roger Scruton, Gordon Brown, Billy Bragg) discuss 'British Identity'.

Now, I am British. I was born in Britain – and, as far as I know, so were most, if not all, of my ancestors – so I am about as British as it is possible to get. But, still I don't know whether I *feel* British. As far as I can tell, I don't know what it means to feel British.

I have – for example – always found the American notion of patriotism rather baffling. The seemingly unreflecting earnestness of it makes me uneasy, uncomfortable. I don't doubt it – or, particularly, want to demean it. But, I have to wonder what this – obvious – PRIDE in one's country means to such people.

So, what can pride in one's country mean, especially in my case of being British?

I have little, or no, time for the monarchy. I am indifferent to them and their activities. As for the current royal kerfuffle, as far as I'm concerned Charlie can marry who – or what (remember he is royalty) – he likes. The only reason that I'm not a rabid anti-monarchy republican is that all the other options for a head of state seem worse than the one we've got. President Blair – or even President Howard (stop laughing at the back) – fills me with... well, unpleasant thoughts at the very least.

As you may have gathered I'm not overly impressed with our politicians either. Britain may claim to be the mother of all parliaments and so on, but I couldn't have anything approaching respect – let alone pride – in the current bunch of incumbents.

The famous British traditions, rites and rituals? The civil service? The aristocracy? No, I can't say that any of those make me feel anything approaching respect or pride, let alone anything approaching that current nonce phrase – *a sense of identity*.

The folks in the *Prospect* discussion mentioned above talk of the 'British traditions': a sense of fair play, tolerance – even the famous stiff upper lip, at one point. But I don't see those things as being particularly, uniquely, British. They are personal attributes – some folk have them, some folk don't. Remember this so-called land of tolerance and fair play also is the home of the *Daily Mail*, Kilroy-Silk and hordes of the hanging and flogging brigade.

British arts and British culture – well, yes. We do have Shakespeare, the Beatles, Monty Python, Newton, Milton, Dickens, Valerie Singleton and all the other names that I can't quite remember – or remember how to spell – at the moment. But there are other folk in other countries that have produced art and culture of equal or greater stature.

But why should I feel a greater pride in Shakespeare because he was born a few miles down the road from where I'm typing this than in – say – Beethoven who was born hundreds of miles away? They were both great blokes, did great stuff and will probably always be remembered for it. What I don't understand is why one should count more to me because of the accident of where he was born.

That's one more thing to cross off the list, then.

So, it is not the institutions that make me feel any sense of 'British-ness', it is not the royal family, it is not the politicians, it is not the culture or the great men.

What does that leave? The people? The place?

The people? Well, the people are the people. Take one aspect – the famous British sense of humour. Now I like a good laugh myself – but Americans, Australians and others have all made me laugh at one time or another. The Germans even laugh at Monty Python – so I don't think there can be anything that special about the 'British sense of humour', or any of the other stereotypical so-called national characteristics. It seems that British people are British people, just, and only, because they are born in Britain.

As for sports, in everything – except football, for some reason I can't put my finger on – I am always pleased when – as usual – Britain, or England, fail, or lose, or whatever. That is mainly because it means we won't be constantly reminded of our great victory at every conceivable – and quite a few inconceivable – opportunity by a suddenly obsessive media.

For example, recently the English team apparently won some rugby match or other, and suddenly everything, the telly, the radio, the newspapers – everything, went rugby mad. But soon, when the rugby team got back to normal and started losing again, rugby went back to being – more or less – ignored.

The same applies to any other international contest or competition, like the Eurovision Song Contest, or the current Olympic bid by London, or how many Oscars the 'British' films or actors will get. None of them stir any great feeling in me, apart from a mild annoyance that I am being bombarded by yet more dull, useless trivia.

So that just leaves place.

I like Britain. I like its scenery. I like its rain (what other countries call weather). But then, I was born here – so it's what I'm used to. Other countries have just as good – if not better – scenery, countryside or whathaveyou. Although, I have never seen a place other than Britain that gets that particular shade of green in the countryside.

I see Britain as just a name on a map, a way of distinguishing one part of the map from another. I don't *feel* anything towards it, except that it is my home, and my family's home and that is why I want to keep at least this bit of it, anyway, in as good nick as possible. But that is all.

The only thing is that Britain is an island (or rather a bunch of islands of varying sizes), so it makes it easier than some other countries to give it a beginning and an end. However, what I can't see is how people can take that... I don't know... call it a leap of imagination, and say all the stuff on this side of the line (or border) is the good stuff, my stuff, our stuff, and that over there is the other – less good – or even, bad – stuff.

After all, despite Britain's island state making it a bit of a special case in this respect, the idea of the nation is a fairly recent invention in humankind's history, perhaps it is only a phase. So, maybe I'm right not to feel anything special towards, or about, it.

There are good things and there are bad things about this country as there are with most – if not all – countries. I am lucky – I know – to live in a place where the good things massively outweigh the bad things. And I do want to keep those good things, and do all I can to improve the bad things, or even make them go away altogether. But I don't think that it only applies to this country – to Britain. I would like the good things to happen all around the world too, and to get rid of all the bad things in the world.

A conclusion? All I can say is – I don't know.

As I said at the start – I don't understand patriotism. I would want to fight for what I think is right, but I know that my country (in the sense of the government, and in the sense of popular opinion) and I don't automatically see eye to eye on what those things are. I don't think I could ever say 'my country right or wrong', I think I would put right and wrong above and beyond country.

For example, if a situation like WWII ever arose again, I wouldn't fight 'for Britain' especially, but – without a moment's hesitation – I would fight *against* fascism.

And I don't know what 'feeling British' means, or rather, I can't find, put my finger on, a 'British' feeling inside me.

So, all I can say is that – for me – the question turns out to be a non-question – meaningless, but not pointless.

So, when any politician, or other member of the great and good exhorts me to do, feel, think or act in a particular way because of my 'British-ness' I will know now that it is just empty rhetoric and can be safely discounted along with all the other attempts at rhetorical manipulation.

But, the only thing that I can think of that would – for me – go some way to defining a sense of 'British-ness' would be a scepticism towards all attempts at defining something as nebulous as such a concept. Theorising about abstractions is something we British tend to prefer to leave to Johnny Foreigner. Maybe that is an example of the famous *British Pragmatism*.

Oh, shit, that's buggered my whole bloody thesis hasn't it?

Stuff and Nonsense
[Deceased... Ed.]

✎ 22 March

‹ED› EVERYONE KNOWS THE ELECTION IS COMING WHEN THE POSTERS START GOING UP. THEY DO NOT ALL MEET WITH A RAPTUROUS RECEPTION, AS THE PSEUDO MAGAZINE POINTS OUT: ‹/ED›

Sorting out the world is a doddle, asshole

When it comes to the bitter observation of a debased election campaign, this guy can't be beat. Usually it's New Labour getting it from both barrels, but now it's the Stupid Party:*

> There are four Tory campaign posters within five minutes walk of my house in the slightly shabby 'burb of Portslade. Two of them are those inflammatory 'handwritten' jobs.
>
> The first is the one that runs 'Is it racist to...' – I can't remember the rest of it, something about 'rivers of blood' and 'nig-nogs', I think. Definitely a pitch to fans of 1970's sitcoms.
>
> The second is one that runs 'How would you feel if a bloke on early release attacked your daughter?' The Tories, you see, want to remove any incentive prisoners have for good behaviour by ending the early release scheme. A better poster would be: 'How would you feel if, under a Tory administration, a bloke attacked your daughter because of the emphasis on punishment not rehabilitation in our prisons and the bloke received no treatment for his violent tendencies?' A bit wordy but nearer the truth I think.

Which reminded me, I have one of these posters just round the corner from my house. Another in the irritating, Post-It style. For a start, hoping my neighbours in

* Taken from *Chicken Yoghurt*: http://chickyog.blogspot.com/2005/03/electionwatch-2005-hove.html

Hackney North will Vote Conservative exhibits the kind of optimism that even Voltaire couldn't have satirised. Anyway, it reads 'I mean, how hard is it to keep a hospital clean?'

Well, to be frank, I'd have thought it very hard indeed. Hospitals are full of sick people, dripping with noxious germs. Many of them are old, some Victorian (the hospitals, not the sick people), others designed and built by the generation that thought tower blocks the cornerstone of a future crime-free society. On top of that, about a third of the supposedly healthy people visiting those sick people are carrying MRSA, and the PFI contract cleaners don't speak English, think you only get legionnaires' in France and are being paid a pittance.

But let's cut Michael Howard some slack. Clearly he has a hotline to the almighty and thinks it'll be a breeze for his team (btw, has *anyone* seen Oliver Letwin recently?) to sort this out. So, I was thinking, perhaps he could sort a few other things out while he's at it. But no point in hiding his light under a bushel. Another poster campaign is in order – and if he's looking for a copywriter, I might just be his man:

> 'I mean, how hard can it be to get those Colombian drug barons to stop shooting each other?'

> 'I mean, how hard can it be to get Christian fundies to put away their leaky pseudo-science and embrace macro-evolution and common descent?'

> 'I mean, that scientist geezer who looks like the lovechild of Seth from Emmerdale and Albert Einstein, he must be some kind of idiot – how hard can it be to land a beagle on Mars?'

> 'I mean, there's all that empty real estate right next to the al-Aqsa mosque – how hard would it be to put up a synagogue and maybe a little chapel, then they could all pray together?'

> 'I mean, nuclear fusion, it's just the opposite of fission, isn't it – how hard can it be?'

Are you thinking what I'm thinking?*

* Just to be clear and avoid ambiguity, I'm thinking: 'What an asshole'.

The Pseudo Magazine
http://pseudomagazine.blogspot.com

🖎 24 March

‹ED› THE AMERICAN BLOGOSPHERE WAS IN UPROAR ABOUT THE TERRY SCHIAVO CASE. REACTION HERE WAS RATHER MORE MUTED, ESPECIALLY AFTER HARRY HUTTON AT CHASE ME LADIES, EXPLAINED IT TO US ALL: ‹/ED›

Hate mail to the usual address

Q. What's the difference between Sven-Göran Eriksson and Terri Schiavo?

A. One's a Swede; the other's a cabbage.

UPDATE! david c points out a possible Unintended Consequence: 'Killing any single American for being an insensible, drooling vegetable could be the thin end of a fairly sizeable wedge.'

Chase me ladies, I'm in the cavalry
http://chasemeladies.blogspot.com

🖎 27 March

‹ED› ONE OF THE FAULT LINES ON THE (POLITICALLY) LEFT SIDE OF THE BLOGOSPHERE HAS BEEN OVER THE IRAQ WAR, BETWEEN THE PRO-WAR LEFT AND THE STOP THE WAR COALITION, KNOWN AS THE STOPPERS. ERIC THE UNREAD HIGHLIGHTS ONE OF THE REASONS WHY HE IS AGAINST THE STOPPERS: ‹/ED›

Stench of the gas chamber

Mick Hartley has drawn attention to North Korea's death camps:*

> A microcosm of these horrors is Camp 22, one of 12 concentration camps housing an estimated 200,000 political prisoners facing torture or execution for such 'crimes' as being a Christian or a relative of someone suspected of

* http://mickhartley.typepad.com/blog/2005/03/north_korean_cr.html

deviation from 'official ideology of the state.' Another eyewitness, Kwon Hyuk, formerly chief manager at Camp 22, repeated to me what he asserted to the BBC: 'I witnessed a whole family being tested on suffocating gas and dying in the gas chamber... The parents were vomiting and dying, but until the very last moment they tried to save kids by doing mouth-to-mouth breathing.'

Two years ago over a million people marched to prevent a war to remove another dictator, no-one marches to help the people in Camp 22.

Perhaps one of the reasons is that the 'peace' activists who organised the marches in the UK are actually on the other side.

If it comes to invasion of North Korea, I'll be with North Korea.

George Galloway, Vice President of the Stop the War Coalition.

we should also be alert to the very real dangers in the Far East and around Peoples Korea. The clear desire of the USA to effect 'regime change' in its second 'axis of evil' target could well provoke an armed clash there, too. Our Party has already made its basic position of solidarity with Peoples Korea clear.

Andrew Murray, Chair of the Stop the War Coalition.

Recently Kevin McNamara MP rather stupidly suggested Michael Howard's proposed clampdown on travellers had the '*whiff of the gas chamber about it*'. However, you need to go no further than the UK's leading '*peace movement*' to find two people in support of a totalitarian regime which appears to have actual gas chambers in use. Still any means necessary, and all that guff, when it comes to pseudo anti-imperialism.

The Stop the War coalition currently has three Labour MPs on its steering committee. Shame on them.

Eric the Unread
http://erictheunred.blogspot.com

APRIL 2005

✎ 7 April

‹ED› BORIS JOHNSON, EDITOR, JOURNALIST, MP, SCOUSE BAITER AND NOVELIST APPEARS NOT TO HAVE ENOUGH OUTLETS FOR HIS WRITINGS, AS THIS PIECE FROM HIS BLOG SHOWS: ‹/ED›

Zimbabwe/GB: Former breadbaskets?

You know I hesitate to assist the mad old tyrant Robert Mugabe, and I only mention this idea because I am sure he has thought of it already. There he is in Harare, luxuriating in another infamous violation of democracy. By force and threats his Zanu-PF thugs have kept thousands from the polls. Pro-Mugabe ballot papers have been magicked into existence, while opposition threats have been systematically destroyed.

To believe that last week's elections were free and fair, you have to believe that the people of Zimbabwe are so in love with Mugabe's policies of chronic inflation and mass starvation that they could think of nothing finer than to give him another five years. The elections were a sham and a fraud. They have been denounced around the world; and that is why, if I were Mugabe, I think I would embark on the following entirely cynical wheeze. I would make a long speech on that very subject; I would harp on about the disaster of electoral corruption, and the eating away of voter confidence in democracy. Then, with a flourish, I would announce that I was sending a team of election monitors to — you guessed it — Birmingham, England. Can you imagine the scenes? The Zanu-PF henchmen would tool around in their Mercs, pompously demanding to interrogate our returning officers, and invoking UN codes on the sanctity of ballot boxes. They would give long-faced press conferences and wring their hands on the steps of Birmingham town hall. Back in Harare, Mugabe would pick up on their findings, renew his hysterical assaults on the Blair government (which he has already denounced, you may remember, as a bunch of 'homosexual gangsters'), and urge his election monitors to redouble their efforts.

And how, in the current circumstances, could we reasonably deny them? We say that there was scandalous ballot-stuffing in Zimbabwe, where opposition election officials were brutally kicked out of polling stations, and where voting was mysteriously closed down early in pro-opposition areas. For instance, in the Kariba district it was initially announced that 16,676 had cast their vote. Then the votes were counted according to party preference. Hmmm. Long pause. Sorr-eee! said the Zanu-PF election officials: actually there were 13,719 Zanu-PF votes, and 9,540 votes for the Movement for Democratic Change. In other words, an extra 7,466 new votes had somehow turned up from nowhere. We in the west say that the whole thing was a fix. At which the Zanu-PF election monitors in Birmingham would feign outrage. A fix! they would say, taking off their shades for extra sincerity. Who are you to call us corrupt? Talk about pots and kettles, they would say. This is just the kind of racist bias we expect from an old imperial power, they would say, and they would point to the amazing way in which the British postal ballot system has been perverted.

And we have to admit that they have plenty of evidence to back up their case. Thousands of ballot papers were nicked, amid scenes of police apathy and general official shambles that belonged, indeed, in Matabeleland. According to Richard Mawrey QC, who presided over the Birmingham inquiry, the entire system is an invitation to fraud and redolent of a 'banana republic'. Mr Mawrey is a brave and good man, and we must hope that his legal career is not jeopardised by his willingness to speak out. And he also, alas, provides Robert Mugabe with the perfect rhetorical opportunity. If I were Mugabe, I would hail Mawrey as a kind of martyr for truth, a lone judicial opponent of political corruption, and I would instruct my British monitoring team to stay for the whole month of the election campaign. That is because if he wants to find evidence of the outrageous pro-government bias of the electoral system, it is there in spades.

We complain that the Zimbabwean system is designed to favour Zanu-PF, not least since Mugabe can pick 30 MPs himself. But look at the way the British system currently favours Labour. We have just started a truly exciting general election campaign. We Tories believe that we deserve to win, and that we could win. We leave parliament today, and hit the campaign trail, with our danders up, our peckers up, and our tails up, if that is anatomically possible. The polls are now putting us level pegging, if not better, with Labour. But consider how the system is skewed against us. Even if we both score 34 per cent in the final shoot-out, Labour would be left with an incredible 142 MORE seats than the Tories, and Mr Blair would still have a majority of 40 over all other parties. Even if Labour and the Tories score 36 per cent apiece, Blair still has a majority of 52 seats. In order to secure a majority of just one seat in the Commons, the Tories would need a lead of about ten percentage points. I am not saying that is impossible; but it means overcoming the kind of ludicrous unfairness that is familiar to the Zimbabwean opposition. How has this happened? There are several reasons, but the most shocking is the way Labour-held seats in the north, and especially in Scotland, have been allowed to shrink and shrink in population, while Tory seats have grown ever more populous. The electorate in Tory seats averages 72,000, with fewer than 66,000 in Labour seats. If the Tories and Labour both achieved 34 per cent, the average Tory MP would have 22,000 votes, while the average Labour MP would have 16,000 votes.

This nonsense cannot go on. if Labour is re-elected, it will be with the help of one of the most gerrymandered systems in the western world. It is time for a Great Reform Act, to redraw the boundaries and clear away Labour's rotten boroughs. The more you study the position, the clearer it is why Jack Straw has been so muted — compared, say, to Washington — in his criticism of the Zimbabwe polls. The awful truth is that the difference between us is not as big as it should be.

Boris Johnson MP
www.boris-johnson.com

‹ED› ONCE THE ELECTION HAD ACTUALLY BEEN ANNOUNCED BLOG INTEREST PICKED UP, ESPECIALLY INTO THE VARIOUS TACTICAL VOTING PROPOSITIONS FLOATING AROUND: ‹/ED›

Cretino-leftism — 1: The *New Statesman*

This week's *New Statesman* comes up with possibly the most idiotic scheme for voting in the general election yet devised: vote against Labour in any vulnerable seat where the sitting Labour MP is not a supporter of Gordon Brown.*

Among the sitting MPs it wants beaten 'to give Blair a bloody nose' are some of Labour's best, including quite a few who used to contribute to the *Statesman* in my time on the magazine.

Sorry, but a Parliamentary Labour Party without Charles Clarke, John Reid, Harriet Harman, Kim Howells, Calum MacDonald, Phil Woolas and Wayne David — to take just a handful of the *Statesman's* chosen victims — would be a lot worse than the one we've got now. Clarke in particular would be a serious loss: he's the only current member of the cabinet who might (in certain circumstances) stand a chance against Brown in a post-Blair leadership contest.

This can't be dismissed as a freak opinion piece: the list was put together by the magazine's editor, Peter Wilby, and one of the contributors he thanks is John

* http://www.newstatesman.com/200504110003

Kampfner, his political editor. As a onetime deputy editor of the *Statesman*, I'm ashamed of them.

Gauche
http://libsoc.blogspot.com

✎ 9 April

‹ED› THIS WAS RESPONDED TO BY ACTUALLY EXISTING: ‹/ED›

The radio did not make a sound

Less than a week in, and things are already getting weird. On Wednesday, I argued that 'we should forget any thought of **differential** protest voting... [trying] to identify the real Blairites and punish them accordingly'. On Friday morning I read that the *New Statesman* had published a weird article listing 35 Blairite Labour MPs (plus 12 Blairite parliamentary candidates) who would be vulnerable to non-Tory tactical voting, and advising its readers to vote against them. Or, er, to vote for them. But not to stay at home, anyway:

> All that said, the only sure way to keep the Tories out is to vote Labour. The **NS** offers this guide in a spirit of public service. We do not recommend anti-Blair tactical voting — but it is better than staying at home and not voting at all.

There's an odd whiff of Prisoner's Dilemma about this: it reads like the result of a deal between Labour loyalists and anti-Blairites at the *Statesman*. It'll suit one group if we vote for Labour candidates and the other group if we vote against them; the one thing they can agree on is that they don't want us to abstain.

Then I read Paul Anderson's reaction to the *New Statesman's* cunning plan. Paul's agin it, on the grounds that the hitlist includes 'some of Labour's best'. In which category he specifically includes John 'friend of Radovan' Reid and Charles Clarke. Yes, **that** Charles Clarke. Speaking as a socialist and a libertarian, I wouldn't feel any compunction about voting against Charles Clarke — in fact, I can't imagine voting **for** him unless the only alternatives were Alan Clark, Petula Clark, Ronald Stark and Mark Park, and even then I'd have to think about it. If this is 'democratic socialism with a libertarian punch', Paul, I'd hate to catch you on an authoritarian day.

In the evening, things got weirder still. Remember the line I quoted from John Lanchester back when, about the possibility of the Conservatives making one final last-ditch move to the Right, in the form of 'an open appeal (as opposed to coded ones) to the Tony Martin/Enoch Powell vote'? Well, the Conservatives have unveiled two new posters, continuing their theme of 'are you tired of pretending not to be an evil selfish bastard?' One says, 'The law should protect me, not burglars'. The other says, 'It's time to put a limit on immigration'. Looks like we're further down the track than I thought.

Friday April 8th: the day the election went mad.

Actually Existing
http://existingactually.blogspot.com

‹ED› IT WOULD APPEAR THAT THE LAW IS NOT WHAT THE LAW SAYS IT IS, BUT WHAT THE LEGISLATORS WOULD HAVE PUT ON THE PAPER IF THEY HAD BEEN COMPETENT TO DO SO. THAT, AT LEAST, IS THE CONCLUSION OF VILLAGE HAMPDEN ON A RULING BY THE EUROPEAN COURT OF JUSTICE: ‹/ED›

The Halifax gets the EU treatment

Here is an example of the way in which European law is incompatible with the principles of liberty. In a tax case heard at the European Court of Justice (sic) [Halifax plc v C & E Commrs (CJEC Case C-255/02) (and related appeals)] Advocate-General Poiares Maduro made the following highly revealing statement in his judgment:

> a person who relies upon the literal meaning of a Community law provision to claim a right that runs counter to its purposes does not deserve to have that right upheld. In such circumstances, the legal provision at issue must be interpreted, contrary to its literal meaning, as actually not conferring the right.

Never mind that it was a case about the operation of tax avoidance schemes, the details of which are only of interest to specialists in that field; look at the general principles being stated. What Maduro means is that even though they get to write the laws, they are under no obligation to say what they mean when doing so. On the contrary, the rest of us are obliged to work out what they mean and obey the law as they meant to write it. I am reminded of a development of the legal profession under the Nazi rule in Germany in which lawyers got into the habit of asking themselves not what the truth about the case was or what the law required, but about what the Führer would think should be done about the case.

I hold it as a fundamental principle of any just legal system that in any dispute between the citizen and the government, the government should be bound by the letter of the law, whilst the citizen may rely on either the letter or the spirit of the law. In this way, the government is constrained when writing laws to say what it means. If not, they will learn the hard way. Remove that incentive and they will become ever sloppier in their drafting. The end result of the system that Maduro is operating will be that the legislators just grunt at a blank sheet of paper and say: well, you know what we mean.

Maduro goes on to say:

> It is true that tax law is frequently dominated by legitimate concerns about legal certainty, deriving, in particular, from the need to guarantee the predictability of the financial burden imposed on taxpayers and the principle of no taxation without representation. However, a comparative analysis of the Member States' legal rules is sufficient to make it clear that such concerns do not exclude the use of certain general provisions and indeterminate concepts in the realm of tax law to prevent illegitimate tax avoidance.

Indeterminate concepts trumping legal certainty, eh! Again the principle is that we must do what they want without knowing for sure what that is. Moreover, Maduro should learn that tax avoidance is by definition legitimate; there is no such thing as illegitimate tax avoidance. It is tax evasion that is illegitimate — specifically, illegal. Of course, in a truly free country, it would be taxation that would be illegitimate.

And more from the great windbag:

> Legal certainty must be balanced against other values of the legal system.

Such as getting the result that the government wants, for example. Maduro is arguing against objective law. He wants subjective law. He is seeking the rule of men (I use the term loosely), not of laws.

> The Sixth Directive should be interpreted as not conferring on a taxable
> person the right to deduct or recover input VAT, in accordance with the
> Community law principle of interpretation prohibiting the abuse of
> Community law provisions, if two objective elements are found to be present
> in terms to be assessed by the national courts. First, that the aims and
> results pursued by the legal provisions formally giving rise to the right would
> be frustrated if the right claimed were actually conferred. Second, that the
> right invoked derives from activities for which there is no other explanation
> than the creation of the right claimed.

The first principle means that if they confer on you a right (not that they or anyone else can confer a right — rights derive from nature) that they do not wish you to exercise, then you must not exercise it — but you presumably still do have the right, just not the right to exercise your right.

The second principle means that it is not permissible to alter your behaviour in response to legislation in such a way as to resist the imposition that they wished to make. That is the problem that has faced socialists for a century; human nature resists being pushed around, and this resistance messes up their plans, and they can thcream and thcream and thcream till they are thick, but anyone with the slightest shred of personal autonomy left will prefer behaviour that lessens the impact on him of the encumbrances of collectivists, and for the same reason that a man with fleas will scratch his head. The authorities in this country have persistently tried to maintain a distinction between transactions carried out for what they term legitimate commercial reasons and those carried out for the purpose of tax avoidance. They overlook the fact that reducing a company's tax burden increases the amount of money it has to apply to its own purposes of buying supplies and equipment, paying its workers and paying dividends to its owners. Tax avoidance is therefore a thoroughly commercial activity — at today's rates, perhaps the most commercial thing possible. At present, they may be stating these principles only in relation to taxation, but this practice will spread. Exchange controls will be an early consequence, as they suffer a fit of pique when the popular response to their reduction of the currency to the status of confetti is to switch to the currency of somewhere more sensible. The end result — admittedly a few years down the line — will be that if they pass laws that you dislike, you must not resist by voting them out of office.

This is what happens under Roman law. The law is treated as the revelation of the will of the legislator, which is therefore prior to and above the law, regardless of how far out of touch with either reality or justice the will of the legislator is. This is the legal system to which we are being handed over. If the people of any country that uses such a system enjoy any degree of freedom, it is in spite of their legal system not because of it. However, modern developments, especially in surveillance and database technology are increasing the ability of governments to apply these ridiculous principles in full.

Maduro himself did not personally write the EU constitution. It would have been a more honest document if he had. Those who did write it have the additional fault of being politicians. You have been warned.

But smile! For that is what they most want to make you unable to do.

Village Hampden
http://villagehampden.blogspot.com

‹ED› ROVER FINALLY WENT BUST AND THE YORKSHIRE RANTER WAS ABLE TO TELL US EXACTLY WHERE THE MONEY WENT AND HOW THE PROFITS WERE MADE: ‹/ED›

The strange death of MG Rover

Well, as if it hadn't been trailed enough, Rover is now an ex-business. 6,000+ jobs are toast, Thatcher's life mission to deindustrialise the UK is complete (you can die now, Maggie, it's done!). I'd like to point up some things about this, some of which I've written about before. Basically, the first thing to remember is that Rover has been run by idiots for years. When the Phoenix team bought it in 2000, they had to hire students to count the cars in stock from satellite photos because BMW either didn't know — *didn't know!* — how much inventory they had, or weren't telling. Which puts all the talk about 'the English patient' at the time in perspective.

Since then, though, we've seen one of the most horrible examples of shameless self-enrichment at others' expense in British history. The restructuring of the Rover complex was conceived to get all the profitable bits of the firm out of the MG Rover Group, the car factory, and into the hands of the Phoenix chaps. This may not seem that bad, until you remember that a sizeable chunk of the original capital was put up by Rover workers themselves. They got shares in MG Rover Group, not Phoenix: so they have now lost everything. Another point: the famous £427 million interest-free loan from BMW was paid to Phoenix (well, actually to another shell company, Techtronic, but this can be collapsed for clarity), not MG. They then charged MG Rover interest on it. What this means has only just dawned on me — as shareholders, the Phoenix group have only the same minimal claim on the assets as the workers who bought in. But as creditors, they are at the top of the heap behind only the Inland Revenue.

Expect a very big supermarket on the site.

They probably think they did a hell of a deal in this, but it turned out they weren't as smart as all that. The other winners, the big winners, are SAIC, the Chinese group they were trying to sell the plant to. SAIC put up £62 million in loans in the winter of 2004, and as a condition of this demanded and got access to Rover's intellectual property. They have already got the drawings for the K-series high efficiency engines (what they wanted all along), the Rover 75, and the right to build it in China — and they also have a claim to recoup their £62 million. SAIC's decision to walk out of the deal neatly avoided taking on any of Rover's liabilities. And, now the Rover engineers and stylists whose heads hold the institutional memory that goes with the drawings are unemployed, they can hire as few or as many as they want.

It is reported that SAIC were spooked when they saw some of the accounts that were far worse than Towers and Co. let on. I don't know if this is the truth, it could be DTI spin, but if so it's an incredible example of that rare phenomenon, someone who really did outwit themselves. Duped by their own chicanery.

Another point what doomed Rover was its inability to finance the development of the new medium car, the long-planned Rover 30. It couldn't fund it because it couldn't shift enough units to generate the cash flow to pay for development costs. When the old British Leyland was about to be savagely restructured preparatory to privatisation, the hard-left union men put out their own counter-plan to the official one. The main critique was that size mattered, and that without a critical mass of production Rover would never be able to keep up technologically.

Who can now say they were wrong?

The Yorkshire Ranter
http://yorkshire-ranter.blogspot.com

✎ 12 April

‹ED› A VERY SHORT AND SWEET ONE FROM CHUNKY MUNKY AT CHOCOLATE COVERED BANANAS: ‹/ED›

Dear My Colonoscopy,

Things you don't want to hear as you slip into sedation:

'Is this the clean camera?'

God Bless the NHS,

Munky

Chocolate Covered Bananas
http://chocolatecoveredbananas.blogspot.com

✎ 13 April

‹ED› ONE OF THE JOYS OF THIS WHOLE INTERNETWEBBIE READING THING IS THE INSIGHT INTO OTHER'S EXPERIENCES. THE MANAGEMENT PRACTICES OF TRAFFIC WARDENS, FOR EXAMPLE, FROM BILL STICKER, OTHERWISE KNOWN AS THE PARKING ATTENDANT: ‹/ED›

Ticking the damn boxes

Got pulled into the office for my 'appraisal' today and got a look at the forms our Management use to keep tabs on our performance. Fortunately I'm reasonably competent at what I do, so the interview only took half an hour.

However, being the 'experienced' person that I am, I learned long ago to read upside down and back to front very quickly. This is a useful skill for rapidly reading rows upon rows of pay and display tickets in car parks without ricking my neck or having to do handstands. Such is the public's predilection for sticking these things every which way up.

The appraisal went okay and the verdict: Bill Sticker gets to keep on walking the streets. Not the fastest booker on the planet but a 'valuable and effective employee', even if Senior Manager wanted to know why I wasn't as fast slapping tickets on windscreens as some of my contemporaries. I responded that I did the job properly as directed in the manner I was taught, then quoted the guidelines back at him verbatim. He couldn't argue with that, seeing as he was the one who wrote the cursed things in the first place. Me, I just kept a straight face and did the nod and smile on cue. One thing I did notice was that the faster bookers have a much higher cancellation and appeal rate than me, so phew, got away with that then.

What amused me was the crude tools they were using to appraise my performance. I shall explain: everything we do is logged on our hand held computers. Every street we visit, every stop to use the toilet (which is logged in the twee little transatlantic idiom of the menu system as a 'Comfort break'), every car we start to book and end up moving on is in the hand held log. The statistics off this are downloaded to industrial strength spreadsheets and turned into whizzy flashy graphs, which mean absolutely dick. What all these graphs and flashy thingies fail to appraise is the human side of the job. Advising worried disabled drivers who are having trouble with some of the more arcane restrictions, giving directions to lost truckers and foreign tourists who have, by some godforsaken fate, strayed off the beaten tourist trail. We do a lot of this. We even get used as 'eyes and ears' for CCTV when some of their reprobates stray out of the camera's field of view. Not to mention fixing damaged pay and display machines. Unfortunately, due to the hand held computer's software, all the aforementioned activities have no menu entry and so do not get recorded. What this means is, if you have a particularly busy day with the helpless and hopeless and your distance and number of streets drop, along with cars booked, then the god of the 'tick box' school of management turns his unwelcome malevolent little eyes in your direction.

As someone else called Bill once wrote: 'Oh brave new world that hath such creatures in it'. Not in the same context of course but I can appreciate the sentiment behind the words.

Walking the Streets
http://parkingattendant.blogspot.com

✎ 18 April

‹ED› HAVE YOU EVER WONDERED WHERE ALL OF THAT GOVERNMENT MONEY GOES? WHY THE ACTUAL WEBSITES ARE SO AWFUL? NEVER TRUST A HIPPIE HAS THE ANSWER: ‹/ED›

Why public sector websites are so dreadful (vol 1)

There are over 400 Councils in England and Wales alone. Almost all of them have built their own websites. They are mostly built from scratch, using a range of different Content Management System (CMS) products, though there is one national open-source project that some councils have collaborated on, as far as I know.

Yet the vast majority of these Councils largely use the same functionality. If they could work effectively together, they could save a fortune in scripts, hosting and software and concentrate on the things that they currently all do appallingly — content, marketing, usability, etc.

But because their IT departments are in charge of this, for the most part, effective co-operation would be a bit like turkeys voting for Xmas. Why concentrate on soft non-techie skills when the finance department (who don't understand how websites are built or how they work) will allocate 99% of the 'new media' budget to the techies?

So, they all go off and 'procure a content management system' (code, 'buy software that our own techies have to implement') and host it themselves (code: 'buy a couple of servers and manage them themselves'). Result? Expensive clunky websites that are badly designed, hard to find anything on, have poor quality copy, are expensive to host and are more likely to be unavailable at weekends.

And ones that have little by way of an upgrade path that isn't costly. Whereas, they could have got together, developed a shared hosted solution and concentrated their budget on usability and copy, etc.

I worked on a big project for the local government association last year. We noticed that NO councillors were getting any help to develop their own websites from their Council (despite £millions spent on e-democracy projects). We worked out that there were a dozen reasons why this was happening (11 of them had nothing to do with the technology and only one of them was the lack of training/manuals) and we came up with a prototype hosted solution.

As a result, the government then made it a condition of getting the 2005 funding that every Council should give their councillors their own sites. Result? — surprise surprise! they're all doing it themselves!

We worked out that 80% of the project was about doing this in a way that councillors are all motivated to update their sites, peer groups, advice on content, marketing, etc. But the government only said that they have to develop them. And because they cost their time differently (we have to charge a figure significantly higher than £100 per day [sic] that we cover our costs, but because of the miraculous way that the public sector are allowed to budget — apparently they can do days of development for the cost that we rack up to do one day's work — even though they pay their staff the same), they will develop it for 'less' than we would charge them to buy into the scheme.

So, the taxpayer pays more, the result is something that is less useable/used, and we wonder why e-government take-up (as opposed to implementation) is so much lower than expected.

calming down now

Never Trust a Hippy
http://nevertrustahippy.blogspot.com

✎ 21 April

‹ED› WITH THE ELECTION NOW FULLY UNDERWAY AND THE FULL LIST OF CANDIDATES AVAILABLE, IAIN MURRAY CASTS HIS EYE OVER THE MINOR PARTIES: ‹/ED›

March of the loonies

The full list of candidates at the election is now available.

One of the features of UK elections is the number of fringe candidates and parties, some of them earnest but weird (making The Daily Show's beloved Candidate Doty look mainstream) and others just plain silly (I well remember the Let's Have A Party standing in '92, I think). This year is no different.

I particularly like the Death, Dungeons and Taxes Party, which sounds like something for the authoritarians to really get behind. The spirit of Commander Boakes appears to live on in the Clause 28 Children's Protection Christian Democrats, although they should add White Resident to get the full effect. Demanding Honesty in Politics and Whitehall must win the prize for the most futile aim ever (followed closely by the Pro Euro Conservatives), while I'd like to find out more about the Imperial Party. The Pride in Paisley Party brings up the image of an Orangeman in drag, while the Publican Party — Free to Smoke (Pubs) would probably get the vote of a large number of my friends.

Most enigmatic is the party label of Stuckist. I asked a friend what this might mean and he replied, 'If I am not wrong (the caveat with which the late lamented Auberon Waugh used to begin his wilder flights of fancy) the Stuckists are a group of musical traditionalists who get together to heckle and disrupt performances of ultra-modern tin-can-and-dustbin-lid composers. As such, presumably to be approved of.'

The election proper has begun. Much fun will be had by all, except the electorate.

The Edge of England's Sword
http://www.iainmurray.org/MT

✎ 23 April

‹ED› WHAT WOULD ANY SELF-RESPECTING BLOGGER DO WHEN STOOD UP ON A DATE? BLOG ABOUT IT, OF COURSE, AS IN ACTUAL FACT DID: ‹/ED›

Cheap meaningless sex

I don't want meaningless, no-strings-attached sex with attractive women.

Now, as you might have guessed, there are a couple of qualifiers to that statement, the most obvious one being that it's blatantly untrue. So would it be better if I said that whilst I wouldn't mind meaningless, no-strings-attached sex with attractive women, I'd much rather have meaningful sex with a woman I loved? It might be more truthful, but would already be setting off the bullshit detectors of some women — after all, that's the kind of thing some guy might say to sound less sordid, without being too corny, with a view to trying to eventually get you into bed for some meaningless sex.

But it gets worse — and for those of you of a gentle disposition, *I really do recommend you stop reading now*. For me, by far the most exquisite feeling is just to wake up next to the woman you love on a Sunday morning, her body pressed against yours — not in an overtly sexual way, just pushed against you in a physical expression of total trust and security. When she gets up to leave for the bathroom, you notice how the sunlight pierces through the blinds, don't ask me why this is important, but it is somehow. When she returns, she'll feel slightly colder and will push back against you in exactly the same position, her back against your stomach, the front of your thighs against the back of hers. You'll inhale the smell of her hair and wrap your arms around her and wish to freeze time, or at least be able to return to that moment of utter oneness whenever you want. *I'm sorry; this really is the most embarrassingly awful tosh.* However, I find that moment, far, far more intimate and, yes important, than sex. Of course, it's not that sex doesn't matter, after all, one of the reasons you're snuggled together so tightly on this side of the bed is because the other half is a mess of congealed bodily fluids, peanut butter, kitchen utensils and a pillow-covered wooden chest (God knows why you lifted that up there, it's bloody heavy, but you seem to remember it having something to do with 'angles' or 'ankles' or possibly both) from the night before. And if she comes back into the room and picks up the whisk with that wild glint in her eye, but you can hear the pattering feet of a small child in the house, you'll decide that 'Dick and Dom in Da Buungalow' is perfectly acceptable televisual entertainment for 3 year olds after all, and lock the bedroom door.

It's a Saturday night and the reason I've had time to type this is because the woman for whom I've cooked dinner hasn't bothered to turn up. I could have written something mean and spiteful, I hope something that made you feel nauseous was an acceptable alternative?

German Phrase For Today: '*Ich werde mich melden, ehrlich.*' — Don't call me anymore, in fact, leave me the hell alone.

In Actual Fact
www.inactualfact.com

<note> As a strategy this seems to have worked. One female blogger was so impressed (whether by the quality of the writing or the mention of the usage of kitchen utensils I haven't had the courage to ask) that she made contact and they now seem to spend their weekends commuting between the two European cities they inhabit. As I was working on the final version of this book in October, news came through from the website that the correspondent had progressed to cleaning his kitchen floor, so obviously a successful relationship was developing. </note>

✎ 26 April

‹ED› A VERY QUICK NOTE FROM MARTIN KEEGAN ON LANGUAGE: ‹/ED›

Saving the subjunctive

I have discovered a new way to save the subjunctive in English: argue that it is necessary to use the subjunctive to 'bring us into line with continental Europe'. Apparently these seven words have a bewitching effect on just the sort of people who think that the subjunctive should be abolished.

Martin Keegan
http://mk.ucant.org

MAY 2005

✎ 1 May

‹ED› ABSOLUTELY ANYTHING AND EVERYTHING ENDS UP ON A BLOG SOMEWHERE. YES, EVEN MORRIS DANCING. ‹/ED›

Jump at the sun

Each day, for as long as any historian can remember, the Earth has turned about itself, and so once every 24 hours or so, the sun sets in the evening and rises in the morning.

It's a little-known fact that, on one day of every year, the fact that the sun rises is all down to the morris dancers.

Quite why they decide to dance, around dawn on May Day, to wake up the sun isn't clear. But if you had to pick a significant day for morris dancers, it would be 1 May. For three centuries and more, the day was treated as a bookmark in the year that showed summer was near. It'd be a festival of celebration, even before it became linked with workers' rights. Morris dancers were part of the festivities.

But that was during the day. Where did dancing *at dawn* on May Day come from? You find out that, like most supposedly ancient traditions, it goes back to time immemorial, or, in other words, to 1923. To 1923 at Oxford, to be precise. For centuries in that city, people have gathered to see in the May dawn. Groups of students, fuelled by adrenaline mixed with alcohol, launch themselves from a high bridge into the freezing river below: all manage to survive with varying degrees of success, in a kind of natural selection for Hooray Henrys. The choir of Magdalen College sing from their bell-tower and welcome May in. So it must have seemed fairly natural for a side of morris men to join in the festivities one year, dancing in the new dawn.

For those taking part, it must have been a fairly arduous tradition to uphold after the first year. Getting up at stupid o'clock in the morning and dancing in the freezing cold and (maybe) rain can't have been many people's idea of fun. But, for whatever reason, dancing the May dawn in has become a fixture of most morris dancers' calendars.

Calendars all over the world, of course. In Australia, May Day dawn is already old news, and even though the start of May there marks more autumn than summer, morris dancers in the country have already danced up the sun. Though, you've heard of a side that preferred to stay in their beds and wait till it was actually dawn in Britain, and you can't say you blame them.

About 20 hours later, the last morris sides to see the new day will probably be in Alaska, where the sun never really properly sets for more than a couple of hours. If they're anything like previous years, the dancers there will probably be staying up all night until the sky lightens. Though they'll still be dancing.

In Britain, it really is as unearthly an hour as it seems to be. You've been up since three in the morning, and soon you'll be jumping in a car and heading off to a straight-up-squire-honest-to-goodness Roman amphitheatre, about 60 miles to your east. It's a very strange thing to do on a Sunday morning, but your conscience is salved somewhat by the promise of dancing outside a cathedral a few hours later, giving if not absolution, at least Anglican semi-approval of what you're doing.

But first, you'll be dancing at dawn, and you'll have to wait and see whether the sun smiles on your efforts. You're fairly sure it should, but then again, you never can tell.

   <note> And does it work? </note>

Out and about (06:03 am, 1 May)

If it's cloudy but dawned, that still counts, right? Right. That must have worked then. Happy May Day.

Nine Days' Wonder
http://www.wibsite.com/wiblog/ninedayswonder

✎ 6 May

‹ED› THE ELECTION IS OVER AND THE ANALYSES START. PETER BLACK (A LIBERAL DEMOCRAT ASSEMBLY MEMBER IN WALES) POINTS OUT THE BASIC UNFAIRNESS OF THE CURRENT VOTING SYSTEM: ‹/ED›

'The electoral system seriously sucks'

In commenting on this post, Australian Senator Andrew Bartlett has a very valid point. He has expanded on it at his place. The fact is that Labour won 35.2% of the vote, amounting to just 21% of the 44 million people eligible to vote, and yet Tony Blair now commands 55% of the seats in the House of Commons.

The Tories, who are only 2.8% behind, have fewer seats than the number won in 1983 by Michael Foot and the Labour Party, in one of the most disastrous results ever experienced by modern Labour. They have failed to break through the 200 seat barrier.

Meanwhile, the Liberal Democrats received just under two thirds of the vote share of Labour and the Tories and yet they have less than a third of the number of MPs won by the latter and 17.5% of Labour's total. As the *Guardian* says, 'For the first time, a majority government in Britain has been elected by fewer people than those who could not be bothered to vote. Labour's 36% share of the vote was lower than the 39% of the electorate who didn't make it to the polling station.'* On last night's results a Labour MP only needed 26,858 votes to get elected, compared with 44,241 votes for a Tory MP, and a staggering 98,484 for each Liberal Democrat MP.

It is because of the distorted nature of this winner-takes-all system that Blair was able to make the outrageous and untrue claim that a vote for the Liberal Democrats will let in the Tories. As was proved by the outcome, even a close run thing, in terms of the popular vote, left Howard floundering way behind.

As Andrew says, it is astonishing that more people are not commenting and protesting about this travesty. The British electoral system is very poorly indeed.

N.B. If you think this post is an argument for proportional representation then you would be right. However, it is vital that any replacement system of voting is properly proportional and retains a constituency link. The Welsh Assembly system conspicuously fails to do this as is illustrated by the fact that Labour won half the seats with less than 40% of the vote in 2003.

Peter Black AM
http://peterblack.blogspot.com

✎ 12 May

<ED> ALFRED THE OK (HE DESCRIBES HIMSELF AS 'NOT AS GOOD AS THE GREAT BUT BETTER THAN ALFRED THE CRAP') STOOD IN THE ELECTION IN ORMSKIRK. POSSIBLY THE BEST PIECE OF POLITICAL REPORTING OF THE YEAR: </ED>

A night to remember...

The big night came. Thursday the fifth of May. Me and the Missus get all togged up in our best election winning gear, slap on the old red and white rosettes, do a double clench fist pose in front of the mirror whilst shouting 'Come and get my seat if you think you're hard enough'... and we're off. We have a date with destiny.

And then we're not.

Because I thought this might be a night to remember — I reckon I'll need my camera to record the great event, the very moment I'm declared a Member of Parliament.

Fantasy over. I'll be made up to get 50 votes.

We arrive at the Civic Hall in Ormskirk. The main players are already in. The Labour crew look like mafia hoods and molls — all grey hair, badly fitting dark suits and chin stubble. The men looked pretty rough as well.

The Tory cadre are typically posh. Tweed, tatty hair-cuts, lots of comb-overs, ruddy cheeks, red fleshy ears and the most enormous blue velour rosettes abound. Amongst the old fogies and blue rinses are a couple of well fit posh totties. I fantasise: riding crops, rounded vowels and shapely, well-filled blouses, tiffin, Ferraris...

Suddenly, a big neon, yellow coated plod ushers us towards the interior of the hall proper. The Lib Dems flounce around in their Hush Puppies, aged slacks and round, penny-collar lemon shirts. They've all got clip-boards and Lib Dem yellow pens — and are trying to outdo each other in officious speed-walking around the hall. They all appear to be called Jeremy, Barry and Isabel...

We stroll in. It's just like the Ringo kid and Mrs Ringo Kid gallooting their way into Dodge City's most notorious Saloon...

We ain't looking for trouble, we've just come in off the trail. We mosey on in.

The entire hall goes quiet.

The Hum stops. The Drum is silenced. Two hundred pairs of politically biased eyes look us over. Think, think think!!!

What would Blair or Howard do in a situation like this?

I check my flies and give a weak as water wavette.

We seek sanctuary in the form of the nearest pair of seats. The spell is broken and counters, tellers, Mafia bosses, Barry, Jeremy and posh totty get back to the business of checking votes.

We survey the activity — and it's frantic. Voting slips are being dumped onto desks and sorted into bundles — it's 11 o'clock at night. It's pretty clear that we are the Electoral Virgins here because we've rather overjudged the dress code — and appear to be the only ones to have bothered to get togged up at all. It looks like tat-central in that place — almost as if a jumble sale is about to start, and the customers are wearing the stuff on sale.

In the middle of the hall, rising like a big, black risey thing with white lettering on the sides, are the ballot boxes. They are stacked higher than a stack of corrupt politicians — and that's high. Now and again, a student is sent over to get another box and tips the contents all over the desks. The counters count. After an absolute age, I check with Alfreda. 'What's the time then?'

'5 past 11'.

It's going to be a very, very long night.

The UKIP candidate saunters over to us. 'What a bloody crap night we're having,' he says. 'D'you know what, I should have voted for you lot, our only policy is to get out of Europe... we're bloody crap.'

His agent nodded in agreement, 'Yeah, UKIP's finished — I reckon you'll be pushing us pretty close tonight, mate. It's a bit of a bummer — we've had a full time crew out canvassing, *full time* in this constituency for a month now.'

I inwardly smirk, smug in the knowledge that these guys are actually worried about little old me and not admitting that since the great ego that is RKS [Robert Kilroy Silk] left them, they've been withering away.

The Labour Don, the boss of bosses, cruises past with his little flotilla of fags. They are handing out real red roses to their team. Righteous indignation takes hold of me. I wanted to say — 'Hey Don-Bollocks, what the bloody hell are you guys hijacking my country's emblem for — got a bloody cheek haven't you?'

Instead, I seethe and decide to twiddle with my rosette flanges. It helps to calm me down.

I think it's about time I strolled around the tables to check that fair play and democracy is being served. I stroll like a Statesman, stiff-legged and hands behind my back; I really do look the bizz —Lord of all I survey.

In spite of my very best efforts I can't find one, not one, voting slip that has a cross next to my name. It's very depressing. And then — I see it. Result, hat trick, loss of virginity and passing driving test all in one gloriously orgasmic moment. And I know it's not the one that I filled in, this one's got a 'tick' next to my name. A tick for God's sake — will they say it's legal? Of course they do! My pile is off and growing! I *am* a Statesman after all. I glide over to Alfreda.

'Why are you walking like a twat?'

'Sorry, I thought I was walking like Prince Charles.'

'Exactly!'

It's now 2 o'clock in the bloody morning. With 200 people in one airless room it's getting hot and stale and manky. Still the counting goes on. I compare piles of votes. The Labour woman has millions, an entire forest worth of paper has been shovelled into the corner called 'winner'. Next is the Tory — he's a decent guy really — and almost local to boot. The Lib Dem is clearly disappointed — he was pretty arrogant throughout this keenly fought contest and this looks like the final straw. His pile wouldn't even start a boy scout's fire. Suddenly, the entire Lib Dem contingent flounce out. Suddenly, there's a lot less yellow around the room. Suddenly, Hush Puppies are silent... Ladies and Gentlemen — Barry, Jeremy and Isabel have left the building.

I catch the eye of the Returning Officer. 'When do you reckon then — the declaration?'

'Oh we should have everything ready for 4 ish'...

Well they weren't ready for 4 ish — more like gone 5 ish actually. We are called over — the Labour manikin wins by miles. Tory second, Lib Dem third, UKIP fourth just — bugger! ?...

And me with 525 voteroonies. I didn't even come last — some indy brought up the rear a good 300 votes behind me.

By the time the Labour manikin finishes her speech of thanks, the audience have obviously had enough — it's light outside and the birds are tweeting. I nervously finger my well-crafted, four-page speech in my pocket. Everyone else is giving short 'n' sharp speechettes. The UKIP guy can't be bothered to say anything he's so pissed off, so it's my turn. I pull out the wad of A4, the crowd sigh.

What would Mel Gibson say at a time like this? Easy, he'd chuck the speech away, thank the Returning Officer, Jane and Anne Marie, his assistants, the counters and his agent. Then he'd shout 'Freedom' at the top of his voice … oh, and 'We demand an English Parliament Tony — or else'?...

Everyone claps. I don't know whether it was the message in my speech or the relief at its brevity. I punch the air, hoping against hope that, just at that moment, Tony Blair had somehow fallen through the ceiling above to meet my well-clenched fist.

The winning Labour candidate, or 'cardboard box' as she is known in this area, looked at the floor. Bloody hell, I'm no Reg Keys but she looked just a little embarrassed there I think. I walk over to her to shake her hand...

'Hi Rosie, congratulations... Oh, and you'll be seeing a lot more of me in the future' ?...

She looked worried. She obviously didn't know that I am a fully paid up member of the awkward squad... But she does now!

Triumphant. I link arms with my agent, my soul mate, my wife Alfreda. We deftly avoid all the no-mark local hacks trying to interview anyone wearing a rosette and saunter past the guard of plod at the door. We stroll out into the weak, watery wet morning light and go home.

The deposit was lost — but it just didn't matter. By standing I had given people in the constituency an opportunity to express their dissatisfaction at the current political system — all 525 of them.

What was it Bill Shankly once said? 'First is first and second is nowhere'...

Well you were wrong Billy boy. Great footy manager you might have been, but you knew bugger all about elections.

First is first is a cardboard box, but 525 is a bloody miracle mate...

Alfred the OK
http://alfredtheok.blogspot.com

✎ 13 May

‹ED› LABOUR'S RE-ELECTION MEANS THAT ALL THOSE BILLS THAT FELL AS A RESULT OF THE DISSOLUTION OF PARLIAMENT CAN NOW BE RE-INTRODUCED. INCLUDING, OF COURSE, THE ID CARDS BILL: ‹/ED›

13 May, 2005: Return to the planet of idiocy

So, as you will have noticed, unless you've been on holiday for the past few weeks or something, we have a new Labour government; depending on who you believe, it may even be a New Labour government. This government has, in the words of Geoff Hoon, been 'elected by a substantial majority in the country', which is what in English we used to call a 'minority', and that means that they're now in a position to '[entrench] progressive politics' in this country, which is what in English we used to call 'invading things and abolishing our civil liberties'.

Now, exactly what the Labour government plan to do is up to them; their immediate plans will be announced in the Queen's Speech next week, but until then we don't know *precisely* what they're plotting. However, it's probably safe to say that the Prime Minister wouldn't have decided to make Andy Burnham MP a Parliamentary Under Secretary with particular responsibility for ID cards unless he plans to have another go at forcing bloody ID cards on us again.

Burnham, whom regular readers will have met here before, has such enthusiasm for ID cards that he advocates making them compulsory-to-carry; without carrying ID cards at all times, he argues, it would be impossible to 'unlock the full benefits of identity cards in fighting crime'. Benefits like, uh, sabotaging the witness-protection programme. Idiot.

Anyway, that means that the ID Cards Bill will very probably be back from the dead in this session of Parliament. The Government didn't take any notice of the responses to the consultation on ID cards or the recommendations of the Commons committee on the Bill last time round, so it's unlikely to make any substantive changes to the previous version of the Bill despite getting a fairly serious kicking from the electorate and being returned to power with the support of only a fifth of the population.

So, we're screwed, right? Well... yes, though it might not look that way right now.

The House of Lords, which is likely to be fairly unreceptive to the Bill, cannot block it because, as Hoon says, it is a Labour manifesto commitment; under the 1945 Salisbury Convention, the Lords can't now kill it off. Of course, if the Government are minded to bring in ID card legislation which isn't as described in their manifesto, the Lords can amend it until it is. Here is what the Labour Party have threatened us with: (from their manifesto, page 52)*

> By 2008, those needing a visa to enter the UK will be fingerprinted. We will issue ID cards to all visitors planning to stay for more than three months. [...]
>
> We will introduce ID cards, including biometric data like fingerprints, backed up by a national register and rolling out initially on a voluntary basis as people renew their passports.

Specific offensive features of the scheme as envisaged in the Home Office's febrile imaginations and thence their Bill, but not stated in the manifesto, include:

- the facility to search for individuals' records in the Register by their biometrics (perhaps the Lords would have to be a little bit autistic to throw that out, but a card carrying a signed statement of the holder's biometric details could actually be somewhat useful under certain circumstances and much less dangerous; the manifesto statement doesn't require that the Register be keyed by iris code, etc.);

- more generally, the particular and extensive list of information which would be stored in each individual's record in the Register, and the power of the Home Secretary to alter this by secondary legislation;

- the compulsion of certain groups of people, except for certain visitors to the country, as above, to register;

- the power of the Home Secretary to prevent people from using the NHS or other public services to which they are entitled unless they register;

*http://www.labour.org.uk/fileadmin/manifesto_13042005_a3/pdf/manifesto.pdf

- the 'audit trail', in which would be recorded every access to the Register or use of a card — for instance, whenever a cardholder visits their GP or uses any other public service, or (in certain government fantasies) buys anything costing more than £200 — and which would be accessible to many officials in the Home Office and the security services, but secret from the cardholder;

- more generally, access by parties other than the cardholder to information on the card or the Register;

- the proposed criminal offences and penalties associated with the card, for instance the power to jail for ten years anybody who has 'false ID', such as that which teenagers use to buy beer;

- the requirement for victims to pay for the card out of their own pocket; and

- any association between biometric passports and ID cards, apart from the coincidental one in the manifesto.

Stripping all of the above out of the ID Cards Bill would not make a bad Bill into a good one. But it would make an extremely offensive Bill somewhat less so.

The reasons why the Labour party are pursuing this scheme are, as ever, unclear. It's big, it's shiny, it's high-tech, it's expensive: a perfect New Labour scheme, some argue. Others suppose that the Home Office have been reading too much stuff from MI5 and have become terrified of terrorism; ID cards, incongruously, are imagined to be the solution. On a different tack, a perceptive article from law firm Pinsent Masons points out that,*

> Details of an ID Card Gateway Review, published on the Office of Government Commerce (OGC) website as a result of a Freedom of Information Act request last month, reveals that the wider 'public service' use of the ID Card database has been an objective of Government for two years. The OGC Review, dated June 2003, states that the ID Card database 'could provide a more efficient basis for administering public services by avoiding the need for people to provide the same personal information time and again to a range of public services'.

*http://www.out-law.com

The OGC Review continues:

> 'There would also be savings for service providers as there would be a single definitive source of information about people's identity and possibly a unique personal number for everyone registered on the system'.

The essentials of the argument:

- the Labour Party has promised to make the public services work better without spending much more money on them; and

- they promise to achieve this by 'efficiency savings'; but

- they don't know how to do that (not surprising: nobody else does either); however

- somebody has told them that, magically, it can be effected using computers; and

- somebody else — very probably a firm of consultants which specialises in building enormous databases at enormous cost — has told them that to do that they would need to have a giant database of everyone in the country.

It's rubbish, obviously. There's no reason to suppose that 'the need for people to provide the same personal information time and again to a range of public services' seriously contributes to the cost of providing those services, or even to the hassle of using them. You might argue that building one central database which all the local databases — at GPs' surgeries, hospitals, benefit offices, etc. — can refer to might save money, but actually linking all those disparate databases to another new database will probably make them *more* expensive to run and will certainly cost a lot of money to set up.

If this is truly what they're based on, I expect Labour's attempts to make the public services 'more efficient' will be a complete disaster — mostly of the 'pissing money down the drain' variety, rather than the 'killing people by accident' variety, though I wouldn't rule out the latter completely.

Anyway, if we believe this theory of What The ID Cards Scheme Is For, we should expect Labour to cling to it through thick and thin, because they believe that their credibility — such as it is — is predicated on efficiency-saving reform of the public services, and that those efficiency savings mean forcing everybody to have an ID card and have all their personal details and all their comings and goings recorded in the National Identity Register. Idiots.

But...

Here is an optimistic possible scenario ('never make predictions, especially about the future'): Labour gets the Bill through the Commons; the Lords then, by amendments, render it relatively inoffensive but impotent for its — unstated in the Labour manifesto — true purpose. Labour resolves to force it through under the Parliament Act, but by the time they've gone through all the relevant parliamentary hoops, their government has dissolved into 1995 John Major-style chaos (or the economy is going down the pan or they're too busy fighting a war in Iran or whatever), and they are left unable to get the Commons to approve the Bill; the idea is dead — for a few more years, anyway.

Well, it looks a bit risky for my liking, but it might just work, right?

Wrong.

In their Manifesto, the Labour party have also promised to emasculate the Lords to the point of irrelevance:

> We will legislate to place reasonable limits on the time bills spend in the second chamber — no longer than 60 sitting days for most bills.

Which I interpret to mean that they intend to further amend the Parliament Act to reduce the extent of the delay the Lords may impose from one year to much less than that. I don't suppose that this crept in purely because of ID cards — it's much more likely to be because Blair and cronies were so enraged by the behaviour of the Lords in trying to protect some of our remaining basic freedoms during the wretched Terrorism Act episode — but basically this means that there will be no effective check on Labour's enthusiasm to fob off on us ID cards or any of the rest of their police state bullshit.

Like I said: we're screwed.

Chris Lightfoot's web log
http://ex-parrot.com/~chris/wwwitter

✎ 17 May

‹ED› NATALIE SOLENT WONDERS WHETHER THERE IS A NEWSPAPER OUT THERE ACTUALLY FIT TO READ: ‹/ED›

Mildly hypocritical, mildly prudish reader seeks newspaper for fun and possible long-term relationship

From the age of ten onwards I read the *Times* every day and learnt a lot from it. I was the sort of child who instructed her elders and betters on any complexities of the situation in South Africa that they might have missed. Having survived being strangled I was on course to be the well-informed person you see today. I remember the *Times*, and particularly the columns written by Bernard Levin, with gratitude.

Decades have passed. My oldest child is twelve. You might think that I would make sure to have a quality newspaper hit the mat each day. We do not. Why not? Several reasons, but to my suprise I find that one of the most important is that they are all too salacious.

Since I am complaining about that I had better mention that there will be some discussion of sex in this post. Nothing the average twelve-year-old hasn't known about for years, but probably mutually embarrassing for parent or child to know the other has read. That's the whole point, actually.

When I was a kid I learned much about the ways of the world — sex, drugs, crime and so on — from reading the paper. The information came in gradually, casually and mixed up with other topics. Good.

However, thirty years ago an article about prostitution, for instance, would be wrapped up in a package of high-minded concern for a social problem. Possibly this concern was fake, mere cover for a way of giving readers a thrill while allowing writer and reader to pretend to be respectable. More likely motives were mixed. Certainly I frequently read such articles in the spirit of one looking up the rude words in the dictionary. But if hypocrisy it was, then so much the better for hypocrisy. It compares well with the crassness of today. A month or two back the *Sunday Telegraph* had an article about that countrywoman who became a prostitute to pay for her daughter's riding lessons. It wasn't the fact that the story was covered that I objected to but the detailed descriptions of her encounters with various clients, including clients who took pleasure in violent abuse. I would rather not have that topic for family discussion over breakfast, thank you.

And that was the *Telegraph* — once upon a time written by respectable Tories. The *Independent* and the *Guardian* are full of writers anxious to assert how comfortable they are with various fetishes. Quite apart from the explicitness, I do not wish my children to grow up to be bores. Should I then go back to my old friend, the *Times*? It's probably the best bet of the qualities, but I find it ominous that David Aaronovitch has joined the staff. I greatly respect Aaro's writing on the Iraq war but every fifth article he wrote for the *Guardian* concerned his relationship with his right hand and I have no reason to suppose he will be any different in the *Times*.

I'm certainly not advocating censorship, just saying that a paper that went back to offering all the news that's fit to print would have my subscription sewn up. I would like it to be a major paper, though. I have nothing against the various Christian papers — I am always happy to learn of a successful Alpha Course in Cheam — but that isn't what I want as a main news source. Too sectional. Too wholesome. Too admiring of Christian Aid. I want the cosmopolitan feel of a newspaper that I know is also read by several hundred thousand of my compatriots at least.

How many other readers are there like me? My guess is that quite a few parents who don't particularly care about sex in the papers on their own account suddenly develop prudish tendencies when their child reads about it. As a result many children may not be getting started on the newspaper habit.

Natalie Solent
http://nataliesolent.blogspot.com

✎ 19 May

‹ED› THE BAG OF BEARS PROVIDES A SCOTTISH VIEW OF THE LATEST REALITY TV SERIES: ‹/ED›

It's all too much

Who are Abi Titmuss and Rebecca Loos, and what exactly is Love Island? And why for the love of a caramel macaroon bar is it on my telly?

Someone somewhere walked into a room and pitched this idea and, presumably kept a straight face whilst doing so. Well it just isn't Scottish. We don't like these things. It's just too, what's the word... it'll come to me in a minute... hang on... yes... sunny. Sunny programmes about damn all are just not our thing.

We need to create Skye TV. Headquartered in Portree it would run an 8-hour rolling news service (except on Wednesday, which is early closing, excluding holidays and on days when the snow is a bit heavier than usual). Reality TV would get a look in as 4 residents are caught on CCTV in the Post Office when the door jams shut, and everyone has to sit on the floor, having a nice cup of tea whilst Mr Doonan pops round with his screwdriver. Weather is easily dealt with by a webcam — if you see a sheep apparantly climbing vertically up the screen it means the web cam's blown over and, ergo, it's windy.

It's got to be done.

The Bag of Bears
http://bagofbears.blogs.com/the_bag_of_bears

‹ED› THE NEW PARLIAMENTARY SESSION ALSO BROUGHT THE COUNTER-TERRORISM BILL BACK. HERE'S THE MILITANT PINE MARTEN'S TAKE ON THE MATTER: ‹/ED›

Queen's Speech: Darth Blunkett's back and so is the notion of sedition

In the aftermath of the latest election, I had hoped that with his greatly reduced – though still healthy — majority and new-found need to actually consult with othe people such as MPs, Tony Blair might tone down his messianic zeal and unshakeable belief that whatever he thinks is right, and that this alone justifies any decision that he may care to take. No such luck. Just to make that point clear to anyone who may have any doubt, he immediately brought David 'Darth' Blunkett out of his retreat to act as the Cabinet Enforcer. Then yesterday, Her Majesty Mrs Windsor came to tell us what the deal is going to be.

I'm not going to go through the entire contents of the Queen's Speech, I'm just going to concentrate on one particular bill in it that gives me the mustelid willies. I refer to the Counter Terrorism Bill (draft), the latest complement to the Terrorism Act 2000, a pretty Draconian piece of legislation that was subsequently superdraconised by the Prevention of Terrorism Act at the end of the last Parliament.

The Counter Terrorism Bill (draft) is thought to introduce the twin criminal offences of 'acts preparatory to terrorism' and of 'glorifying or condoning' acts of terrorism. Now I don't want anyone to start thinking that pine martens are particularly in favour of blowing up innocent people as a means to bring about an ideological end; however, these notions are vague enough to be causes for high levels of concern. But I am worried that these offences, and particularly the latter, could be an open door to reintroducing the notion of sedition into English Law.

An often heard quote from an anonymous source is that 'one man's terrorist is another man's freedom fighter' (just think of everything that's been said about Nelson Mandela over the years), so presumably, in Law, there is a clear definition of what is meant by the word '*terrorism*'. A good place to start you'd assume, given the international scale of the problem, is the UN. So what does the UN, which is after all the main source and guarantor of international law, have to say on the matter?

From the UN Office on Drugs and Crime website:*

> The question of a definition of terrorism has haunted the debate among states for decades. A first attempt to arrive at an internationally acceptable definition was made under the League of Nations, but the convention drafted in 1937 never came into existence. The UN Member States still have no agreed-upon definition. Terminology consensus would, however, be necessary for a single comprehensive convention on terrorism, which some countries favour in place of the present 12 piecemeal conventions and protocols.

*www.unodc.org/unodc/index.html

Or in other words, there's still a fair amount of poetic licence allowed in individual states' legal definition of who is or isn't a terrorist. Never mind, I'm sure that good old English Law can help us for domestic purposes. Let's see what the Terrorism Act has to say:*

(1) In this Act 'terrorism' means the use or threat of action where —

(a) the action falls within subsection (2),

(b) the use or threat is designed to influence the government or to intimidate the public or a section of the public, and

(c) the use or threat is made for the purpose of advancing a political, religious or ideological cause.

(2) Action falls within this subsection if it –

(a) involves serious violence against a person,

(b) involves serious damage to property,

(c) endangers a person's life, other than that of the person committing the action,

(d) creates a serious risk to the health or safety of the public or a section of the public, or

(e) is designed seriously to interfere with or seriously to disrupt an electronic system.

(3) The use or threat of action falling within subsection (2) which involves the use of firearms or explosives is terrorism whether or not subsection (1)(b) is satisfied.

(4) In this section-

(a) 'action' includes action outside the United Kingdom,

(b) a reference to any person or to property is a reference to any person, or to property, wherever situated,

(c) a reference to the public includes a reference to the public of a country other than the United Kingdom, and

*www.hmso.gov.uk/acts/acts2000/00011—b.htm

(d) 'the government' means the government of the United Kingdom, of a Part of the United Kingdom or of a country other than the United Kingdom.

(5) In this Act a reference to action taken for the purposes of terrorism includes a reference to action taken for the benefit of a proscribed organisation.

Now I realise that this is a load of Legalese; however, what it boils down to, in conjunction with the proposed Draft Bill, is that the UK Government can prosecute anyone in the UK for acts against any organisation that it likes anywhere in the world. Saying that, when all's said and done, Palestinian suicide bombers may have a point worth listening to, for instance, would probably qualify as 'condoning terrorism', and therefore be a criminal offence.

To summarise, this reintroduces the legal notion of a crime of opinion. It opens the door to reintroducing sedition, a Common Law offence that was declared obsolescent by Lord Denning on the grounds that it was too broadly defined and inhibited too much the free and full discussion of public affairs, as a criminal offence. It makes openly holding certain opinions illegal. This is a stunningly illiberal legislative proposal.

Maybe I'm wrong. After all, I'm not a lawyer, I'm a pine marten, albeit possibly a seditious one. But just because I'm paranoid, it doesn't mean that I'm wrong.

Militant Pine Marten
http://militantpinemarten.blogspot.com

✎ 20 May

‹ED› GUIDO FAWKES APPEARS TO HAVE FOUND
THE LABOUR PARTY INDULGING IN ILLEGAL
PRACTICES DURING THE ELECTION. IT'S ALL
OVER NOW, OF COURSE, NOTHING WILL COME
OF IT, BUT INTERESTING NONETHELESS: ‹/ED›

Labour broke e-laws during election campaign

This post has been in gestation for a month and has been held up for various reasons, including Zack Exley threatening to sue Guido. It has been edited down to what can definitely be stood up in court — Zack has seen it and whined extensively about it. Despite being invited to make corrections, he has failed to point out any specific errors. There is a lot more to this (Zack, the comments section is open).

There is evidence of law-breaking by the American left-winger George Bush dubbed the '*garbage man*' and who Labour hired to create its sophisticated e-mail campaign. Zack previously worked at the anti-Bush, Soros-backed MoveOn.Org campaign. He also worked on Kerry's campaign. All the Labour Party campaign e-mails designed by Zack made bold references to the Privacy Statement on Labour's website, which states

> You may be asked for personal information if you complete one of the forms on this site. Please see below the information we ask for and what this information is used for. In each case we will only use the information about you for the purpose for which you provide it. The Labour Party does not sell or disclose this information to outside organisations or individuals, nor transfer it outside the United Kingdom.

It is a criminal offence under the Data Protection Act to obtain information by misrepresentation. Guido has evidence that data collected by the Labour Party was in fact, contrary to their privacy claims, disclosed to an outside private corporation. The corporation is Email Reaction, a firm usually hired by banks and similar mass marketers. The Labour Party's e-mail campaign utilised Email Reaction to embed unique Spyware links in the e-mails to identify who opened an e-mail. Link-tracking systems can analyse signals sent back from embedded software code in the e-mails to report who clicked on a link in an email and when. The Spyware is sophisticated enough so that individual histories for each individual can be compiled showing their full history (e-mails sent, clicks, opens, donations made). The Labour party collected postcode details when it collected e-mail addresses for its database, which could be used to tie in with the data available from the massive Mosaic consumer database.

David Naylor, partner, Technology Transactions Group at global technology and finance law firm, Morrison & Foerster, points out that

> the Directive on Privacy and Electronic Communications 2002 introduces new laws across Europe controlling the use of cookies and other tracking technology used on websites as well as location-based data.
>
> These laws were brought into force in the UK on 11 December 2003, under the Privacy and Electronic Communications (EC Directive) Regulations 2003. Companies and other data controllers that ignore these laws may be subject to regulatory investigation and fines, civil liability and, in some circumstances, criminal liability. In certain circumstances, criminal sanctions may be imposed for breaches of data protection laws not only against a company that acts as a data controller, but also against its directors. You should note that the regulations apply to all cookies and tracking devices, whether or not they are used to store personally identifiable data.

During the campaign Guido had been digging into this for a few weeks when he exchanged e-mails with Zack Exley and challenged him on this issue. Despite initial denials, when presented with proof he later admitted that the links were in the e-mails, but denied they were utilised and claimed they were an oversight by the outside software supplier Email Reaction. He tried to put Guido off the scent, eventually threatening that he would '*cut you off for life*' if Guido disclosed this information. (Guido will cope.)

Subsequent campaign e-mails sent out by the Labour party did not contain the unique identifiers. The press office and the legal department will not respond to any information requests. Failure to disclose the Spyware and failure to offer opt out facilities are criminal offences under the Data Protection Act and the Privacy and Electronic Communications (EC Directive) Regulations 2003. Melanie Onn, the Constitutional and Legal Officer for the Legal and Financial Compliance Taskforce for the Labour Party stonewalled on giving answers to all questions and requests prior to 5 May. Applications and requests under the Data Protection Act were ignored — in breach of the law. But breaching the Data Protection Act by not supplying blogging applicants such as Guido and Tim Ireland with the information they are obliged to supply, in the time they are supposed to do, is the least of

Melanie Onn's worries. *Guido understands that privacy advocates are contemplating legal action in what would be a test case, who better to test the laws against than the governing party that introduced them?*

Guido Fawkes
http://5thnovember.blogspot.com

✎ 29 May

‹ED› AS YOU WILL HAVE NOTED THERE HAS BEEN, OVER THE YEAR, QUITE SOME OPPOSITION TO THE ID CARDS SCHEME. IN FACT, I HAVE BEEN UNABLE, OVER THE COURSE OF THAT YEAR, TO FIND A SINGLE BRITISH BLOG THAT ACTUALLY CARES TO DEFEND THE SCHEME IN ANY WAY WHATSOEVER. CHRIS APPLEGATE TRIES TO WORK OUT WHY IT IS EVEN BEING PROPOSED, GIVEN THE TECHNOLOGICAL PROBLEMS IT FACES: ‹/ED›

Identity cards...

I know, let's talk about ID cards. I've been itching to for ages.

Identity cards, as they are being proposed, aren't actually identity cards. In fact they have very little to do with identity. This may seem a little strange, but let me explain: there is a difference between identitfication (i.e. who we are and where we have come from), and verification (i.e. whether we actually are who we claim to be). Identity is a highly complex concept, which is innately interwoven with our own sense of self; it varies depending on which context you are in — when writing a blog entry, I assert my identity in very different ways from when I am at passport control, for example.

In this case, the government is trying to introduce a verification mechanism aimed at linking our identity, as it is regarded as within the context of transactions, with the state —claiming benefits, crossing borders, being stopped and searched. These data are quite dry and factual, and only form a minor subsection of our whole identity. In fact the old 'entitlement cards' name was a far better and more apt name for what is at the end of the day a verification mechanism.

In fact, the 'cards' bit isn't very accurate either; since the most important factors in the system aren't the cards, but the biometric scanners and the data about you that are being held on the national identity register.

Anyway, when providing your identity within a context, you often have to supply verification. Computer networks often use usernames and passwords; cash machines use cards (which store your account number) and PIN numbers. In both cases, we have two separate devices; the identification device that is unique but not very private; and the verification device, which is secret but probably not unique. Together, they work to say 'I am X and I can prove it by showing you Y'.

The problem with identity cards is that people confuse these two concepts; thanks in no small part to the 'wonders' of biometrics. A biometric is a digital representation, based on the unique patterns of our irises or fingerprints. But this suffers from a horrible confusion — just because your fingerprint is unique, it does not entail that your biometric is. The representation is only an approximation; as a result it would be entirely possible for a scanner to say you're not who you are (a false negative), or for two people with similar patterns to share the same biometric data (a false positive). Given that fingerprints and irises are both analogue and highly similar, there is no way a system of digital biometric representation can ever be proven to be unique for every person. This is not to say biometrics are useless (although even iris scans only have a 96% success rate) but just as it is stupid if we only had to type a 4-digit PIN to access our cash, it is stupid to rely just on biometrics to 100% guarantee our identity. A system that assumes verification = identification (and the Home Office far prefers to use the latter over the former in its papers and bills) runs the risk of blind faith in something which is in actual fact quite fallible.

Now, up till now I've said biometrics are the same as PIN numbers. But they're not; there's a big big difference, and it makes biometrics far worse. If we think someone else might know our PIN and we want to stop them, we can change it to something else. But we can't do that with the biometric — we can't change our irises or fingerprints, so we can't change the verifier either. Biometrics truly are the worst of both worlds — more than one person can have the same one, and we can't change it if we find out.

Bad so far? I haven't even considered what happens when there are *deliberate* attacks on the system, rather than accidental errors. And believe me, it is a certainty the register will be successfully broken into and subverted: the sheer size of the national ID register, and the number of people who will have to be able to access it in order for it to run, means that it won't be too hard to find someone with insider access who can be bribed or threatened into fiddling it on someone's behest. As well as the means, there is the will — for a government that continually warns us of this alleged multi-billion identity theft industry, it hasn't stopped for one second to realise that fraudsters are going to try their damnedest to get their hands on fake cards, which being 'unfakeable' and 'unique', will be worth their weight in gold.

So we have non-unique verifiers that are being touted as unique identifiers, which are unchangeable and unrevokeable, and a system that will be far less secure than touted. So there will be duplicates and mistakes, there will be fraudulent entries. Some people will be denied services they are perfectly entitled to, others will slip through the net totally unseen. And it will be very difficult to fix these problems. Fine. One or two people dying of cancer because they're not given the treatment they are entitled to, or a known terrorist gaining access to an airliner, would be an acceptable risk if, overall, the benefits outweighed the costs.

Except that the benefits are not clear. There has been no analysis on how ID cards will cut terrorism, or crime that is not identity-related. As for the menace of identity fraud which it purportedly costs the UK £1.3bn a year (in what is not much more than a bad guesstimate). As identity fraud is just a catch-all for a highly varied set of crimes, many of which are borne by the private sector and do not involve personal transactions — such as Internet fraud or false postal applications for credit cards. There are no figures on how much the specific crimes that ID cards could stop actually do cost the economy every year, but it is bound to be only a proportion of this figure.

Still, this figure is in the hundreds of millions, possibly. But given that the system could cost as much as £18bn — which is three times the government's estimate, but this is more or less the going rate for government IT projects — that's a lot of money for saving a few hundred million a year.

Oh yeah, the loss of civil liberties. Forgot that (just like Charles Clarke in fact...). Anyway, the most nauseating statement that can be said on the matter, and one that instantly marks the speaker as being fundamentally mentally defective, is 'If you're innocent you have nothing to worry about'. This is bullshit. It is precisely because we are innocent that we should worry. There is a fundamental principle that we should be presumed innocent rather than guilty; that suspicion should not fall on us as a blanket measure. The ID cards bill compels compulsory ownership and thus compulsory use; the police will be given powers to make you present yourself with ID if they don't like the look of you — this will inevitably be misused against the poor, and the marginalised just as stop and search and other measures have been in the past, regardless of actual guilt.

Right — that's all I'm going to say for now on why ID cards are rubbish — if you want more, there's plenty of other literature out there from respected writers and academics like Bruce Schneier and David Lyon who write a fair bit on the subject, and better than I can.

A final question — despite little supporting evidence for the benefits, overwhelming and rapidly rising costs and significant public opposition, still the government pushes a national identity scheme forward as an essential measure. I mean, £6bn is a lot of money; £18bn even more so. Which really demands the question — why? Why risk fucking up so much? I've thought of several reasons but none of them are that satisfactory:

- The government are a bunch of technology fetishists: Plausible, but why not just pick yet another NHS or social security IT project instead of something so tricky?

- They're being heavily pressured by IT providers to come up with another reason to line their pockets in exchange for an inferior product: I like this less than the first one; also, again, why pick such a difficult project?

- They're part of the masterplan along with imprisonment without trial, implementation of postal voting, etc., to slowly turn the UK into a dictatorship: I really don't like this option one bit.

- They want a prestigious project to show competence and effectiveness: Maybe... but why not spend that money on something obvious and simple that no-one will object to like more policemen or hospitals, rather than a controversial and difficult project?

- They're just plain stupid: Depressingly enough, this is the most plausible and the least worst option of the lot.

Dunno about you, but I'm now scared.

www.qwghlm.co.uk
www.qwghlm.co.uk/blog

JUNE 2005

<ED> LIVE 8 AND GLENEAGLES. THERE WERE THOSE WHO THOUGHT THAT THIS WAS NOT, PERHAPS, THE MOST FABULOUS EVENT EVER, EVEN THOSE WHO DID NOT QUITE ENTER INTO THE SPIRIT OF THE THING – CHICKEN YOGHURT FOR EXAMPLE. </ED>

Live 8: The point being *what* exactly?

I'm probably in a (soon to be vilified) minority here, but what exactly is the point of holding another Live Aid concert if it's not going to be a fundraiser?

The set list for the Hyde Park concert is a mixture of some of the most monstrous egos on the planet (Madonna, Robbie Williams, Elton John) and the worst of anodyne nonentities (Muse, Razorlight). It reads like the playlist for the iPod I'm going to be forced to wear when I'm finally consigned to Hell.

The opportunity to appear before an audience of millions of course has nothing to do with mediocrities like the Stereophonics signing up. I notice 'Sir' Bob Geldof is on the list as well. I suppose him being the organiser it would be churlish not to let him groan through 'I Don't Like Mondays' one more miserable time.

And why the hell are Coldplay, Keane *and* Snow Patrol on the bill? Don't they cancel each other out in the maudlin, piano-driven, why-do-the-nice-girls-hate-me angsty shiteness stakes? Two of these bands are redundant for the purposes of this concert. Can't they draw straws and two of them stay at home and the winner play three sets — it'll be no different from what you're going to get anyway. Or why not combine them into a beige, ulcer-inducing supergroup. And do you know anybody who actually likes Dido? Everybody who owns one of her albums was bought it as a present by an unimaginitive relative.

There's nothing more unedifying than multi-millionaire popstars lending their talents for free. Like the ubiquitous charity record, if this isn't about bolstering their careers then why can't they just chuck in a few spare million quid each into the kitty and stay at home?

Geldof, in actual fact, says the concerts aren't to raise cash but awareness and political pressure instead. Which still isn't a good enough excuse. If this isn't about feeding already bloated egos then why can't Elton John, Madonna, McCartney et al. put their money where their mouths are and pay for a massive advertising campaign instead. Think of the television slots, internet ads, radio ads, mailshots, newspaper pages, billboards, magazine ads, text messages and emails they could buy. It'd have a much bigger, widespread and sustained effect than a one-off event. No doubt a lot of people will find the concert an ecstatic moment of communion but it'll get coverage for one day, a few headlines the next day and then turn up again on the 'I Remember 2005' shows in a few years.

But without the concert our entertainers would be denied their great big back-slap while us mere mortals are pushing our noses up against the screen. As it happens, 150,000 proles will be generously allowed to be in Hyde Park in person on the day. Tickets are to be allocated via some convoluted mobile phone lottery (which excludes Elton John's fanbase for starters). £1.5m of the funds raised through the competition are going to that well-known famine relief charity, The Prince's Trust. The rest will be spent on the event itself so that no massively wealthy popstar will be out of pocket.

The naivety behind the venture that thinks any of this is going to sway the G8 would be hilarious in any other setting. Almost as naive (and hilarious) as Tony Blair thinking he's going to be able to have a similar effect.

I also wonder if Elton John and his peers are going to march on the G8 meeting at Gleneagles as Geldof is exhorting the rest of us to do. The security at the conference complex is going to be airtight. The marchers will be lucky if a single delegate hears them let alone sees them. People power hasn't had a great record for bringing about change in our leaders' thinking of late and the merest whiff of trouble at Gleneagles is going to get heads busted. I somehow doubt Madonna will be there getting tear-gassed. Are George Bush's bodyguards going to ask for shoot-to-kill privileges as they did (but didn't get) when Bush made his state visit? Only then would I be pleased to see the sludge of popular culture, arms-linked, at the head of the march.

In a final analysis, if people in general didn't need to be coaxed and emotionally blackmailed into showing human feeling for their fellow man, there'd be no need for this and Bono would be polluting our lives just a little bit less.

Those who care are already engaged in some fashion. If starving black children sold as many papers as copulating celerities, Africa would be quids in.

UPDATE 02/06: And another thing. The set list for Hyde Park as it currently stands features white artists only. Black and Asian culture features not at all. With rumours of the Spice Girls reforming for the event, it looks like they might be able to shoehorn one black face in, if only one who's most recent impact on popular culture was three years ago. It's also worth noting that the seven people sitting around the table at the Live 8 launch press conference were all white, middle-aged men. I doubt it's intentional but the continuing white man's burden schtick is just ugly.

UPDATE 02/06: *The Times* — Concert line-up attacked for being all-white

> Organisers say privately that there are not sufficient British black artists who can deliver ticket requests in volume and meet the expectations of a global audience of two billion.

Message to black artists: try to be more whitebread — white artists like Eminem are allowed to appropriate black culture (it sells better to white middle-class wannabes if it comes from the likes of him) but the black man needs to be more like Chris Martin. Wait, there's more. How about this for an unsourced, unsubstantiated smear:

> It is believed that some urban artists requested payment for appearing, which the organisers said was a demand that they could not comply with.

'*It is believed*'. By who? The journalist or the organisers? *The Times* didn't have the balls to say which urban artists or just who has this 'belief'. No names so no libel but the message is clear: there'd be black artists on the bill if those that have been asked weren't grasping bastards.

Chicken Yoghurt
http://chickyog.blogspot.com

✎ 6 June

<ED> THERE WAS A CERTAIN AMOUNT OF NOTICE
(AS ABOVE) TAKEN OF THE FACT THAT THE LIVE
8 LINE UP WAS LACKING IN A CERTAIN MEASURE
OF RACIAL DIVERSITY... 'HIDEOUSLY WHITE'
ACCORDING TO ONE COMMENTATOR.

THE JOY OF CURMUDGEONRY REALISED
THAT THIS WAS NOT LIMITED JUST TO THIS
ONE EVENT: </ED>

New report finds Britain is 'hideously white'

All socially aware people have long suspected it, the line-up at the upcoming
Live 8 concerts has highlighted it, but now a report to be released today by
the Committee on Racial Affairs has confirmed it: Britain is 'hideously white'.
The report found that up to 91% of the population of Britain is white. 'This can't
go on,' said Dr Donald Watkins, who co-authored the report. 'I find it offensive
that in this day and age so many people in Britain are white. It is a disgrace.'

Institutions such as the BBC have been reprimanded before on precisely this
issue. The new report, however, makes it clear that the problem is not confined
to institutions: the problem extends all the way down into wider society.
Indeed, the hideous whiteness of institutions is an accurate reflection of society
at large. As Prof. Tetherton, a sociologist at the University of East Anglia, explains,
'Because 91% of the population is hideously white, it means that the institutions
naturally tend to take on the same horrific hue. If we are serious about tackling
the problem, we must eradicate it at the root. Only this way can we create a
freer, more equal society.'

Chris Martin, of the popular beat combo Coldplay, was unsurprised by the
findings: 'Most of my teachers at school were white, most of the people in
my street were white, even my parents were white. I think it's disgusting.
People don't seem to realise just how offensive it is. And when you consider
that most shareholders are white, well, then we know we are dealing with the
most unspeakable evil.'

The report comes after weeks of mounting pressure on the government to make known its understanding of the extent of the problem. 'It seems there has been a lack of will on the part of politicians to tackle this issue,' said Emily Burton, spokeswoman for the independent think-tank Totalitas. 'But now the government cannot ignore it.'

The report also places greater pressure on the organisers of the Live 8 concerts to change the racial constitution of its performers. 'The thought of old white people playing guitars makes me physically sick,' said one activist.

The Joy of Curmudgeonry
http://curmudgeonjoy.blogspot.com

✎ 9 June

‹ED› MORE PROBLEMS FOR THE NEW LEGISLATIVE PROGRAMME: ‹/ED›

Sympathy for the Devil

Paul Goggins (silly name, silly man) has announced that [...] his new incitement to religious hatred bill will protect Satanists.

I wonder how an outburst like this would fare under his new law?

> Ye are of your father the devil, and the lusts of your father ye will do. He was a murderer from the beginning, and abode not in the truth, because there is no truth in him. When he speaketh a lie, he speaketh of his own: for he is a liar, and the father of it.

Our caller, of course, is Jesus from Nazareth (John 8:34), addressing the scribes and Pharisees. Which raises the intriguing prospect that, should Christ return to Earth, he will be prosecuted by New Labour.

No wonder the Evangelical Alliance has come out against Mr Goggins' bill.

Liberal England
http://liberalengland.blogspot.com

🖎 17 June

‹ED› THE SERIOUS ORGANISED CRIME AND POLICE ACT 2005 WAS NOT, ON THE WHOLE, WELL RECEIVED. THE CREATION OF THE EXCLUSION ZONE (OR NO DEMONSTRATING ZONE) AROUND PARLIAMENT WAS CONSIDERED TO BE SOMETHING OF A SLEDGEHAMMER TO CRACK THE NUT THAT IS BRIAN HAW.

BLOOD & TREASURE MANAGED TO COMBINE THE WAR, LIVE 8 AND THE ACT WHILE BRINGING US THE DESCRIPTION OF THE HOME SECRETARY AS 'CHARLIE THE SAFETY ELEPHANT', WHICH IS HOW HE IS GENERALLY KNOWN IN THE BLOGOSPHERE THESE DAYS: ‹/ED›

Princess Tony and the Ugly Face Man

Hello children. Are we sitting comfortably? I'm going to tell you a story. It's the story of Princess Tony and the Ugly Face Man.

We all know about Princess Tony don't we? Yes, we do. We all know about how Princess Tony likes to fly all over the world bringing smiles to people's faces. Do you remember what the place was called that Princess Tony went to with his friend Crazy George? The place where he made all the children happy by arranging a big firework display and lots of finger painting?

Yes, that's right. It was Iraq.

Anyway, this time Princess Tony and his other friends Hairy Bob and Nobbo the Little Rock Star went to Africa. Now Africa is a place where all the children play with guns and nobody has any money except a few people who have all the money, and they take it and put it in a bank in a place called Switzerland. And there aren't any Milky Ways or Smarties or Turkey Twizzlers and everybody has to eat mud.

Well you know what Princess Tony did? Princess Tony and his friends Hairy Bob and Nobbo the Little Rock Star made all the children put their guns away and then they gave them strawberryade and kinder eggs and lots and lots and lots of current buns. And he made the people with all the money take it away from the place called Switzerland and give everybody pocket money so they could buy Milky Ways and Smarties and Turkey Twizzlers. And all the Africans jumped up and down and said Thank you Nobbo the Little Rock Star! Thank You Hairy Bob! And especially big Double Thankyous and hugs and kisses Princess Tony!

It made Princess Tony happy to see all the little smiling Africans. But when he got home, he wasn't happy any more. Do you know why, children? It was because of the Ugly Face Man.

Nobody knows where the Ugly Face Man came from. Perhaps he has no home. Because every time Princess Tony came back from making people happy somewhere he would see the Ugly Face Man sitting outside the place where he and his friends work, pulling ugly faces and shouting rude things. And he had posters with nasty horrible things written on them about Princess Tony.

You know what the Ugly Face Man was, don't you children?

That's right. A nutter. Can you pull a face like the Ugly Face Man? Ooooh, horrible!

Seeing the Ugly Face Man made Princess Tony unhappy. He didn't like it when people pulled ugly faces at him and shouted rude things when all he wanted was for people to smile and sing and say how wonderful Princess Tony was. Tony's friends, the parliamentary pixies, didn't like it either. The parliamentary pixies are little men and women who run around all day and all night constantly having ideas that make all our lives better in a thousand and one ways. But it's hard to have wonderful ideas when there's an Ugly Face Man sitting outside pulling ugly faces and shouting all day.

When he heard that the Ugly Face Man had made the parliamentary pixies sad, Princess Tony got red in the face. 'It's nasty and horrible and just not fair!' he said And Princess Tony stamped his little feet.

Suddenly Charlie the Safety Elephant appeared in a puff of bureaucracy. 'Don't worry, Princess Tony' he said. 'I'm here to protect you and all your little chums. And I'm going to make a law. I like doing that!'

'What kind of law are you going to make, Mr Safety Elephant?' said Princess Tony.

'It's a law that says 'go away Ugly Face Man' said Charlie. 'And it means that he can never come back and nor can anyone who thinks like him and wants to say nasty things and make life hard for Princess Tony and his little friends. And everyone will be able to go round making Africans smile and having wonderful ideas that improve all our lives in a thousand and one ways and there'll be nobody to say nasty things about them or interfere in any way at all.'

And so it was done. And Princess Tony and the parliamentary pixies all lived happily ever after.

Blood & Treasure
http://bloodandtreasure.typepad.com/blood_treasure

✎ 19 June

‹ED› AS THE DETAILS OF THE ID CARDS BILL ARE DIGESTED OPPOSITION CONTINUES TO GROW. TALK POLITICS PROVIDED A THOROUGH EXPLANATION OF JUST WHY WE SHOULD FEAR THEM: ‹/ED›

Where the truth becomes a lie

One of the more interesting and illuminating books I've read in a long time is Tim Slessor's *Lying in State*, which through a range of examples, some familiar (Hutton, Belgrano, Gulf War Syndrome) and some maybe not so familiar (the Chagos Islanders, Chinook ZD576), explores the way in which Whitehall routinely lies, dissembles and obfuscates in order to limit our exposure to the truth of what our Government and the State get up to — supposedly in our name.

One of the more interesting tactics in common use is, interestingly enough, actually to tell the truth — but in such a way that even the truth fails to tell the full story and becomes, instead, misleading as in this example from Home Office Minister, Tony McNulty in a written answer to Sadiq Khan MP (Tooting, Lab) —

> Since the publication of the Identity Cards Bill on 25 May 2005,
> 21 representations have been received from members of the public.
> No representations have been received from any organisations or official
> bodies. The representations took the form of both letters and e-mails,
> and they expressed concern that the Identity Card Scheme would infringe
> civil liberties.

> The Government believe that the Identity Cards Scheme will support civil liberties and human rights. The scheme will be bound by legislation such as the Data Protection Act, Human Rights Act and the Disability Discrimination Act. The Identity Cards Bill also contains a number of important safeguards such as setting limitations on the information that may be held by the scheme and its use. Only Parliament would be able to change the statutory purposes of the Register or the type of information which could be held and only via primary legislation.

To understand what's happening here let's look at two specific points where the literal truth of the Minister's answer fails to encompass the full reality of the ID cards debate.

First we have:

> 21 representations have been received from members of the public. No representations have been received from any organisations or official bodies.

That may indeed be true but, as should be obvious, it fails entirely to reflect the widespread and detailed debate that is actually taking place on the subject of ID cards and the National Identity Register. If fails to acknowledge the existence of the NO2ID campaign, the LSE's [London School of Economics] analysis of ID cards which was widely reported in the media and their subsequent work on developing an alternative system which would be both substantially cheaper and far less intrusive.

To the Home Office, in responding via a Minister to a Member of Parliament, none of this exists as it has not been reported directly to them even though this entire debate is being conducted openly and in full sight of the public in the media and on the Internet.

This, as Slessor notes on several occasions is classic Whitehall, where civil servants will decide what information is and, more often than not, isn't relevant to the question being answered and draft a response accordingly. Indeed a key element of the credo of the Government is that in response to Parliamentary questions it should provide the minimum information necessary to answer a particular question and nothing more, as giving additional detailed information invariably spawns further, usually unwelcome, questions — thus we get comments like this one;

> It was apparent to me that if we were to moved down the route of following the detailed analysis which was being requested, we would end up with yet more requests for yet more information.

That comment was made to a Parliamentary Select Committee by the then Defence Minister, Michael Heseltine, in relation to a detailed analysis of the circumstances of the sinking of the Argentine warship *Belgrano* prepared by Clive Ponting. Ponting, as you may recall, was subsequently arrested, prosecuted and finally acquitted of breaking the Official Secrets Act after leaking elements of his report, which he was asked to compile by the Foreign Office, to a Member of Parliament, Tam Dalyell.

Knowing, then, that the provision of answers which are factually correct but incomplete is very much a standard tactic in Whitehall when Ministers and their civil service advisers are seeking to obscure the truth, what of Tony McNulty's other key statement?

> Only Parliament would be able to change the statutory purposes of the Register or the type of information which could be held and only via primary legislation.

This is, again, a factually true but extremely limited statement which does not encompass the full extent to which data may be added to the National Identity Register or how that data may potentially be used.

First of all it needs to be understood that while this apparent stricture, requiring primary legislation, i.e. a full Act of Parliament, to extend the Register applies only in circumstances where Government is seeking to extend its purpose or the type of information it holds, might reasonably lead one to believe that an Act of Parliament would be required to add any additional information to the Register, over and above what is already specified, this is in fact not the case.

The Act defines two clear statutory purposes for which the Register may be used:

(i)   Provision of a convenient method for individuals to prove their identity; and

(ii) Provision of a secure means of identifying individuals where that is in the public interest.

And goes on to define the *public interest* as encompassing:

— National security;

— Prevention and detection of crime;

— Enforcement of immigration controls;

— Enforcements on prohibitions on unauthorised working or employment; and

— Efficient and effective provision of public services.

As you can see this is already a pretty broad definition to begin with, particularly if one considers the full scope of information that might conceivably be incorporated into the Register just on the basis of these definitions alone.

The full list of information which will be included, right from the outset, is not in the Bill itself but in Schedule 1 of the Bill — for those unfamiliar with legal terminology, think of a schedule as being like an appendix — about which the Government's own explanatory notes have this to say:

> **Schedule 1 may be amended by secondary legislation following a resolution in both Houses of Parliament to add to the list of information that may be recorded on the Register.** However, any additional information must be consistent with the statutory purposes of the Register. So, for example, this power to amend Schedule 1 could not be used to include criminal records in that Schedule without further primary legislation as recording previous criminal convictions is not covered by the definition of registrable facts and so is not consistent with the statutory purposes of the Register in clause 1

Ah, so in actual fact, an Act of Parliament would be required *only* if the Government wished to do something completely different with the Register from what's already been specified — if all it wishes to do is extend the range of information in the Register within its existing purposes then only secondary legislation, a statutory instrument, needs to be passed.

An Act of Parliament would not, therefore, be needed to add a DNA profile to personal data held about individuals within the Register as, obviously, recording such information would be entirely consistent with its use in the detection of crime. What wouldn't the Police and its forensic scientists give for access to a national DNA register?

The same argument could also be made in relation to recording information about an individual's bank accounts and other financial records as an aide to the detection of 'white collar' crime, fraud and money laundering and, therefore, this too would be entirely permissible without a full Act of Parliament just on the existing definition of the Register's purpose.

This, then, is the first — of three — ways in which the Minister's statement, which factually correct, succeeds in providing a misleading and incomplete picture of the full extent to which the Register may impact on our daily lives.

The second misleading *absence of information* is closely related to the first and exemplified by the statement, in the Government's explanatory notes to the Bill, that:

> for example, this power to amend Schedule 1 could not be used to include criminal records in that Schedule without further primary legislation

In simple terms, what the Government is saying is that it would require an Act of Parliament to include details of an individual's criminal record on the Register — and, of course, by implication, one can extend that same stricture to other records, medical records, tax records, welfare benefit records, etc.

Now, as anyone who understands how databases work will tell you, the first and most obvious thing about this statement is that [the] mere idea of compiling things like criminal records into the Resister is, for simple and practical reasons, a total nonsense — for no other reason than that the sheer amount of data that would have to be stored in a single system in order to do this would make the Register so unwieldy as to be almost useless. It would simply collapse under the sheer weight of information it was being asked to hold.

The Government can, therefore, quite happily make this idea subject to the requirement that [a] full Act of Parliament should be passed to make it possible simply because it [has] no intention of ever doing it anyway.

The second thing to note — and the basis of my original article 'Unlocking the Register' — is that in order to use the National Identity Register to access things like medical records — the Government is currently spending around £6 billion on computerising record keeping in the NHS — tax records and criminal records, which are or will be held on different databases, you do not need to store those records in the Register itself. All you need to store in the Register is the information needed to locate this information in the database in which it is already stored.

To use the example of your tax records. In the tax system each individual is identified uniquely via their National Insurance Number — if you have someone's NI Number you can search the tax system for their individual records and locate them very easily. So as long as you record someone's NI number in the Register — which the Register will as this is already included in Schedule 1 — then the information the Register provides will, in turn, provide you with the information you need to locate and examine an individual's tax records provided that you have the authority to do so.

However, don't make the mistake of thinking that the Identity Cards Bill will go so far as to identify who might use the contents of the Register to access your data or in what circumstances they may be able to carry out such an examination. Such powers, some of which already exist, are, or will be, defined in a range of different primary and secondary legislation, making it nigh on impossible to identify who might have access to what without a detailed and time consuming trawl of the statute books.

This, then, is the unstated purpose of the National Identity Register, it acts as an index, and as a 'skeleton key', to locate and unlock a vast range of information about individuals which is held across government and in a wide range of other databases and, indeed, will include from the outset a number of index references — what in database terms are called 'keys' — to other systems including your passport and driving licence numbers as well as your National Insurance Number.

In order, therefore, to link your medical records, or even your criminal record, to the Register it's not necessary to store that information in the Register itself, only its location — another database — and the unique identifier — the key — required to identify and isolate your individual records from everyone else's. And this information can be added to the Register at any time not by Act of Parliament but by secondary legislation, by a statutory instrument which is not, generally, subject to anything like the same degree of scrutiny or debate as a full Act.

In fact, if you look at when and how many statutory instruments are debated and passed, especially ones which may be somewhat contentious as those extending the Register could be, you'll find that a little Parliamentary 'trick' usually comes into play in which debates on statutory instruments are scheduled to take place on a Friday afternoon, at a time when the majority of MPs have already left for their constituencies and are, therefore, not present for the debate. It's fairly easy, therefore, for secondary legislation to slip in under the radar with the minimum of debate and without the public, for the most part, even realising it has happened.

The third and final deceit regarding the National Identity Register is rather less obvious than the other two yet, in many ways, potentially the [most] intrusive and the most damaging to civil liberties inasmuch as it enables personal information and data to be linked to the Register without anyone even realising it.

In order to locate a specific piece of information in a database you need a 'unique identifier', a piece of information held in the database which is unique to that information — and when it comes to identifying information which relates to a specific individual, the Register provides just such a unique identifier, your National Identity Registration Number.

Now, if and/or when ID cards are introduced, one of the pieces of information which will be disclosed to anyone making a request to verify your identity will be your National Identity Registration Number, the number which uniquely identifies you — and once that information has been disclosed there is nothing in the Bill to say how it may then be recorded or used. The only protection, in law, you will have will be via the Data Protection Act which, when it comes to issues of privacy, is far from watertight.

In fact, its highly likely that a wide range of third parties will make use of and record your National Identity Registration Number as a matter of routine — one can envisage from the outset that the financial services industry will be amongst the earliest adopters and that, before very long, banks, building societies, credit reference agencies, insurance and pension companies and others will all be tagging every single piece of information they hold with your Registration Number and using that number to exchange information about you and your finances. Once your National Identity Registration Number gets out 'into the wild' it can be used for a wide range of purposes outside of those specified in the Bill and with few controls on its use. More often than not, you may not even realise that it's being used.

Moreover, because the Register incorporates an 'audit trail' which records each and every time a third party accesses the Register in order to verify your identity, when this happened and, most importantly of all, who was doing the asking, the Government then has a complete record of everyone who is using the Register and your National Identity Registration Number — so if the Government did, for any reason, want to know what you've been doing — or even where you were at a particular time — the audit trail will tell it exactly where to look...

...and it already knows what to look for — any information to which your National Identity Registration Number has been attached.

It should be noted that, on its own, the National Identity Register does not create a 'surveillance state'. It does however put in place the means [to] create such a state by providing a mechanism which enables a wide range of personal information held in a variety of locations, not all of them in government by any means, to be connected together to form a comprehensive 'picture' of who you are, where you are and, more importantly, what you've been doing.

I've now written maybe three or four full articles on the subject of ID cards and more specifically on the National Identity Register and the 'deeper truth' of these proposals, which go far beyond anything that the Government or the State will openly discuss or admit to.

Much of what I've had to say in those earlier articles — which are all categorised under 'Civil Liberties' if you wish to review them — tended to be quite technical in tone, a fact noted obliquely by Vicki Woods, writing in yesterday's *Telegraph*,* in pointing out that she didn't quite understand the concept of 'foreign keys' for 'Unlocking the Register'. In fact she can be entirely forgiven for having difficulty with that concept, [as] it is difficult unless one possesses a solid technical understanding of databases and database design, and it [is in] recognition of [this] that I sat down to write this piece in the hope that I could provide a less technical explanation of the extent to which the National Identity Register may quietly infiltrate every aspect of our daily lives.

I, therefore, owe Vicki a debt of gratitude for showing me, perhaps without realising it herself, the need for a less technical examination of the Register and a debt of thanks for recognising, in the mainstream press, not only my own work but the work of other bloggers on this issue. It's good to see the mainstream press starting to pick up on what's going on out here in the blogosphere and, in particular, recognising that increasingly much of [the] detailed work of unpicking government policy and identifying what Whitehall is really up to is going on out here on the Internet. Good for us, certainly, but also, I believe, good for democracy as out here on the electronic frontier is where you'll find many of the debates which government would rather we didn't have and which they clearly would like to ignore; not just about ID cards and the National Identity Register but on electoral reform and PR, and also on Europe, which above all others has been the debate which dare not speak its name in either of the two main political parties for the last few years.

Oh, and lets not forget NO2ID in all this, for leading the campaign against ID cards and tackling so many more issues than I've personally had time to deal with.

*www.telegraph.co.uk/opinion/main.jhtml?xml=/opinion/2005/06/18/
d01802.xml&sSheet=/opinion/2005/06/18/ixop.html

What I also hope I've demonstrated here is how, in the hands of a politician or civil servant, even the truth can be misleading, incomplete and downright disingenuous, although I should note my belief, in this case, that it's doubtful that the Minister in question, Tony McNulty, is even aware of just how far from the full truth his statement, quoted in the article, is. The ID Cards Bill is a highly technical bill which creates a highly technical system of interlocking databases and records, the full extent of which is most probably understood only by those within the Civil Service charged with the development of this system. In short I doubt even those politicians most closely involved in bringing forward these proposals, first David Blunkett and, more recently, Charles Clarke, understand anything more than what they are told by their Civil Service advisers.

As Slessor's book — which I heartily recommend to anyone interested in understanding how Whitehall operates — demonstrates on several occasions, what even the Minister knows may quite easily be some considerable way short of the full truth, even though it is the Minister who 'carries the can' should it be discovered that they have misled Parliament, even having been misled themselves by Whitehall. And even were I, as a member of the Labour Party, inclined to trust my fellow party members in Government, that trust does not extend to the legions of unelected and unaccountable minions of the State, the civil servants who are busily constructing this reprehensible system and who, should it come into being, will be the ones to administer and make use of it and its almost unrestrained ability to intrude into our personal lives.

And it's for this last reason that I believe that we should, indeed we must, resist the introduction of ID cards or, if we are to have them, to have them in a form which does not, in turn, require anything near such an extensive and centralised identity register — such a system is not only possible but eminently workable and far cheaper to install and administer than the monstrosity being proposed by this current government, yet the government seem unwilling to even admit to such a possibility, let alone debate its merits openly and in public.

Governments, ultimately, may be held to account. We have the ballot box as our ultimate weapon, our means of exacting a little payback on a ruling party who we see to be acting against our interests as citizens.

But when it comes to the State, to the people who build, administer and ultimately make use of such systems, the people who could most directly intrude on our personal lives through use of the Register, then we have no such weapon and no means of holding them directly to account — and it's that about which we should be most nervous and most watchful, because when we ask Juvenal's question, 'Quis Custodiet Ipso Custodes' — 'Who will guard the guardians' — the answer is **no one but themselves**.

Talk Politics
http://talkpolitics.users20.donhost.co.uk

✎ 27 June

‹ED› ID CARDS, AS WE HAVE SEEN, HAVE BEEN A CONSISTENT TOPIC OVER THE YEAR. THE LATEST WAS THAT WE NEED TO HAVE THE BIOMETRIC IDENTIFIERS BECAUSE WE NEED TO HAVE THEM ON PASSPORTS ANYWAY. REALLY? CHRIS LIGHTFOOT RESPONDS: ‹/ED›

More passportery

Not a proper post, but a factlet for those who may be confused by the government's claims about biometric passports, and specifically that much of the cost of their ID cards programme would have to be spent anyway on biometric passports.

The ICAO biometric passport programme requires only that passports be equipped with a 'smart-card' style chip containing information about the bearer (the same stuff that's printed in the machine-readable zone on the bottom of the back page of your passport in an angular OCR font), plus a digitised photograph and a cryptographic signature.

This is all that is needed to implement the new ICAO passports standard. How much will it cost?

- in Germany, the cost of a passport will increase by 36 Euros, or about £23;

- in Australia, the cost will go up by $19, or about £8;

- whereas here in Britain the government plans to charge everyone **an additional** £51 on the current £42 fee for a new passport.

What's actually going on here is a fairly simple scam. The idea is to add lots of bits of the ID cards programme (like the database that records every transaction you have with the public sector) into the cost of passports to make the cost of ID cards seem more reasonable, and then lie that these expenses are actually necessary under our international obligations. Fuck that, frankly.

Chris Lightfoot's web log
http://ex-parrot.com/~chris/wwwitter

JULY 2005

✎ 1 July

<ED> THE GLAZERS FINALLY SUCCEEDED
IN THEIR PLAN TO TAKE OVER MANCHESTER
UNITED. BOBBY CHARLTON APPEARED TO BE
IN FAVOUR, AT LEAST AS RECORDED BY
THE NORTHERN IRISH MAGYAR: </ED>

Charlton pleased with the Glazers

Having met the Glazer Brothers on Wednesday, United legend Bobby Charlton had this to say:

'I'm like any other football fan. I've been waking up in the night wondering what was going on,' said the World Cup Winner.

'But they allayed a lot of my fears. I asked them questions about the future of the club — and the future of people who were wrapped up in the club. I'm happy with their answers, I'll continue to receive a fat salary for doing diddly squat and will not be affected by the ticket price hike.'

I may have employed a bit of poetic license with one of the sentences.

The Northern Irish Magyar
http://nimagyar.blogspot.com

<ED> ONE OF THE THINGS THAT DRIVES BLOGGERS
UP THE WALL IS THAT HERE WE ARE, TURNING
OUT REAMS OF COPY (OF VARYING QUALITY, TO
BE SURE) YET VERY FEW SEEM TO BE GETTING
PICKED UP BY THE MAJOR MEDIA. OCCASIONALLY
'THE THUNDERER' IN THE TIMES IS BY SOMEONE
NOTED FOR THEIR BLOGGING (PETER BRIFFA,
PERRY DE HAVILLAND ARE EXAMPLES), SALAAM
PAX AT THE GUARDIAN, BUT THAT SEEMS TO BE
ABOUT IT. YES, LOTS OF US WOULD LIKE TO BE
WRITING FOR THE NEWSPAPERS AND IT WOULD

BE THAT LITTLE BIT LESS ANNOYING IF WE
THOUGHT THAT ALL THOSE WHO WERE WERE IN
FACT BETTER AT IT THAN WE ARE. THE AMOUNT
OF INVECTIVE DIRECTED AT THE DAY'S NEWS
REPORTS AND COMMENTATORS SHOWS THAT,
CLEARLY, WE DON'T. CLIVE DAVIS EXPLAINS
FURTHER: ‹/ED›

Media class — 1

The *Sunday Telegraph* ran a story last weekend about the news that Tony Blair's
son Euan had landed a stint in DC. The item (which doesn't seem to be on-line)
posed the question, 'Is Euan incredibly bright? Or is his coveted internship in
Washington a result of being incredibly well-connected?'

I don't know the answer to that, but I wonder if anyone on the editorial staff
harboured similar thoughts about the paper's new op-ed columnist, Anna
Stothard, who just happens to be the daughter of the former Times editor, Peter
Stothard. (I couldn't help smiling at the final line of her column about the
Dreaming Spires: '*Oxford may have its mad rules, but as far as accommodation is
concerned, it's a mad lottery — just like the outside world.*') I also noticed that page
four of the paper's Review section that day carried a piece by Daisy Waugh
(daughter of Auberon) while page five plugged a new fine-arts company set up
by John Mortimer's daughter, Rosie.

There are lots of other examples I could mention from across the world of
journalism in general.

Everyone knows about media nepotism, but it's not a subject that's aired often
outside the pages of *Private Eye*. We all know it happens, but it's considered bad
form to dwell on it. I've been a journalist for more than twenty years [*he said,
puffing on his pipe*] and I've never ceased to be amazed at how incestuous the
London scene is — on the Left as well as the Right. What's even odder is that the
people involved assume that it's quite natural. The idea that there's another world
beyond NW1 or SW4 rarely occurs to them.

I was discussing this with a colleague recently. He's a fair bit younger than me,
has risen high up the ladder (from a modest background) and has a sharper sense
of London's social currents. Slightly to my surprise, he agreed with me about the

claustrophobic atmosphere. Even more surprisingly, he thinks it's grown worse over the last decade. That's my impression too, only I'd assumed I was simply being over-sensitive. Which left us with one question: how do you raise the subject without appearing to have a chip on your shoulder? We couldn't think of a way. Perhaps it's just not possible.

Clive Davis
http://clivedavis.blogs.com/clive

✎ 6 July

‹ED› LONDON WINS THE OLYMPICS 2012. THE FOLLOWING IS FROM NEVERATOSS: ‹/ED›

New Olympic sport suggestion

I just rang up Lord Coe to be the first to congratulate him and to nominate a new, typically British, Olympic Sport — War! We're very good at it and the French are, quite frankly, merde! Germany are pretty good but lack a decent finish, the Italians don't quite get the '*half time no changing sides*' rule and Argentinians are rubbish even when playing at home.

Did I miss anyone out?

Neveratoss
www.neveratoss.co.uk

✎ 7 July

‹ED› THE LONDON BOMBINGS. THREE TUBE TRAINS AND A BUS WERE HIT BY SUICIDE BOMBERS DURING THE MORNING RUSH HOUR. MAJOR ORGANISATIONS LIKE THE BBC, THE GUARDIAN AND THE TIMES WERE POSTING PHOTOGRAPHS FROM PEOPLE'S MOBILE PHONES. BLOGS WERE USED TO SPREAD THE NEWS OF THE ATTACKS, PEOPLE POSTED THAT THEY WERE OK AND UNHARMED (THE MOBILE PHONE

NETWORKS WENT DOWN UNDER THE WEIGHT
OF TRAFFIC) AND SEVERAL BLOGS DID WHAT
IS KNOWN AS 'LIVE BLOGGING'. WHATEVER
RUMOUR, SPECULATION, SCRAP OF FACT OR
FANTASY THE WRITER COMES ACROSS GETS
POSTED UP ON THE WEB FOR ALL TO SEE. PUT
THAT WAY IT SHOULDN'T WORK IN ANY WAY AT
ALL BUT IT DOES, FOR READERS, COMMENTERS,
OTHER BLOGGERS, DISCUSS AND CORRECT THE
INFORMATION AND AT THE END OF THE PROCESS
WHAT COMES OUT IS RELIABLE. IT'S VERY
SIMILAR TO WHAT HAPPENS WITHIN A
NEWSROOM AS JOURNALISTS GRASP AT
ANYTHING AND EVERYTHING AND THEN ATTEMPT
TO VERIFY WHATEVER IT IS THAT THEY'VE
HEARD. THE DIFFERENCE IS THAT WITH BLOGS
ALL OF THIS IS TAKING PLACE IN PUBLIC, WITH
THOSE BEING REPORTED PROVIDING MUCH OF
THE EDITORIAL AND FACT CHECKING. THREE
MAIN BLOGS FOLLOWED THE STORY
THROUGHOUT THE DAY: NOSEMONKEY AT
EUROPHOBIA, ROBIN GRANT AT PERFECT.CO.UK
AND TIM WORSTALL AT HIS EPONYMOUS BLOG
(COUGH, COUGH, WELL, YOU KNEW I WAS GOING
TO PUT AT LEAST SOMETHING OF MINE INTO
THIS BOOK, DIDN'T YOU?)

THE FOLLOWING IS AN EXAMPLE OF LIVE
BLOGGING FROM ROBIN GRANT (NOTE THAT
BLOGS WORK ON THE PRINCIPLE OF LATEST
POST FIRST OR REVERSE CHRONOLOGICAL
ORDER): </ED>

12:19 pm

I'm alive, as are my immediate family and friends. Edgware Rd tube is approximately 200 m from my office, and I imagine around half of the people at work use the station during their commute.

The attacks, although seemingly very well co-ordinated (including targeting buses after the initial attacks on the tube system, likely packed with displaced commuters), do not seem as bad as our worst nightmares. Blasts are confirmed at Kings Cross, Tavistock Square, Russell Square, Edgware Road, Liverpool Street, Moorgate and Aldgate, and yet so far the fatalities seem to be fairly low — confirmed figures are below 10. This figure could easily rise significantly — especially if there have been incidents underground that have been hard to reach and evacuate. Let us all hope that this is not the case.

12:01 pm

Police have now upped the figure to 7 blasts — Tony Blair making statement now – he doesn't seem to know any more than us. He's coming down to London for a few hours — but the G8 will carry on.

11:40 am

The news sites seem to be catching up — I'll be adding links to all the coverage above.

11:16 am

The Metropolitan Police Chief says there have been at least 6 explosions — and other reports that 3 of these were on buses, 90 casualties at Aldgate east, a number of fatalities and the Army is on the streets of Covent Garden.

perfect.co.uk
www.perfect.co.uk

‹ED› 6 BLASTS? 7? THIS ISN'T A FAILURE OF ROBIN'S OR OF BLOGS. THOSE WERE THE FIGURES THE POLICE THEMSELVES WERE GIVING OUT. AT TIMES LIKE THIS NOBODY ACTUALLY KNOWS WHAT'S GOING ON.

THOSE OF US WHO WERE WRITING THESE BLOGS ON THAT DAY WERE FLOODED WITH EMAILS AND COMMENTS, EXPRESSING SYMPATHY, ANGER ON OUR BEHALF AND OFFERING PRAYERS FOR THOSE DEAD AND INJURED. MY REACTION TO ONE OF THESE: ‹/ED›

> Oh, tears came to my eyes when I turned on the television this morning. All my memories of September 11 came flooding back. I love London so much, and am so sorry that these dirtbags have attacked you.

Many thanks for the kind words and to those who have emailed offering condolences and prayers. I have a prediction to make: that tomorrow we'll find out whether Britons are, still, in fact, Britons. Many years ago I was working in The City and there were two events that made travel into work almost impossible.

The first was a series of storms that brought down power lines, blocked train routes and so on. Not surprisingly, the place was empty the next day. Why bother to struggle through?

The other event was an IRA bomb which caused massive damage and loss of life. Trains were disrupted, travel to work the next day was horribly difficult and yet there were more people at work than on a normal day. There was no co-ordination to this, no instructions went out, but it appeared that people were crawling off their sick beds in order to be there at work the next day, thrusting their mewling and puling infants into the arms of anyone at all so that they could be there.

Yes, we'll take an excuse for a day off, throw a sickie. But you threaten us, try to kill us? Kill and injure some of us?

Fuck you, sunshine.

We'll not be having that.

No grand demonstrations, few warlike chants, a desire for revenge, of course, but the reaction of the average man and woman in the street? Yes, you've tried it now bugger off. We're not scared, no, you won't change us. Even if we are scared, you can still bugger off.

*(That last paragraph rather went round the world. My Mother received a clipping of it from her aunt in New Zealand from a Christchurch paper with a small note. 'Is this **your** Tim?')*

Tim Worstall
http://timworstall.typepad.com/timworstall/

‹ED› NOSEMONKEY AT EUROPHOBIA: ‹/ED›

13:01 — God, us Brits are great. Hardly any panic — more just getting pissed off that it's going to be a bugger getting home. I love this country sometimes.

14:05 — I tell you what, if this is an 'Islamic' terrorist attack, they're doing a piss-poor job. The pubs are all packed out, people sipping their pints happily, all a tad pissed off, but basically fine with it. Nice one, al-Qaeda — you profess to be from a teetotal religion, and you've given the pub trade a massive mid-week boost. Result.

17:43 — a message to our sensible American friends (and others from around the world), many of whom are posting in the comments:

Cheers for the messages of support. London's grateful. And we're going to keep our heads. Stiff upper lip and all that — wouldn't do to get all emotional. Hardly British — and if we stop being British about it, the bastards have won. So we'll have a few beers, make as many sick jokes about it in pubs up and down the land as we can, and get on with our lives as normal. Other than causing the grief of too many innocent people, these cunts will have achieved precisely fuck all. We shall not be moved.

Europhobia
http://europhobia.blogspot.com

‹ED› NEVERATOSS NOTED EXACTLY THE SAME SORT OF BEHAVIOUR: ‹/ED›

The bulldog spirit

Went to the pub at lunchtime to see the latest new on events in London. Three young guys were sitting directly in front of the TV as details of a major terrorist attack on London were emerging — all three avidly reading the *Sun's* account of the Steven Gerard/Liverpool fiasco.

Neveratoss
www.neveratoss.co.uk

‹ED› ANDREW SULLIVAN COMMENTS UPON THE ABOVE: ‹/ED›

The Brits and stoicism

Here's one cultural difference between Brits and Americans. Brits regard the best response to outrage to carry on as if nothing has happened. Yes, they will fight back. But first, they will just carry on as normal. Right now, a million kettles are boiling. 'Is that the best you can do?' will be a typical response. Stoicism is not an American virtue. Apart from a sense of humor, it is the ultimate British one.

[...]

Do not mistake this attitude for indifference. It's a very English form of determination.

Andrew Sullivan
www.andrewsullivan.com

‹ED› ANDREW AT NON-TRIVIAL SOLUTIONS WAS ON A TRAIN IMMEDIATELY BEHIND ONE THAT WAS BOMBED. HIS REACTION: ‹/ED›

An open letter

To the terrorist cunts who tried to kill me today:

Fuck you. You missed me. Better luck next time.

Update: I am coping with the shock as only a Brit (and maybe an Irishman...) knows how — I'm getting well and truly pissed.

Update 2: Thanks for all your thoughts and words, everyone. Going to get a shower, get dressed and then get the tube into work. Life goes on.

Update 3: Back home, safe and sound. Can't thank everyone enough for visiting and leaving their thoughts. One last word: Please — no politically charged comments at least until they've dug out the bodies of those Londoners still buried 100 ft underneath King's Cross in a tube carriage. Time to grieve, not score points.

Non-trivial Solutions
http://nontrivialsolutions.blogspot.com

‹ED› JOHN BAND PROVIDED THE FIRST GOOD JOKE ON THE SUBJECT: ‹/ED›

Tomorrow's *Daily Mail*

Asylum Seeker Terror Attacks Hit House Prices

John Band
www.stalinism.com (site no longer exists)

‹ED› IT COMES IN PINTS? USED THE THEME SONG FROM TEAM AMERICA TO PROVIDE A HOOK FOR A POST: ‹/ED›

For our British friends

This is not to be callous in light of the horrors that happened today in London, but I thought our British friends could use as many gestures of support as possible. If you want to read further, check the extended entry and feel free to add anything to the list that you like.

Bangers! FUCK YEAH!

Mash! FUCK YEAH!

Goofy hats! FUCK YEAH!

The Queen! FUCK YEAH!

Boddingtons! FUCK YEAH!

The MI-5! FUCK YEAH!

Monty Python! FUCK YEAH!

Blood pudding! ER... fuck yeah!

Mad Cows! FUCK YEAH!

Scotland! FUCK YEAH!

The Royal Navy! FUCK YEAH!

The Beatles! FUCK YEAH!

PG Tips! FUCK YEAH!

Page Three Girls! FUCK YEAH!

Black taxis! FUCK YEAH!

Beefeaters! FUCK YEAH!

The Union Jack! FUCK YEAH!

> *<note> This was then added to by well over 1,000 people, listing what they thought great about these isles. Probably the longest comments section in the history of blogging (yes, I know, all five or six years of it). </note>*

P.G. Wodehouse! FUCK YEAH!

Barbara Woodhouse! FUCK YEAH!

Horatio Hornblower! FUCK YEAH!

The Secret Garden! FUCK YEAH!

Hugh Grant (had to hear it again)! FUCK YEAH!

Freddy Laker! FUCK YEAH!

Sir Robert Morley! FUCK YEAH!

Arthur Conan Doyle and Edgar Rice Burroughs! OH FUCK!! FUCK YEAH!

Judy Dench! FUCK YEAH!

The Black Watch! FUCK YEAH!

Kilts! FUCK YEAH!

Shagging! FUCK YEAH!

Tolkien! FUCK YEAH!

Trafalgar Square! FUCK YEAH!

Pound coins! FUCK YEAH!

Christopher Marlowe! FUCK YEAH!

Calling fries 'chips'! FUCK YEAH!

Eddie Izzard! FUCK YEAH!

Alfred Hitchcock! FUCK YEAH!

Spice Girls! FU — wait, what?!?

Neil Gaiman! FUCK YEAH!

The Common Law Tradition! FUCK YEAH!

Geoffrey Chaucer! FUCK YEAH!

The Jam! FUCK YEAH!

The Wilton Diptych! FUCK YEAH!

Withnail and I! FUCK YEAH!

Chips and curry... FUCK YEAH!

Magna Carta: FUCK YEAH!

Salt and vinegar crisps! FUCK YEAH!

Orange squash! FUCK YEAH!

Rounders and netball! FUCK YEAH!

Prime Minister's Questions! FUCK YEAH!

Boiled Veg! FUCK YEAH!

Singing 'Who ate all the pies?' when you see an overweight supporter for the other team in a football match! Fuck Yeah!

   <note> I think that gives a flavour? Last two: </note>

As an Englishman, might I be permitted to add:

pride at the length and contents of this list. Gosh, yes!

   <note> Was followed a few minutes later by: </note>

Englishmen who say 'Gosh, yes!' FUCK YEAH!

My British boss who actually greets people with 'What ho, fishface' a la Bertie Wooster FUCK YEAH!

It Comes in Pints?
http://www.secondbreakfast.net/

✎ 8 July

‹ED› SEAN THOMAS HAD A SMALL TALE FROM ONE OF HIS FRIENDS: ‹/ED›

A friend of mine visits a strip pub, once a week, down by the Gray's Inn Road. Despite the bombs, he went along this afternoon, as usual, and was the only guy with four strippers. But, he told me, he had to go — 'otherwise the terrorists would have won'.

Thetoffeewomble
http://toffeewomble.blogspot.com

🖉 17 July

‹ED› ONE OF THE NAUGHTY THINGS THAT
BLOGGERS DO IS CORRELATE. LOOK AT WHAT
SOMEONE HAS SAID ON A SUBJECT IN ONE
PLACE AND COMPARE THAT TO WHAT THEY SAY
ON THE SAME ISSUE IN ANOTHER. AS LABAN
TALL NOTES, THIS CAN LEAD TO THE
OCCASIONAL EMBARRASMENT: ‹/ED›

Cake wanted — to have and to eat

'The once-concealed symbols and attitudes of hardcore porn are now flooding mainstream culture' complains 'Flic Everett' in the *Guardian*.

Er ... would that be 'Flic' Everett, author of *Sex Tips for Girls, How To Be A Sex Goddess, Fantasy Sex*, and *The Sexy Bitch's Book Of Doing It, Getting It and Giving It?*

'*...it alarms me that we have bought into the culture of porn as readily as the 1950s salary man bought into the culture of domestic bliss...*' tut-tuts the '*Mirror*'s sex-pert' who brought us *Find Your Sex ID* and *Spice It Up* (and whose knowledge of the 1950s seems to come from 'I Love Lucy'. There were few salary men in 50s Britain — we still had a thing called industry).

> There is no voice of dissent — TV, music and magazines conspire to imply that women require no stimulation beyond a lustful male gaze...

Not true, 'Flic' — as shown by responsible magazines. Like Cosmo.

> Cosmopolitan magazine (UK) is looking for couples to talk about the turn-on that always works for them; foreplay, position, prop, whatever. It involves a phone interview and a small picture. Your time will be paid for. Interested? Contact Flic Everett asap.

UK Commentators
http://www.ukcommentators.blogspot.com

✎ 21 July

‹ED› THE SECOND BOMBINGS. FROM NOSEMONKEY: ‹/ED›

14:14 — more reports of the bomber at Oval being a fucking pussy, dumping his bag (big black rucksack) and legging it. These guys are pathetic. If you're going to blow us up at least have the guts to blow yourself up too.

14:42 — two weeks ago we were asking 'is this the best they can do?' Well, no answer to that one yet — but it appears it certainly wasn't their worst. This is — from currently available information — likely to go down in history as the most half-arsed terrorist attack ever.

16:48 — this is getting to the 'move along, nothing to see here' stage.

Pah — back to the cricket. (Oh, and the job, obviously...) I'll keep an eye out for any more developments, but looks like this was a bit weak.

Only two suspects reported as being in custody that I'm aware of so far, though, so there's likely to be a couple still on the loose.

In summary? Amateurs.

15:55 — 39–5? What the fuck? That's almost as pathetic as these bombs.

   <note> (Yes, he'd noticed the score in the first Ashes Test.) </note>

Europhobia
http://europhobia.blogspot.com

‹ED› IT DIDN'T TAKE LONG FOR PEOPLE TO START JOKING ABOUT THE INCIDENT. ERIC S ADDED A COMMENT: ‹/ED›

Pint glass shattered in terror blast

LONDON (Reuters) — London is reeling in panic after a terror blast reportedly shattered a pint glass at the Angel in the Field pub on Marlyebone High Street. Police cordoned off the end of the bar where the blast occurred, temporarily forcing three customers to relocated to a table.

Pubgoers contradicted the police report, saying the glass was merely cracked, not shattered. One eyewitness, who only identified himself as 'Nosemonkey', choked back the tears as he said 'the glass had only just been topped off – it was a FULL PINT, dammit! The glass wasn't actually broken, but the entire pint was lost. LONDON WILL NOT STAND FOR THIS!'

By Eric S (Washington DC), at July 21, 2005 4:34 PM

Europhobia
http://europhobia.blogspot.com

✎ 22 July

‹ED› TODAY SAW THE SHOOTING OF JEAN CHARLES DE MENEZES, A BRAZILIAN ELECTRICIAN MISTAKEN FOR A SUICIDE BOMBER. ANGRY CHIMP DID NOT AGREE WITH THE 'ERRORS WILL HAPPEN' LINE, PROVIDING THE TEXT OF A TONY BLAIR PRESS CONFERENCE FROM ANOTHER UNIVERSE: ‹/ED›

We believe we now know the identity of the man shot at Stockwell Underground Station by police on Friday July 22, 2005.

It is certainly true, that it would have been a huge help if we'd known the identity of this man before we murdered him, but we can't be expected to get everything right. We are all under a massive amount of pressure here, and small mistakes will happen from time to time.

It has taken a little while to formally identify the man, this is because our well-trained officers managed successfully to shoot his face off. In which case we can make allowances for the delay.

Tragically, the man was a tax payer, although fortunately he was not a native born Britain. So we are able to state categorically at this time that although there was a fatal shooting in Stockwell Underground Station, no Britons were involved. Which is frankly a silver lining.

Obviously, our officers are highly trained to identify a potentially life threatening situation. Moments prior to the shooting – in that 1 or 2 second crisis time – they would have had to use their experience and training to take the course of action they took.

In the case of this incident the officer involved will have mentally gone through a checklist similar to this:

1. Is the suspect a darkie of some description?

2. Does he run when a group of random strangers start to shout/scream at him and wave guns around?

3. Does he have a terror deployment device – or rucksack, as they are also known?

4. If he does not have a TDD, is he wearing something that could cover up a bomb? Such as an item of clothing?

5. Does he look guilty (e.g. panicky/sweaty/scared when an undercover officer sticks a shooter in his mush)?

6. Is he a darkie of some description?

7. How many bullets will it take to shoot his face off?

8. Will it be just like Counterstrike for the PC?

9. If we shoot him, can we get away with it?

The only point open to question is point 9. Seeing as how the officers involved shot this fella in front of a tube load of commuters, they have made it a tad tricky to cover up, hence this press conference.

Following this embarrassing incident, I believe that there are now two major questions facing us.

The first is: do we count the man the Police incorrectly executed as a score for the terrorists or one for our side? – There will be debate surrounding that issue for sometime I imagine, not least of all with the victim's family.

The other question is around our current shoot-to-kill-a lot policy.

Well, this goes back to the suspects involved in the terrible incident on 7/7 – which incidentally I coined as a new brand – 7/7 – a brand this Government has pledged will help elevate Britain in the terror bombing attack league to at least Madrid level.

Definitely ahead of Bali and more recently Egypt, which, although tragic, did involve a number of 'dark skinned' people, and not really that many Brits — hence it's relegation to 2nd or 3rd item of news on the day it happened. You want a story to be No.1 — here's a tip — make 'em White or make 'em Brits, preferably both.

We've learnt a lot from the criticism over the Guildford 4 and Birmingham 6, or was it 5 and 7? Oh I forget.

Anyway, the point is we have learnt that if you are gonna fit up some poor bastard, better choose someone who was tragically killed in the incident itself. Far less chance of them protesting their innocence later. You want a patsy that will stick. The last thing this Country needs is to open wounds later with a load of 'Grassy knoll' nonsense.

But as I said before, our officers were tactless enough to 'kill to death' this innocent man in front of 'too many to silence' witnesses.

This is a mistake we certainly hope not to make again in the future.

Ironically, the man slaughtered by our Police hailed from Brazil, a country that has itself become an expert in 'back alley' government sanctioned death squad murdering.

Anyway, I would like to conclude in my now traditional manner. This will be by making an empty statement regarding our need to remain vigilant in the face of a threat which I will reduce to purely ideological and/or simply Evil, in a Judo-Christian way, obviously.

This of course will be a veiled attempt to distance myself from blame, and to increase your fear and paranoia, which will ultimately keep you easy to control and a piece of piss to lie to.

So here goes:

The terrorists are attempting to attack our very way of life and our freedom. I say to them, with your blessing, that they will never change our way of life.

And if preserving our way of life and our freedom means we have to impose new restrictive freedom of movement legislation, allow our Police to stop and search anyone who looks slightly Asian or 'funny looking' without good reason, have undercover coppers executing the occasional 'innocent' darkie or indeed generally become a crypto fascistic 1984 Big Brother style society; then so be it.

You will never change our way of life, which is based on freedom and a huge pile of bullshit.

Britain will prevail.

Angry Chimp
http://angrychimp.blogspot.com/

✎ 25 July

‹ED› THE DILPAZIER ASLAM CASE. SCOTT BURGESS AT THE DAILY ABLUTION NOTES SOMETHING INTERESTING ABOUT THE BACKGROUND OF THE WRITER OF A GUARDIAN COMMENT PIECE. THIS LEADS TO THE SACKING OF THAT REPORTER, THE RESIGNATION OF THE EXECUTIVE EDITOR AND, WELL, LET SCOTT TELL THE TALE: ‹/ED›

L'Affaire Aslam: *The Ablution* responds

I'm back!

Warm thanks to all those that have emailed and commented in these eventful few days — I'll be wading through the contents of my mailbox, and trying to respond, in the next couple of days. I'd also like to express my deepest appreciation to the guest posters for keeping the blog going.

There are of course times when a dignified silence is an appropriate course of action, and this may be one of those times. However, I'm sure that readers will understand that it would require superhuman discipline not to respond to the *Guardian's* recent comments about certain reactionary elements of the blogosphere. And anyone who knows me knows that discipline isn't exactly my forte.

For those unfamiliar with the story, there's copious background in past Ablution posts but, briefly, I exposed a *Guardian* trainee journalist as a member of an extremist Islamist organisation, and asked the *Guardian* what they were going to do about it. The story got picked up in the MSM and made quite a stir in the British blogosphere.

On Friday, the *Guardian* announced that they had fired the journalist in question, and published no fewer than three articles about it. One of them addresses the role of bloggers in the affair, and that's the one I'd like to examine a little more closely.*

Aslam targeted by bloggers

By a staff reporter

This is extraordinary. In fact, a search of the *Guardian* archives indicates that, within the last 3 years, a total of only three stories have been published completely without attribution. Two of these involved memorial services for individuals associated with the newspaper, and one was filed from Zimbabwe by a reporter with very good reasons for anonymity.

One really can't help but wonder why the reporter wishes to remain unidentified. My hunch is that it's not so much simple cowardice (although that may play a part), but that it's because the article is written by a recognisable name who wants to get in some low blows without accountability. Sadly, we'll probably never know.

> Rightwing bloggers from the US, where the *Guardian* has a large online following, were behind the targeting last week of a trainee *Guardian* journalist who wrote a comment piece which they did not care for about the London bombings.

'Rightwing bloggers from the US'! And so the Guardianista is prepared for a tragic story of injustice and retribution, brought about by the evil that stalks the dark corners of cyberspace. Sadly, the assertion misleads in the extreme.

As it happens, *Harry's Place*, a blog usually characterised as left-wing, and with no American contributors (as far as I know), played a role at least as significant as mine in promulgating the story after it was broken.

There's no point in asking, even rhetorically, why the *Guardian* did not note the contribution of *Harry's Place* in developing the story. Pointing out the critical role left-wing Brits played in the episode does not add the proper, er, *tone* to the piece.

> The story is a demonstration of the way the 'blogosphere' can be used to mount obsessively personalised attacks at high speed.

*All extracts from the *Guardian* article can be found at
http://media.guardian.co.uk/site/story/0,14173,1534497,00.html

Note the emotive language — 'obsessively personalised'. Then read my posts, or the posts at *Harry's*, and see if you find the characterisation appropriate. In light of what follows in the article, the reader can't help but find the 'staff reporter's' use of the phrase rather ironic.

> Within hours, Dilpazier Aslam was being accused on the internet of 'violence' and belonging to a 'terrorist organisation' — both completely untrue charges.
>
> One blogger appealed for 'some loyal Briton to saw off your head and ship it to me'. Another accused Aslam of being guilty of 'accessory before the fact to murder'.
>
> These ravings were posted alongside more legitimate questions as to whether a newspaper should employ a reporter who belongs to a controversial political group linked to the promotion of anti-semitic views.

All true. Unfortunately, nowhere in any of the *Guardian's* coverage do readers learn of the most legitimate question of all, concerning Mr Aslam's reporting of a court case (see *Harry's Place*) in which the organisation to which he belonged played a critical role — one which is never mentioned in the piece, which constitutes little more than propaganda for the Islamist group in question.

> Aslam's comment piece was about the attitudes of angry young Muslims in the north of England and headlined 'We rock the boat: today's Muslims aren't prepared to ignore injustice'.
>
> It did not mention that the author was a member of the radical but non-violent Islamic group Hizb ut-Tahrir, proscribed in Germany and Holland as anti-semitic.

And they *are* radical. In fact, as the *Guardian* itself pointed out in 2003, they constitute '*Britain's most radical Islamic group, banned across the Middle East*'.

> Scott Burgess, a blogger from New Orleans who recently moved to London, spends his time indoors posting repeated attacks on the *Guardian* for its stance on the environment, its columnists such as Polly Toynbee, and its recent intervention in the US presidential election campaign.

I wonder how they know when I moved to London — I don't think I've ever mentioned it here. The intent of painting me as a recent arrival to these shores seems to be to emphasise my American-ness, with all of its negative (to

Guardianistas) connotations. In fact, I moved here over 6 years ago. To call my presence 'recent' is akin to referring to the 'recent' opening of the Millennium Dome, i.e. ridiculous.

'Spends his time indoors'? Can someone explain to me what this is supposed to mean? As for the balance of the paragraph, I plead guilty with pride and without reservation — although I might append the phrase 'as well as its blatant misstatements of fact'.

> He pitched into Mr Aslam, who as it happened, beat him to the traineeship on the Guardian.

This is where the fun really begins. 'As it happened' I did indeed 'apply' for the traineeship — as a means of providing ironic entertainment to my readership (thanks very much Jackie D. of *Samizdata*, for your spirited and welcome defense). My 'application' succeeded very well in its goal, becoming a running *Ablution* joke.

Honestly. Given that I 'spend my time indoors posting repeated attacks on the *Guardian*' (as I was doing long before my spurious 'application') how can anonymous really expect people to think that I was serious?

Actually, I should thank the *Guardian* for being so impressed with my investigative skills. In their view, I went from never having heard of Mr Aslam to my discovery, two days later, of exactly which trainee position he was occupying. Perhaps the *Guardian* has room for a reporter of such ability — I understand they have a slot open. [*NB — the last sentence is intended ironically.*]

> Another blogger, Laban Tall, wrote enthusiastically that Burgess' coup 'has resounded across the blogging universe like a shockwave from a supernova'.
>
> He said: 'I bet the Guardian wish they'd given him the job now, not Mr Aslam. Scott applied for the job in June 2004. Mr Aslam got it. They say revenge is a dish best eaten cold.

'Resounded across the blogging universe like a shockwave from a supernova'? Hmm — perhaps Mr. Tall overstates the case somewhat. But thanks, Laban.

> Googling the 27-year-old Muslim's name, Mr Burgess picked up some articles the journalist had openly written in the past for Hizb ut-Tahrir websites and denounced him on his blogspot, The Daily Ablution, saying: 'He is on record supporting a world-dominant Islamic state.'

Well, yes. And, in fact, he *has* publicly recorded that view. As he put it, referring to the need for young Muslims to be educated in the sciences, mathematics, etc.:

> we will have to run an Islamic state which must lead the world, economically, militarily and politically.

Returning to the *Guardian* article:

> Mr Burgess fished out a website article written by Mr Aslam before September 11 for Hizb ut-Tahrir. He quoted one line: 'Establishment of Khilafah [the worldwide Islamic caliphate] is our only solution, to fight fire with fire, the state of Israel versus the Khilafah state.'

Reporters *dig*. Right-wing American bloggers *'fish out'*.

The *Guardian's* keenness to point out that the article in question was written before September 11 strikes me as odd. It is, after all, an article of faith among the Guardianista ilk that the actions of the US and Britain since that time have radicalised Muslim youth. By that logic, Mr Aslam's views are probably even more extreme now.

> A fellow blogger, Dsquared, promptly accused him of using quotes out of context.

It's hard to avoid this charge without reproducing entire articles, which is perhaps why outclassed commenters are so often tempted to raise it. That said, let me try to provide some context.

The context of Mr Aslam's remarks was that of the official organ of an organisation that, according to the BBC*, '*promotes racism and anti-Semitic hatred, calls suicide bombers martyrs, and urges Muslims to kill Jewish people.*' Mr Aslam's comments were made in the context of his membership of a group that — according to a particularly prescient Muslim leader quoted in the 2003 BBC report — must be stopped '*politicis[ing] and pollut[ing] the youngsters' minds and other gullible people minds,*' lest:

> what will happen in effect is that these terrorism acts and these suicide bombings that we hear going on in foreign countries, we will actually start seeing these incidents happening outside our doorsteps.

Mr Aslam was writing for this group until at least last June.

It is more than four years old, written when the author was a teenager, before 9/11 and during a really nasty episode early in the intifada. How many people posting on this blog would like to have their teenage scribblings used as an assessment of their politics as an adult?

Mathematically astute readers will note that Mr Aslam was about 23 when the piece was written; and, again, was writing for Hizb until at least last June. As for dsquared's question, it would in fact be more apposite were Mr Aslam on record as publicly repudiating the views in question. In fact, not only has he failed to do so, but, *given the choice between a* Guardian *job and membership in an organisation that calls for followers to 'kill* [Jews] *wherever you find them,'* the 27-year-old Mr Aslam chose the latter.

The way you've used these excerpts is a bit spintastic and if this is the worst you can dig up, I don't think the *Guardian* can be blamed for not rumbling him.

But they did, ostensibly because:

the *Guardian* considered that Hizb ut-Tahrir had promoted violence and anti-semitic material on its website and that membership of the organisation was not compatible with being a Guardian trainee.

So Hizb is a 'non-violent Islamic group' that promotes violence.

The *Guardian's* stated reason for releasing Mr Aslam raises the most interesting question of all. The *Guardian* seems at first to have denied all knowledge of Mr Aslam's affiliation. As the *Independent* put it:

It is understood that staff at the *Guardian* were unaware that Mr Aslam was a member of Hizb ut-Tahrir until allegations surfaced on 'The Daily Ablution', a blog run by Scott Burgess.

However, an article published Friday by the *Guardian* states quite clearly that the fact was well known, even among senior editors:

Subsequent to joining the *Guardian*, Aslam made no secret of his membership of this political party, drawing it to the attention of several colleagues and some senior editors.

It seems that the explanation given for Mr. Aslam's dismissal should be rewritten a bit, in the interest of accuracy:

the *Guardian* considered that Hizb ut-Tahrir had promoted violence and anti-semitic material on its website and that membership of the organisation was not compatible with being a *Guardian* trainee, **if noticed by outsiders**.

But meanwhile, New Jersey undergraduate Joe Malchow [aka Joe's Dartblog] was writing on his own blog: '*Guardian* employs known member of terrorist organisation.'

Fantasies like this zoomed round the world and soon seeped into the paper's mainstream rivals.

An anonymous reporter quoting undergraduate websites to make their easily refuted point? How very sad.

Perhaps the most extreme blog was posted by 'dreadpundit', a right-wing New Yorker using the name 'Bluto'. He wrote:

Okay, Dilpazier, I've decided to bow to your 'logic' — sauce for the goose and all that. That's why I'm issuing a secular fatwah and asking for some loyal Briton to saw off your head and ship it to me (use Fed-Ex, please, so I can get a morning delivery, and do remember the dry ice, also, a videotape of the 'execution').

I have to say that I'm not a fan of this kind of rhetoric. Not only is it unfunny and sophomoric, it should be avoided for reasons that the *Guardian's* use of this excerpt makes clear — it simply provides ammunition for terror apologists and their employers, who are of course more interested in attacking an easy target like 'Bluto' than addressing the cogent points so intelligently raised at *Harry's Place*.

In the *Independent on Sunday*, Shiv Malik, also briefly a *Guardian* intern, accused the hapless Aslam of mounting 'a sting by Hizb ut-Tahrir to infiltrate the mainstream media.

Hapless!

To put it bluntly, the accusation made against Mr Malik is a lie. Here's the quote, directly from the *Indy* article:

Speculation is mounting that it may have been a sting by Hizb ut-Tahrir to infiltrate the mainstream media.'

Either the anonymous *Guardian* reporter believes that the phrase 'speculation is mounting' is tantamount to an accusation, or they're being shamelessly deceptive. I don't think it's the former.

And in the tabloid *Sun*, their attack-dog columnist, Richard Littlejohn, took the opportunity to claim:

| A *Guardian* journalist has been unmasked as an Islamist extremist.

Tabloid! Attack dog! Claim! And yet the claim is true, as the *Guardian's* action with respect to Mr. Aslam makes clear.

> Many bloggers repeated Malik's untrue assertion — made in the *Independent on Sunday* — that the Guardian was 'refusing to sack' Aslam.
>
> The episode was a striking illustration of the way that blogs and bloggers can heat up the temperature and seek to settle scores — as well as raise legitimate concerns about journalism and transparency — when something awful happens in the streets of London.

'Seek to settle scores' — there it is again; the implication that I discovered (in just two days) that Mr Aslam held a position for which I had ironically 'applied', and attacked him for that reason. At first I found this rather amusing, but the more I think about it, the angrier I get. Is this actionable?

| as well as raise legitimate concerns about journalism and transparency

Thank you. And now, speaking of 'journalism and transparency', would the author of this article please make themselves known?

The Daily Ablution
http://dailyablution.blogs.com/the_daily_ablution/

> <note> *The reason this gets so much space is because this is the first time that British blogs have made a real impact upon the mainstream media. In the US there have been a number of cases, Trent Lott resigning as Senate Majority leader after praising Strom Thurmond's stance on desegregation was stirred up by blogs (many of them right wing by the way), Dan Rather's use of forged documents to show that George Bush had avoided active service, shown to be forged within hours of the broadcast, Eason Jordan of CNN resigning over allegations that US troops were targeting journalists... this is our first time on this side of the pond.* </note>

‹ED› SCOTT WENT ON TO SHOW FURTHER LINKS BETWEEN ASLAM AND HIZB UT TAHRIR. TIM BLAIR GIVES US THE TIMELINE: ‹/ED›

The Burgess effect

Doubt the power of blogging? Consider:

October 2004: Dilpazier Aslam is hired by the *Guardian* under its 'diversity scheme'.

13 July, 2005: The *Guardian* publishes an opinion piece by Aslam in the wake of the London bombings; Aslam asserts that younger Muslims are 'much sassier with our opinions' and don't much care 'if the boat rocks or not'.

13 July: Scott Burgess — an indoor-based blogger — uncovers Aslam's support for a global Islamic state.

15 July: Burgess exposes Aslam's membership of extremist Islamic group Hizb ut Tahrir.

16 July: The *Melbourne Age* publishes Aslam's comment piece.

17 July: The *Independent* reports: 'The *Guardian* newspaper is refusing to sack one of its staff reporters despite confirming that he is a member of one of Britain's most extreme Islamist groups.'

19 July: The *Guardian* fires Aslam, considering his membership of Hizb ut Tahrir to be 'not compatible with being a *Guardian* trainee'.

22 July: An insanely bitchy and cowardly piece ('by a staff reporter') in the *Guardian* claims *Sassygate* is 'a demonstration of the way the 'blogosphere' can be used to mount obsessively personalised attacks at high speed'.

29 July: Albert Scardino, *Guardian* executive editor for news, resigns.

3 August: Mockery of the *Guardian* spreads.

5 August: Prime Minister Tony Blair **bans Hizb ut Tahrir**.

Tim Blair
http://timblair.net/

✎ 29 July

‹ED› THE BIG NEWS AT THE END OF JULY WAS THAT THE IRA HAD AGREED TO END THE ARMED STRUGGLE. TWENTY MAJOR WAS ABLE TO BRING US THE FIRST DRAFT OF THAT HISTORIC SPEECH: ‹/ED›

IRA Statement

Dear cuntos,

Yes, I know we've been blowing people up willy-nilly for years now and justifying it with some tired old shite about a united Ireland. You, me and the wall know that's never going to happen so we, the IRA leadership, have decided to throw down our arms.

We realise that the international support we've received, especially from America, is going to be hard to maintain when the world and his mother are affected and appalled by the terrorism being perpetrated by those Muslim lads. As terrorists ourselves it makes it very difficult for us to throw grand gala fundraisers in New York and Boston and makes it difficult for our Irish-American benefactors to chuck us the cash we need for our guns, bullets, explosives and other devices of murder we've used throughout the campaign.

We decry the actions of these Muslims for ridding terrorism of its cuddly image, its shileleagh and its bejaysusness. Long gone are the days when Mickey Rourke would be seen dead in the same snug as us. Christ, look at the state of Mickey now though, 'tis better for our image he forgot about us and went mad for the plastic surgery.

Anyway, after lots of amicable discussions we've decided that in order to prolong the political careers of Gerry and Martin, who by the way have nothing to do with us at all, all volunteers will be dumping their arms, ditching their balaclavas and will never more bother the people of the UK by exploding them, their buildings or places of work.

Oglaigh na hEireann will strive for political solutions to... pfffff... sorry, something got caught in my throat there... political and peaceful... bwa ha ha... er...*cough*... political and peaceful something or other. It's not really important right now.

The important thing is that we make this statement, that you fall for it believe it like you believed us when we said we didn't rob that bank at Christmas time and we can continue our work as smugglers, dealers, loan sharks and keep running the protection rackets that keep us filthy fucking rich.

Tiocfaidh ár lá agus póg mo thon.

your old chums,

The 'Ra.

Twenty Major
http://twentymajor.blogspot.com

AUGUST 2005

✎ 2 August

‹ED› BLOGGERHEADS WAS RATHER ANGRY
ABOUT THE ABOLITION OF THE RIGHT TO
DEMONSTRATE PEACEABLY IN PARLIAMENT
SQUARE. SO ON THE FIRST DAY THAT IT WAS
ILLEGAL TO DO SO WITHOUT PRIOR PERMISSION
OFF THEY WENT TO DO SO: ‹/ED›

The thick blue line

Gawd bless those men in blue for enforcing an unenforceable law... or at the very least making a very good show of things.

Who'd be in the army these days, eh? Or the police force, for that matter. What a thankless bloody task that is.

Think about it. With Tony Blair, Jack Straw and Charles Clarke off on holiday (crisis or no crisis, these men deserve time with their families, damn it) who's in charge of home affairs? Hazel Blears, that's who.

And if the shit really hits the fan, who's in charge? John Prescott, that's who.

Now, you can say what you like about Blair, Straw and Clarke, but they know how to stifle dissent — or at least how to make a convincing 'tut tut tut' noise when others go too far on such matters — but Blears and Prescott couldn't organise a shitfight in a sewer.

Yesterday, as 300 or so people gathered in Parliament Square either as part of Brian Haw's demonstration or in open defiance of the very new, mostly secret and generally stupid law banning spontaneous protest at the heart of our democracy, the police handed out flyers warning us that:

> We believe that you may be, or are about to be, involved in a demonstration located within an area subject to the provisions of the Serious and Organised Crime and Police Act 2005. The map on the reverse of this leaflet clearly defines the area concerned.

So, without reading further, I turned to the map — and then discovered that people could not keep and read this notice without being willing accomplices to a violation of the Copyright, Designs and Patents Act 1988.

Yes, the police had lifted their map entirely from StreetMap, which is a copyright work (© BTex Ltd 1997, 1998, 1999, 2000, 2001, 2002, 2003, 2004). The lack of any notation suggested the work had been lifted without permission.

Now, I'm man enough to admit my wrong-doing. If BTex Ltd wish me to withdraw my version of their map from The Interwebs, I will do so.

But I'm not a police force using a copyrighted image without permission with the intention of enforcing a law with it, now am I?

I'm also not a police force with instructions provided by the Home Office and sent forth with a map that's so poorly executed (by the Home Office) or so poorly publicised (by the Home Office) that even those 'in the know' can't find it or see fit to use it.

On the face of it all, it would appear that Bloggerheads.com — while admittedly (and reluctantly) being in violation of copyright — has been doing a superior job to that of the Home Office in its interpretation and publication of area-sensitive legislation.

But wait... it gets better:

The police ran out of warning flyers!

Maybe...

I'see, they 'ran out' about 5 minutes after I advised Superintendent Malcolm Simpson of the small copyright problem and then advised the crowd of the problem via the 'open mic' megaphone. But they were back on the case about 10 minutes later, after a *very* speedy copy-run... or a quick phone call to head office.

Either way, we wuz Warned. There were already plenty of 'nice' policemen in the square, plus two mini-buses full of 'do the jobbers' doing laps... and another four mini-buses on stand-by in Great College Street. (So many police and not enough warning flyers... what gives?)

In this glorious tension-filled lull, I approached the 'open mic' megaphone yet again.

Whether or not you accept that I've been an active member of Brain Haw's protest since 15 May 2003 there was no denying that — by taking a ballpoint pen and showing the crowd how to apply it to a piece of paper with a certain amount of pressure and manoeuvre that pen in such a way as to make a clearly recognisable smiley-face — I had organised and taken part in a completely different (and totally unauthorised) demonstration.

I did this in full view of dozens of police officers (and their cameras), the media (and their cameras) and about 300 witnesses (and their cameras).

Even though this was in direct violation of the new Serious Organised Crime and Police Act 2005:

> Any person who —
>
> (a) organises a demonstration in a public place in the designated area, or
>
> (b) takes part in a demonstration in a public place in the designated area, or
>
> (c) carries on a demonstration by himself in a public place in the designated area,
>
> is guilty of an offence if, when the demonstration starts, authorisation for the demonstration has not been given under section 131(2)

(Note — In case you missed the significance of this, I was demonstrating the correct use of a ballpoint pen. In clear violation of the new act, which appears to have been drafted by a 7-year-old.)

But no-one arrested me.

Instead they chose to arrest an elderly woman. And then about 4 other people. But not under the new legislation, it would appear.

No, I have the sneaking suspicion that these people were threatened with arrest under the new law, but actually arrested for resisting arrest, verbal assault, littering, or the usual nonsense.

Why do I think this?

Because I approached Superintendent Malcolm Simpson and asked if arrests were being made under the new law. Actually, a journalist beat me to it by about two seconds, but he was informed that he should contact the press office.

But I had the same question. And I pressed him on it.

Those of us assembled — whether we had taken part in copyright infringement or not — had a right to know if arrests were being made for this 'offence'. Remember that their official warning in the form of a leaflet read:

> We believe that you *may* be, or are *about* to be, involved in a demonstration located within an area subject to the provisions of the Serious and Organised Crime and Police Act 2005.

Were we so involved? Had that time come?

Were these arrests being made under this new legislation?

His answer? I'll give it to you verbatim:

> What do you think?

Now, please remember that this man is a Superintendent in charge of police, not school prefects or cub scouts. Your general officer of the law may get away with snarky and disingenuous comments like this, but a superintendent?

I asked again, and was rewarded with the Ignore side of his face.

This is what has me thinking that yesterday's arrests were a bluff. A few 'show' arrests on any pretext available that would allow the police — who appeared to be operating on uncertain ground and/or with poor instructions — to scatter the crowd and discourage others without actually putting the new law on the line.

But I guess for the official poop, we'll all have to wait until morning.

loggerheads
http://www.bloggerheads.com

✎ 4 August

‹ED› THE TINBASHER IS A BUSINESS BLOG.
NOTHING TO DO WITH TECHNOLOGY, MARKETING,
PUBLIC RELATIONS OR ANY OF THE BUSINESSES
YOU WOULD THINK WOULD BE AT THE
FOREFRONT OF THIS NEW COMMUNICATIONS
METHOD. NO, THEY'RE EXACTLY WHAT THEY
SAY ON THE TIN, TINBASHERS, PEOPLE WHO
WHACK HELL OUT OF BITS OF METAL. THEY'RE
ALSO, AS HARRY'S PLACE POINTED OUT BACK
IN FEBRUARY, ONE OF THE MOST SUCCESSFUL
OF THE BUSINESS BLOGS IN THE UK‹/ED›

What happens when you don't give up on your blog

John managed to stop up way past his bedtime last night to give me the lowdown
as to what is happening at Butler Sheetmetal at the moment.

His typing skills are such that it took him infinitely longer than it would any
ordinary mortal, but it appears that we're rather busy quoting for jobs that have
come via the internet. I know I mentioned this a couple of weeks ago, but it's
definitely going from strength to strength.

And you know something else? It seems that we're getting one or two of the
jobs as well.

Yes, I know this is what should be happening, but I'd just like to point out that
before I started with the Butler Sheetmetal site I had no idea about website
building, or SEO [Search Engine Optimiser], or anything relating to web presence
at all. And everybody at BSM HQ had even less of an idea than me.

To say I didn't have a clue about blogs would also be a slight overstatement.

Now I'm still no expert, but something we've done has worked somewhere along
the line. Either that, or we're extremely lucky bastards. I've also worked harder
than I ever have in my entire life for less reward than I ever have done in my entire
life — other than the sheer enjoyment, of course.

It is possible to take obscure, non-tech related businesses that wouldn't know the back end of a blog from the back end of a bus and create a viable and profitable web presence for that business.

But, it's not a time to rest on one's laurels as there's plenty I still get wrong and plenty I still don't know and could probably be doing a damn sight better. For example, the main Butler Sheetmetal site hardly even integrates the blog in any way, shape or form, and that needs addressing.

We also don't sell nearly as many of our planters as we should, but we would seriously struggle and have to make some serious decisions about expanding if we did.

As experiments go, it's been rather interesting.

Nobody expected any of this to actually work apart from me, and I didn't know what I was talking about.

Anyway, give it a couple of months and there might just be a little case study to celebrate one year of the Tinbasher.

The Tinbasher
http://www.butlersheetmetal.com/tinbasherblog

> <note> At another point Paul points out that sales have risen 35% since he started the blog. Pretty good going for one guy and a computer. </note>

✎ 7 August

<ED> ENGLAND AND AUSTRALIA, THE ASHES SERIES, THE SOUND OF LEATHER ON WILLOW, AN EVOCATION OF A TRADITIONAL BRITISH SUMMER. AS POOTERGEEK POINTS OUT, THINGS DO CHANGE: </ED>

The Tebbit Test

Cambridge Sony Shop. Saturday. Your host Damian 'Ebony'n'Ivory' Counsell and a Sony employee of Asian descent who's darker than a sideboard are wincing at the fall of cheap England wickets in their second innings. Mr Sony even goes off on one about a particularly shoddy piece of umpiring in the Aussies' favour. Meanwhile all the white people are looking at MP3 players.

PooterGeek

www.pootergeek.com

✎ 11 August

‹ED› PETER BRIFFA CHANNELS SOME FAMOUS NAMES: ‹/ED›

Thursday, August 11

Okay, so, it's a matter of when not if there is another terrorist attack on London's financial and transport systems. Indeed, according to a report in the *Indy*, there are thousands of Anglo-Iraqis who don't go a bundle on Freddie Flintoff, the Queen Mum, and Coronation Street. In the light of this, I contacted a bunch of ou most compassionate columnists to see if any of them had got anything cooling on their PCs in anticipation of the forthcoming carnage. And, if they did, would they be kind enough to send me a paragraph or two. And what do you know, a whole bunch of them wrote back...

Simon Tisdall:

If there is one thing more sickening than the bombs that ripped through the tube trains of London yesterday, killing scores of commuters in the process, it is the grotesque overreaction to these events by certain sections of the tabloid press. Where is the measured calm, the careful analysis of what happened?

Blair's refusal to countenance any sort of dialogue, let alone compromise, with the bombers, is in a way as morally obtuse as the very fundamentalists he claims to oppose. With his simple-minded adherence to 'democracy' and 'the rule of law', one could be forgiven for wondering who is the civilised party here.

Simon Jenkins:

I walked into London yesterday, and stood feet away from the bomb victims. Curiously, I have never felt safer in my entire life. And, I am happy to say, away from the hysterics of the bleeding and the wounded, my fellow Londoners greeted the events with commendable placidity and equanimity that made one feel proud to be British.

Polly:

Yesterday's bombs were as predictable as they were unnecessary. Predictable, because of the growing gap between rich and poor, unnecessary, because of the war on Iraq.

Indeed, the real threat to this nation doesn't come from the Islamofascists at all. They are merely a distraction from a revived Tory party. If David Davis gets elected leader, he will be a suicide bomber for the free market, icily prepared to walk into the nearest hospital and sacrifice himself and destroy as many doctors as possible in the cause of fundamentalist capitalism.

Yazzmonster:

No, I thought. Not again. And please let it not be Asians. Anything but Asians. Please, let it be a renegade branch of the Countryside Alliance. The IRA. Anyone but Muslims. But no, it was true. For those of us dreaming of a multicultural nation we have suffered yet another withering blow. I hugged my daughter, and pleaded with my husband never to let her travel by tube again. 'She might get lynched by white people,' I explained.

Seamus Milne:

The fact is, irrefutable and unavoidable, that some of their demands are more than reasonable. Indeed they are just. A fully-functioning democratic Palestine; the troops out of Iraq; Saddam Hussein restored to his Presidency; a sixty foot statue of George Galloway in Columbia Road Flower Market. These are essential political rights whatever the behaviour of the terrorists, and if Tony Blair really were the statesman he aspired to be, rather than the Bushite poodle his critics accuse him of being, he would accede to them forthwith.

Jackie Ashley:

Most people in Britain now are brought up in safe environments, and have no idea what it is like to be a suicide bomber. Yet instead of understanding, all we hear, as we switch on our radios and televisions, is righteousness and indignation. Naturally, there is a place for this. But there is also a risk, namely, that we could be in danger of demonising the young bombers. Indeed, in persecuting them like this, there is a very real danger of a backlash.

Joan Smith:

In all the acres of newsprint spent analysing the events of last week, and the supposed motives of the perpetrators, one salient fact has been all the more noticeable by the fact that not one of the great and good has so far had the bravery to mention it. Truly, it is the terrorist equivalent of the elephant in the drawing-room.

All of the bombers were men.

Matthew Parris:

For those brought up on a diet of compromise, and whose idea of radical political change is stuffing leaflets through mailboxes every four or five years, there was something refreshingly direct about the bombs that blasted through central London last week.

That is no way to diminish what happened, let alone justify it. Yet I don't suppose I am alone in getting a slight visceral thrill from the news. In a lacklustre summer where England's cricket team has performed so badly, and after a disappointing series of Big Brother, perhaps this might wake the capital up from out of its current torpor.

Gary Younge:

Mike Tyson. OJ Simpson. Michael Jackson.

Yesterday was payback time.

Libby Purves:

Nobody wants to return to the dark days of the Fifties, when Britain was a conformist, dull, classbound society. But in many ways what we have replaced it with is worse. A spoiled, self-indulgent, sexually-obsessed, deeply materialistic world where our young people are offered no spiritual nourishment at all. Given these circumstances, who can be surprised when they turn to suicide bombing as the only outlet for their misery?

Michael Gove:

Yesterday he was at his most magisterial. Nothing gets the best out of Mr. Blair like a crisis, and there it was once again, centre stage. The frown was back, the pauses for breath perfectly timed, the hesitation and the quivering lip were positively Olivier-like in their command. The man has an uncanny grasp of the public mood and once again he seized it, reminding us all how right we were to re-elect him as Prime Minister at the last general election.

Tariq Ali:

Now is the time to consider the plight of the real victims of yesterday's atrocity. A superficial reading might see that as those hospitalised and murdered, but what about the innocent Muslims, like Hassan Ali, 18, a bricklayer from Dalston who is now too afraid to leave his home after his car was vandalised by BNP supporters? Or Asif Habib, 22, an unemployed bomb-maker from Luton?

Alice Miles:

All the talk these days in the Westminster village is of Tony Blair and exactly how long he intends to go on. Yet the real winner of yesterday's incident does indeed live in Downing Street and it isn't Gordon Brown. No, this week it's Cherie who's been striding down the corridors with a great big grin on her face. 'I'm afraid Tony gets like this whenever there's a war on,' a former cabinet minister explained to me last Monday over a liquid lunch. 'He's like Errol Flynn on viagra. Poor old Gordon has to sleep on the other side of the house, while Cherie's going at it hammer and tongs, screaming like a banshee.'

Nick Cohen:

Once again, the bombs go off, and once again the key, if unspoken, question in London's dinner parties, at least the parties I get invited to, among the quiche-eating trendies that stalk the wine bars of South Islington is, was Enoch Powell right?

Moonbat:

It's worth remembering that, yesterday, in the hour between the two bombs, fifty people were being murdered in Detroit, five species of beaver became endangered, twenty-seven thousand acres of Brazilian rainforest were reduced to timber, 18 oil wells were drilled in Southern Iraq, 20 thousand SUVs will have been sold worldwide, and 48 schoolchildren will have died of passive smoking in Scotland alone. I make these points not to trivialise what happened, but to put it all in perspective.

Will Hutton:

Yesterday was a day of disaster for Britain. A watershed for us all. None of us is innocent, and in that sense, we are all terrorists now. Yet there are thorns among the roses. The police, the health service, and the schools all played their part. As did the BBC, with its courageous refusal to bow down to the general squeamishness, and its fearless demand for asking probing, searching questions.

Unlike the privately owned and outrageously partisan Sky News, which operates like the thicker, inbred cousin of its American counterpart Fox News, the BBC was steadfast.

The BBC coverage of yesterday's disaster was worth the licence fee alone.

Jonathan Freedland:

Of course, it would be easy to castigate yesterday's bombers as terrorists, extremists, and all the rest of it. After all, they are. But, whilst it is perfectly understandable to do so, there is nonetheless a worrying strain of Islamophobia underlying the reaction of so-called 'ordinary people' to the latest wave of bombs which swept through the capital yesterday. One wonders if there would have been the same degree of condemnation had these acts been performed by middle-class white boys from the Home Counties?

Vicki Woods:

We were told that invading Afghanistan would make us safer.

We were told that invading Iraq would make it easier for us to sleep in our beds.

Who feels safe now, I wonder?

Madeleine Bunting:

It's happened again. And, my first reaction this time was to wonder about the spiritual malaise of whoever it was who did this. Were they unemployed, were they homeless, were they gay? Had they come to this country, desperate to belong, only to be confronted by a British media whose only interest lies in Ipods, Personal Videorecorders and the sex lives of b-list celebrities? Was it really the case that, for these poor lost souls, the only option available to them was to strap bombs to their jackets, go on a packed tube train and kill dozens of commuters?

Karen Armstrong:

There is something quite disturbing, and culturally imperialistic to boot, about the almost unanimous outpouring of condemnation following the recent bombings, with little attempt made to see things from the perpetrators' point of view. Indeed, there appears to be very little comprehension that suicide bombing, far from being an aberration, lies at the very core of moderate Islam, and for many is a rite of passage as intrinsic and important to contemporary Muslims as the hazing that American teenagers practise on university campuses. Imagine, if you will, the outcry that would happen if Western liberals were to denounce those in Southern Italy who force their children to undergo baptism.

Aaro:

I remember the first terrorist I ever met. It was the long, glorious summer of 1976, and I was living in a squat, scribbling editorials for Trotskyite Weekly. I was a fresh-faced 18-year-old, in my gap year before going off to Exeter University to do PPE. There I was, standing in the toilets, sweating like a pig, dousing my hair with water, when out of one of the cubicles came Dymphna, clutching a well-worn copy of Ulysses. Of course, I didn't know she was a terrorist then. Perhaps she didn't even know it. At any rate, when I first knew her, Dymph the Nymph seemed to have other preoccupations, of a distinctly earthy kind.

Even today, I can still remember her pert buttocks, impenetrable accent, and conical breasts.

Public Interest.co.uk
http://publicinterest.blogspot.com

‹ED› SCARYDUCK PROVIDES US WITH A PERSONAL MEMORY OF THE LATE PRINCESS DIANA: ‹/ED›

Lucky bag

The 'Having-it-done-for-real' Remix.

The year was 1997. Mrs Duck and I sat down and earnestly decided that we had had enough Scaryducklings for one lifetime, and that, for various practical reasons, I should go and have The Snip.

I would present myself at the hospital and allow a perfect stranger to cut a hole in my ballbag and do strange, unnatural things with my plums until they didn't work any more. It seemed totally fair at the time, after all Mrs Duck had gone through the pain of child birth twice AND endured a lifetime of marriage to me.

Following a visit to the doctor (who actually tried to talk me out of it), I put my name on the list, and waited, knowing full well that such was the state of the Health Service, it would be upwards of two years before they got round to me.

Six weeks later, I got a cunningly worded letter asking me to present myself at Battle Hospital in Reading, and don't forget your gonads. Arses.

Despite my morbid fear of blood (my own) and incredible pain, I bravely faced up to my ordeal. I am, after all, the son of a doctor and a nurse, so what did I have to worry about? An entire lifetime of regular supplies of *The Lancet*, the journal of the medical profession, for starters. Every month it would flop through our letter box, and every month I was introduced to a new kind of skin condition, hideous disease or bizarre injury, all in glorious Technicolor. It put me right off following in my father's footsteps, and I have steadfastly pursued a career path that has taken me as far away from these knife-wielding goons as possible. And now I was going to let one of them loose on my bollocks. Doom.

Bright and early I awoke on that Monday morning. I showered. Then I shaved. And shaved again, a process done with the utmost care so as not to cut any more holes in the scrote than was absolutely necessary. All this was done in a bathroom resembling Piccadilly Circus, with people from a five-mile radius bursting in to use the lav, surreptitiously checking out how I was getting on with the 'nads.

With the kids packed off to relatives, I took the short journey down the road to the Battle Hospital. It was deserted. Not a soul to be seen. Like the Marie Celeste, there were signs of habitation, a half drunk cup of coffee, a coat on a hook, but no-one present. Eventually, after a search of the hospital's empty corridors, I collared a passing nurse and asked where everybody was. She told us.

It was Monday morning. Princess Diana had forgotten to do up her seatbelt during a frenzied Saturday night in Paris, metamorphosing from 'Sex-Crazed Royal Tart flounces round Europe's capitals with Egyptian Boyfriend' in the early editions of Sunday's papers to 'We'll Never Forget You, Princess of all our Hearts. Oh, and Dod as well' by the following lunchtime. The entire hospital staff was allowed the day off to go and have a good cry over it.

'Even Dr Norris?' I asked.

'Especially Dr Norris', she replied, 'Though I suspect he'll be remembering Diana with eighteen holes of golf.'

It was all the excuse I needed. I took to my heels and ran, Mrs Duck struggling to keep up. I got out of the hospital building, and kept running until I reached the car. My gonads were safe. Dr Norris was hacking about with his mashie niblick on the golf course instead of hacking away at my crown jewels, which was a situation I could live with for the rest of my natural life. I jumped into the car and sped away, never to return. Except to go back and pick up Mrs Duck.

After all the national grieving, the crying, the media hyperbole and the fucking awful Elton John song, I feel the time has come to finally pay my respects to Her Royal Highness Princess Diana of Wales, who died saving orphans, poor people, kittens an' stuff:

'God bless you, Your Highness', I say, 'You saved my bollocks.'

A fitting tribute to a great, great woman. It's what she would have wanted.

Scaryduck
http://robberrabbit.blogspot.com

✎ 12 August

‹ED› THE WASHINGTON POST NOTICED THE NIGER FAMINE AND IN THE OPINION OF ONE AID BUREAUCRAT (CURRENTLY ON SABBATICAL) WERE COMPLETELY WRONG IN ALMOST EVERY DETAIL: ‹/ED›

An article in Thursday's *Washington Post* by Craig Timberg claimed that 'the rise of a market mentality' has contributed to the famine in Niger. As you would expect, this has provoked a strong reaction from free market bloggers, such as Don Boudreaux at *Cafe Hayek*, Melana Zyla Vickers at *Tech Central Station*, Craig Newmark at *Newmark's Door* and Anthony Batty at the *Globalization Institute*, who claim that the problem has been caused by price controls, excessive government regulation and the unintended consequence of well-meaning donor intervention.

In this polarised debate, both ideological extremes are wrong. This is a reality-based blog, so here is the middle ground.

First, Timberg's claim that market liberalization has led to this famine is painfully misguided. He says:

> In a country adopting free market policies, the suffering caused by a poor harvest has been dramatically compounded by a surge in food prices and,

> many people here suspect, profiteering by a burgeoning community of
> traders, who in recent years have been freed from government price controls
> and other mechanisms that once balanced market forces.*

This does not make sense. Surely he cannot believe that food production would
be higher, and more food would be available in Niger, if food prices were lower,
for example as a result of government price controls. Rising food prices create
incentives for higher production, marketing of stockpiled food, reduced exports
and increased imports. If Niger has too little food, then an increase in food prices
is exactly what is needed to increase the supply.

Timberg offered himself up as a free hit for the right-wing commentators, which
they duly took. But seeing the world through ideological blinkers, they headed
off over the reality horizon in the opposite direction.

Notably, Melana Zyler Vickers misunderstands Amartya Sen's *Poverty* and *Famines*
claiming that Sen finds that 'command-controlled, totalitarian and authoritarian
regimes have regularly bred famine'. Actually, this wasn't Sen's point. His analysis
showed that some (but not all) famines are caused not by a lack of food
production, but by a failure of *entitlement*, which occurs when some members of
the population lack the resources to buy the food they need. It is true that Sen
pointed out that excessive state interference might contribute to the failure of the
market to ensure that food reaches people who need it. But his central conclusion
which Ms Vickers conveniently ignores, was that even in free markets with
sufficient food production, it is possible that an imbalance in the distribution of
economic resources might lead to hunger and famine. Sen pointed out that, in
these circumstances, the best approach might be for aid donors to make cash
grants to those who need food, to enable them to buy it in markets and so feed
themselves while increasing incentives for the production and distribution of
food. So on Sen's analysis, the conclusion is that rich countries should provide
increased resources for Niger, provided in the form of un-hypothecated cash
grants to the poor (basically, dropping dollar bills out of a helicopter). But of
course Ms Vickers (and the corporate interests that fund *Tech Central Station*)
are ideologically opposed to government assistance, and would prefer any US
aid that does sneak under the radar to be tied to US corporate interests such as
agribusiness, so this wasn't the conclusion that Ms Vickers reached. She prefers
instead to blame the

> failure of the socialist-style economic players — within Niger and around it —
> to allow its people to feed themselves.**

*http://www.washingtonpost.com/wp-dyn/content/article/2005/08/10/AR2005081001946.html
**http://www.techcentralstation.com/081105H.html

So to be clear: Timberg is wrong that a move to less regulated markets has reduced food production; but Ms Vickers is wrong that food shortages are the result of excessive government regulation and intervention. (Incidentally, Ms Vickers also makes the bizarre claim that most of the population in sub-Saharan African 'lives under command-controlled economic conditions' — which is complete balderdash.)

Cafe Hayek also has a crack at the donors:

> Perhaps if the U.N. weren't in Niger, traders would be selling food directly to starving people rather than waiting for well-meaning westerners to buy it.*

It would be right to criticize the UN and other donors to the extent that they are importing surplus food from western countries and dumping it in Africa, so driving Africa's own food producers out of business. We don't have the figures yet, but I have no doubt that some of this is going on, and it is a scandal. But using aid funds to buy food locally, which is what *Café Hayek* criticizes, is exactly what the donor should be doing, as it supports local food producers and increases production. *Café Hayek's* idea that increasing the demand for locally-produced food is likely to result in a restriction on the production and supply for food in Niger is just as absurd as Timberg's converse ideological argument that lack of food production is caused by higher prices. (I am not saying that it is logically impossible; just that it is highly unlikely and an allegation made with no evidence whatsoever.)

Craig Newmark (the economist, not the geek who runs *Craig'sList*) is closer to the truth. He is right to dismiss Timberg's claim. But he too ignores the point that even in free, otherwise well-functioning markets, famines can occur when some people are too poor to buy the food they need.

Overall, this was dismal reporting by Timberg which should never have got through quality control at the *Washington Post* (why didn't someone like Sebastian Mallaby spike this before it reached the paper?). But the ideologically-driven outpourings of the right-wing bloggers were no closer to reality. **The problem here is not market regulation or aid, but poverty, and that is something that we can and should do something about.**

Owen's Musings
www.owen.org/blog

✎ 15 August

‹ED› SCARYDUCK TELLS US MORE ABOUT THE RERUN OF THE OPERATION: ‹/ED›

Inappropriate things to say during a vasectomy operation

1. 'Ooh! That tickles! Do it again!'

2. 'Did you hear the one about the Irish circumcisionist?'

3. 'I love you.'

4. 'No, I think you're wrong there. The movement of capital will only have a negative effect on the bourgeois/worker relationship.'

5. 'I'll give you any money if you stop now.'

6. 'I've had your wife.'

You know you're addicted to your weblog when...

...shaving yourself for a vasectomy operation you're thinking 'what could I write about this?', followed closely by the startling revelation that you are prepared to tell the world about the shaving of your knob in a pithy, humorous manner. Still, it's never stopped me before.

Here's a hint, though: don't use one of those new Gilette vibrating razors — send all the wrong signals.

Scaryduck
http://scaryduck.blogspot.com/

✎ 17 August

‹ED› AND THE AFTERMATH: ‹/ED›

Nads update

The best weblogs tend to gravitate towards a theme, for which they become an authority. Fraser has become world famous in Cricklewood for his skill at the exotic end of the culinary arts*. Gert is THE blogging authority on Opera and the art of performance. Tim Ireland has documented the paucity of government and our descent into the surveillance society.

I, on the other hand, write about my testicles.

Now that I am on the long, potholed road to recovery, let us examine the cut-out-and-keep instructions given to me by Dr Shipman ('Calm down madam — now you've signed these insurance doc... errr... consent forms, it's time for your vitamin injection. Yes. Your non-fatal vitamin injection.').

According to the sternly worded leaflet 'So You Want To be a Jaffa', I've got to send two samples for analysis to make sure the op's been a success. That's two huge jars, to fill to the brim and cart ten miles to the Dorset County Hospital, with my trousers round my ankles and my face still in the hideous rictus of the vinegar strokes within two hours of scraping the man gravy off the ceiling.

Beforehand, I've got to clean out the old system to ensure that none of that nasty baby-making sperm is present. 'The best method of doing this' says Dr Shipman's leaflet, 'is through masturbation. This will take up to forty ejaculations and up to two months.'

Forty? FORTY? **TWO MONTHS?** One week down the line, and I'm just about used to pissing out of it, let alone getting myself geared up for a two month hand shandy marathon. Christ on a bike, unless I get used to multi-tasking, I'll hardly have time for anything else; and I am certain this could dangerously deplete world scud supplies at a crucial point in the global war on terror.

Also: 'Avoid intercourse for three days before submitting the specimen. Keep the specimen under your armpit.' They were laughing when they wrote that, the bastards.

Pray, then, not just for me and my hairy palms, but for the law enforcement community of this proud country. Y'see, I only ever get quality time to myself in the car these days, and, well, you know what I said about multi-tasking. What could possibly go wrong?

*As a matter of fact, I really ought to suggest sauteed gonads by way of celebration of my hideous ordeal.

Scaryduck
http://scaryduck.blogspot.com/

✎ 19 August

‹ED› THE SHOOTING OF JEAN CHARLES DE
MENEZES ON THE TUBE CONTINUES TO CAUSE
OUTRAGE AS FURTHER DETAILS COME OUT ON
THE ACTUAL EVENTS. HE WASN'T CARRYING A
RUCKSACK, WAS NOT WEARING A BULKY
JACKET, DID NOT LEAP THE TICKET BARRIER,
DID NOT RUN FROM POLICE, WAS UNDER
RESTRAINT WHEN SHOT… IN SHORT, EVERYTHING
THAT WE WERE TOLD IN THE IMMEDIATE
AFTERMATH WAS WRONG. THIS HAS LED TO AN
ATTEMPT TO CREATE ANOTHER GOOGLEBOMB.
THIS TIME, LINKING THE WORD 'LIAR' TO THE
HOME PAGE OF SIR IAN BLAIR, THE
'COMMISSIONER OF POLICE OF THE METROPOLIS'
(AND WHEN DID HE GET THAT ORWELLIAN TITLE?
WHAT WAS WRONG WITH CHIEF CONSTABLE OF
THE MET?). THE AIM IS THAT WHEN SOMEONE
ENTERS 'LIAR' INTO GOOGLE AND THEN HITS THE
'I FEEL LUCKY' BUTTON, SIR IAN'S WILL BE THE
MUGSHOT STARING OUT. THE FOLLOWING
IS AN EXAMPLE OF THE STRONG FEELINGS
ON THE SUBJECT FROM PAUL DAVIES AT
MAKE MY VOTE COUNT: ‹/ED›

Don Blairo and modern-day Omerta

Some days in particular, you just never know what's going to happen. The world's
messed up like that — confused, illogical and unstructured. The evidence is on this
very blog. Having taken my A levels a good few years ago, I'm in the position to
know that this is the fifth posting on this here blog today. Conversely, the only
thing posted yesterday was stolen from somewhere else.

don't know how busy 22 July 2005 was for Jean Charles de Menezes, but I bet the poor bastard didn't know how it was going to end up: shot in if not cold, then no-higher-than-room-temperature blood, while being restrained on a tube train.

At the time, the prevalent mood was one of mild shock mixed with a feeling that it must have been excusable in some way, just make sure it doesn't happen again. This was fuelled by a swarm of speculative soupçons of information, designed to make the execution appear somehow less wrong, all of which we now know to be bollocks.

The atmosphere now is one of growing, or rather maximised, disbelief. This man really didn't have to die, in the name of safety, national security, or anything else. The unfortunate Brazilian got knocked off by incompetence, ineptitude, and, one suspects, a bit of panic — how do you miss three of eleven shots when fired from a few feet away? Even GIs can do better than that.

At the centre of the controversy is Met chief Ian Blair. The new liar.

Now we're told that the person responsible for making him look like a shameful it has been suspended for breaking Blair's own Omerta, which, given that Ian is till knocking around, doing his job, saving us from terrorists, etc., means that letting the public know what's going on is worse than overseeing the biggest botch-job in history.

There's no need for me to elaborate here, Robin's summed it up perfectly well already. Don't be surprised to never hear from the leaker again, he's clearly messed with the wrong dude.

The poor sucker probably won't even see it coming.

From *The Times*:*

A CLERK at the Independent Police Complaints Commission (IPCC) was suspended last night for allegedly leaking secret documents about the Stockwell Underground shooting of an innocent man to a television station.

Sir Ian yesterday rejected demands for him to resign. He said: 'I'm not going to resign — I have a job to do.'

Sir Ian replied that he raised the role of the IPCC because it would have to disclose information to the families of those affected and he questioned how this would work during a counter-terrorism operation.

http://www.timesonline.co.uk/newspaper/0,,174-1741475,00.html

N.B. (in case not obvious) exaggerated tone... police do a wonderful job under incredibly difficult circumstances and I'd be shit at it... but this is just sick.

Make my vote count

www.makemyvotecount.org.uk/blog

✎ 22 August

‹ED› THAT THERE'S SOMETHING WRONG WITH THE ASYLUM SYSTEM IS WELL KNOWN. THAT WE SEND PEOPLE BACK TO A COUNTRY WHERE THEY WILL BE HANGED FOR THEIR SEXUALITY SHOWS THAT IT IS WORSE THAN MANY THINK. THE FOLLOWING IS FROM MUSINGS FROM MIDDLE ENGLAND: ‹/ED›

Blood on our hands — remembering Hussein and Israfil

When I stayed in Eastbourne years ago it pretty much lived up to its stereotype. Walking along the front I saw fleets of coaches disgorging hundreds of elderly people on zimmer frames and in wheelchairs — they probably still call them Bath Chairs in Eastbourne.

I almost expected that the hotels they shuffled into would be displaying not the Tourist Board star symbols but rows of zimmer frame symbols: the coveted 5 zimmers if they chop all the food up into tiny pieces, and have a stairlift and walk-in baths in all rooms.

Posters for the local theatre advertised an old music hall star who I'd assumed had been dead for at least 20 years.

Actually, the night I was there something really exciting happened and the local paper debated whether to bring out a special morning edition. A shop window got smashed. But nobody was sure whether it was done by a drunken hoodie or one the visitors who'd had too much Bristol Cream and cocked up a three point turn on their zimmer.

In the morning, I gazed out of my hotel window on to the beach and a cold, grey sea. It wouldn't have been surprising to see the ghosts of the Eastbourne Home

Guard patrolling that beach and scanning the horizon with opera glasses borrowed from the local theatre, ready to repel the Nazi hordes, to keep Britain a beacon of freedom and democracy and allow Eastbourne and places like it to slumber on into the 21st century — genteel, dowdy and slightly comical.

I wonder if Hussein Nasseri looked out on to that cold, grey Sussex sea in June 2004 as he made his way to an activity centre.

Did any of the elderly residents and holidaymakers squint at him, or even automatically smile at him in the way old people often do, as he passed them on the street?

If they did, he probably didn't notice.

He went into the activity centre car park and shot himself between the eyes.

Hussein, 26 years old, was a gay man who fled Iran and came to Britain. He had already spent three months in prison in Iran for being gay and feared execution if he was sent back.

In June 2004 the Home Office refused to grant him asylum and was going to send him back to Iran.

So he killed himself.

A private death in an Eastbourne car park was preferable to a public hanging in an Iranian square.

The Coroner said the asylum refusal was the 'obvious motive' for his death.

The year before, Israfil Shiri, another gay Iranian, died six days after setting himself alight in the offices of a refugee charity in Manchester. His asylum application had also been rejected. Unlike the mythical asylum seekers described in the tabloids, living the high life on state handouts, Israfil was both homeless and penniless, often sleeping in a wheelie bin. He was also in constant pain because, following his asylum refusal, he was unable to get medical treatment for a bowel complaint.

Now another gay Iranian man has been refused asylum and faces being sent back to almost certain death. In this case, the words of the judge who approved his removal have caused justifiable outrage. He described his sexuality as 'predilection', referred to 'his coterie' of fellow gay men and spoke of 'unseemly activity'.

It's the language of an Eastbourne Colonel (Retd.), circa 1950.

This July two gay teenagers were publicly executed in Iran and it is believed another gay man suffered the same fate in August.

One Iranian gay rights group estimates that the Iranian Government has executed at least 4,000 homosexuals since 1979.

Our Prime Minister has stated that Britain went to war with Germany to stop the Holocaust, the mass slaughter of Jews, homosexuals, gypsies and people with mental and physical disabilities, and that was why the butcher, the baker and the candlestick maker were patrolling the beaches of southern England in the early 1940s.

It's nonsense of course. Tony's grasp of history is as shaky as his grasp of human rights. And, given that gay men were imprisoned in the Britain of 1939, I doubt that their treatment at the hands of Hitler, had it been known at the time, would have motivated the tradesmen of Eastbourne to spend their nights patrolling the beach. Nor was Britain particularly keen to welcome the Jews who were fleeing Nazi Germany before the war.

You may also recall that, when no weapons of mass destruction were found in Iraq, the reason for the war was suddenly transformed into concern for Saddam's abuse of human rights and his slaughter of his own people. Many crocodile tears were shed by Blair and his allies for Iraq's dead (the ones killed by Saddam, not by us, naturally), although it wasn't Blair and his friends who campaigned about abuses in Iraq at the time that we and America were happily selling Saddam arms.

Today our Government, like others, is making a lot of noise about Iran's nuclear fuel programme and the possibility that they may be seeking to build nuclear weapons. This concern, we are led to believe, is because of the nature of the Iranian regime, vividly illustrated by what I have written above. Our gay teenagers get bullied at school. In Iran, boys like 16-year-old Mahmoud Asgari are hanged in a public square.

Yet our Government is determined to send young, gay Iranians back to almost certain death.

A Labour Government.

A Government that put human rights at the top of its agenda.

A Government that once boasted of an ethical foreign policy.

A Government whose Prime Minister sermonises and emotes with moist eyes and quavering voice about poverty and famine in Africa.

A Prime Minister apparently inspired by the ideals of Christian Socialism and who vows to defend an idealised concept of 'Britishness'.

Is it possible that some of the small number of gay Iranian men who have escaped to Britain had looked at the *Visit Britain* website and read this enthusiatic invitation:

> Awash with rainbow pride, Britain is a nation of excitement, history, talent and understanding... The UK has one of the largest populations of gay and lesbian folk in Europe, we also have equal age of consent laws (set at 16), partnership laws and even legal commitment ceremonies in some of our major cities. As for marriage, it'll just be a matter of time!
>
> So whether you're gay, lesbian, transsexual, bi-sexual, in or out, be yourself in Britain!... With our proud gay history, cutting edge culture and fashion, flamboyant cities and pulsating nightlife, isn't it time you came out... to Britain!

It would surely be only fair and sensible to add the words:

We've put all this exaggerated, self-congratulatory, and in places sickening, nonsense on our website because gay tourism has been identified as a key niche market for the British tourist industry. Pink pounds? We can't get enough of them! But if you're from a country like Iran, don't even think of outstaying your welcome because we'll send you back to certain death before you can say Old Compton Street.

In the hours before their suicides did Hussein and Israfil feel just black despair or did they also experience puzzlement and a sense of betrayal? They had every reason to.

If I could speak to them now I'd say this:

I'm not responsible for the actions of my Government any more than you were for the actions of yours. But I still feel a deep sense of shame for something done in the name of my country.

The horror of what happened to you is that you escaped from one nightmare only to be plunged into another.

You died here not because of religious fundamentalism but because of political expediency and the callous inhumanity of politicians, judges and others.

Your stories and your deaths were mostly unreported in the British media. Sponging 'bogus' asylum seekers sell papers. Penniless, dead, gay, asylum seekers don't.

A small number of people will read about you here and some of them may share my anger at what this country did to you and may yet do to others.

I and some others may even find the time in our *exciting, pulsating* lives in this *rainbow nation* to write to the Home Secretary and our MP to try to prevent your tragedies being repeated.

A blog post is as quickly forgotten as most human lives, not least by the person who writes it. But, Hussein and Israfil, I'll try to remember you and how your deaths affected me. Sentimental, perhaps, and ultimately pointless. You were betrayed by my country and my country is stained by your blood. Remembering you and mourning your deaths won't change that but it's better than indifference.

And there's not much else I *can* do or say — a thought that's as depressing as the cold sea rattling the shingle on Eastbourne beach and warm blood spilling on to the concrete of a deserted car park.

Musings from Middle England
http://goinguphill.blogspot.com

SEPTEMBER 2005

✎ 1 September

‹ED› HURRICANE KATRINA AND THE FLOODING OF
NEW ORLEANS BROUGHT THIS REMINISCENCE
FROM A LONDON BASED AUSSIE, SALTATION,
AT HIS BLOG FARTING THROUGH MY FINGERTIPS:
‹/ED›

Katrina and the waves

The reports from New Orleans of the deaths caused by the flooding, and then the amount of the looting, and the rescue helicopters being grounded due to looters firing on them — all these I find saddening and sad.

My deepest sympathies and condolences to all who have lost property or livelihood or persons to Hurricane Katrina.

But...

At the risk of sounding insensitive...

I am a little bewildered.

Not by the looting, etc. — that's just a function of the USA's disturbingly actively deliberate social stratification. Those weird invisible social shells that Londoners create for themselves, such that they can Live and Work with but never really Mee people outside that invisible shell (*we used to describe it as 'Londoners spend their lives running through glass tunnels'*), are a country-wide feature of the USA.

So the looting and shooting's no surprise — bluntly: there's been no real change there for at least the last century.

No, I mean I'm bewildered by the deaths and chaos from the flooding.

Or rather, by the literally surreal and literally hysterical behaviour of the population of New Orleans, with regard to the hurricane and the flooding. Apart from the mid-hurricane wind damage, there should have been no deaths, and there sure as shit should have been no major problems from the flooding.

And here's why I'm bewildered:

I grew up in an environment fairly similar, physically, to New Orleans: the Gold Coast in Australia. Over and above the summers of 90+% humidity and average 30–40° temperatures (86–104°F), we get hit by hurricanes every few years.

In 1974, we got hit by a doozy. Not just your common or garden cyclone, oh no. This was a big 'un.

Floods.

BI-IIIIGGG floods.

Floods that make New Orleans's last week look like a summer thunderstorm.

The coast was flooded for about 50+ miles inland along at least a strip of coast from above Noosa to below Coolangatta (I'm just going from a 7 year old's memory of people complaining — it could have been further), which is, what, about 150 miles. And Brisbane's population alone (the city halfway between those points) would be the same as New Orleans (back then: it's about twice as big now).

And when I say 'flood', I don't mean like wading knee-deep through water. I mean some serious inundation action.

Our two-storey house stood atop a slope that dropped 2–3 storeys down to a tidal canal, about a mile and a half from the sea as the crow flies and about 5 miles as the water flowed. The floodwater came up ~4–5 feet into the ground floor of the house. So that's what, a rise of ~40 feet of water *at the water's edge*. (By comparison, going by the overwhelming bulk of published photos at this point, New Orleans' average seems around 5 feet *inland* with one single media quoted maximum of 'up to' 20 feet. Note nearly all photos of streets show the door lintels clearly visible above the water.)

But rather than demanding immediate restoration of normal life, the Aussies just grabbed tins and food and tinopeners and camping stoves and hurricane lamps and blankets and climbed onto the roofs or were offered other peoples' second storeys (we billeted next-door) and waited a few days till the waters went down.

People with boats had mostly prepared by putting out sufficient rope slack; then after the water had risen, swam out to them and used them to help ferry people round after the storm passed. *(Every boat left tied up normally either sank or broke (or their jetties did).)* We used surfboards and kayaks to get to the shops — they'd pulled as much food as they could onto their roofs and there was no reason for us to not buy the bread and milk while it was still fresh.

The waters went down to the point you could walk through them after a couple of days. I was kinda disappointed. It was fun! Sitting on the outside steps looking at the brown swirling through the open downstairs door. Dad pulling the kayak out of the garage. The delight of the world turning a new colour and a new shape as far as I could see. Mum told me (I never saw it) that a pool up the road had had a little shark left in it.

We got over 10 metres of rain (33 feet) in a week and some serious wind.

And people didn't die, people didn't panic, people didn't demand internet access or mobile phone coverage, they didn't even demand electricity, let alone phones.

They accepted that the real world could affect their lives.

And they took action to prepare, to ensure that they themselves could cope reasonably, to prepare themselves so that they wouldn't be dependent upon anyone else, at least for a reasonable while. And then they helped the other people around them.

In Australian language:

'They just got on with things.'

(An amusing observation just now: I'm not sure that any nonAustralian will read that last sentence correctly. In all other English-speaking cultures I've had useful experience with 'get on with' as a responsibility-avoiding pure amelioration verb (-al phrase) confined to social interaction. 'Oh, it was tense. But we managed to get on with them after a while.'

In Australia, it's a driving, active, punchy, Achievement-Driven verb.

For example: 'Get on with it!'

Or: 'The building burnt down and then exploded and then sank into the swamp and then disintegrated before being swallowed up by the earth's core. So it needed rebuilding. So we got on with it.')

It seems less physically dramatic in New Orleans. From the one-eyed or half-eyed perspective I can get from the TV and the papers and the web, including all the 'on-the-spot!' pseudobloggers (many Americans and all journalists seem to (want to) confuse the word 'blogger' with 'amateur journalist'), Katrina did some serious wind damage initially, but the real problems have come from the flooding. Yet the flooding is not dramatic.

nd some things particularly stick out in my mind.

People are dying. Not in extreme conditions, merely unusual conditions.

People are *demanding* to be rescued, including screaming abuse at boats that go past them, too overloaded to stop.

The various media are filled with earnest reports of people's worthy strivings to solve the 'desperate need' for locals to have full and uninterrupted mobile phone coverage and internet access.

Self-obsessed emails/posts to major public websites and 'emergency blogs' all caterwaul their own personal emotional responses to other people's personal emotional responses.

nd I can't help seeing these as all just different aspects of the same social nvironment, the same learned culture of both behaviour and conditioned erception of self versus others versus 'the authorities'.

hat is, the same conditioning that underlies the second two, created the learned elplessness that underlies the first two.

arting through my Fingertips
ttp://go-blog-go.blogspot.com

2 September

ED> IN THE AFTERMATH OF THE 7/7 BOMBINGS OSEMONKEY AT EUROPHOBIA WAS CONTACTED Y ONE OF HIS READERS TO ASK... WELL, LET IM TELL THE STORY: </ED>

urophobia's St John Ambulance thank-you piss-up — success!

ell that went pretty well.

all started thanks to the insane number of visitors my liveblogging of the 7th ly bombs managed to attract. The following evening I received an email from meone (who wishes to remain anonymous) who'd read the coverage and had een really impressed with the calm way that London (initially, at least) reacted to xplosions in our midst.

Rather than make regular charity donations, they were wondering how they could buy someone in London a pint — pretty tricky from the other side of the Atlantic. They bunked me £50 via PayPal to distribute as I saw fit. Despite me being some anonymous guy on the internet about whom they knew basically nothing. Within a few days, other readers had chipped in to the tune of a good couple of hundred, and it continued to grow.

I started to get worried, and asked for advice on how to proceed. At this point a volunteer from the St John Ambulance Brigade left a comment pointing out that they had attended all the bomb sites (met the chap last night — good bloke).

Now most people, when they think of St John Ambulances, think of the people at the village fete or at football matches, waiting around in case a small child grazes their knee or gets an asthma attack. I don't think that any major news organisation mentioned the fact that, on 7th July, they acted not only as vital back-up to the regular emergency services (attending non-terrorism related emergencies, manning the phones, helping co-ordinate the response, etc.), but also attended the various scenes of the blasts.

One chap I met last night, who was also interviewed on BBC London News with me, was one of the first medics on the scene after the Tavistock Square bus bomb, tending the injured for several hours. Other St John volunteers walked into London through the chaos to help out, and stayed on duty not only throughout the day, but for several days on end — right through the following weekend and beyond.

You will doubtless find it hard to believe, but few organisations take emails from someone calling themself 'Nosemonkey' very seriously. Jenny from the St John press office, bless her, did. Over the last few weeks, with various emails back and forth, we managed to set a date, and she was able to contact the volunteers. Last night a bunch of them turned out to a pub near Edgeware Road tube (where a few of them had helped treat the injured on the 7th), and we had a good old-fashioned piss-up courtesy of *Europhobia's* generous readers. (At this point I will admit that did have a couple of pints on the fund — but only a couple, and at their insistence — I bought the rest myself.)

These people did a fantastic job, most for no money as the vast majority are volunteers. Some of them encountered things that no one should have to, many have been left traumatised by their experiences. This thank-you piss-up was, apparently, the first time that any of them can remember the public showing their thanks in such a way. One St John worker couldn't think of anything similar happening in the 27 years she's been in the job.

This was genuinely appreciated. To all those who donated — you've done this here nterweb proud.

As an added bonus, BBC London News were in attendance (camera crew and the works), giving some much-needed publicity to the fact that these guys were doing a gruelling job for no money and — pretty much until now — no recognition. You can watch them interview me and the St John hero of the day for the next week via this handy video feed (it's about 17 minutes or so in from Thursday's early evening news).* There was also a reporter from *The Times* who will hopefully be able to get a write-up in Saturday's edition, and Rafael of *Observer* blog fame was also in attendance (not to mention my *Sharpener* colleague Katie bringing a donation). A long-time reader of *Europhobia* even turned up briefly to whack an extra £20 over the bar.

n short, damn good stuff.

And from henceforward I shall be known as 'Internet Website Master Nosemonkey, as seen on TV'. Or not.)

Blogs can do some good, even if most people on this side of the pond still don't know what they are. And as there is currently a massive, co-ordinated blog appeal or help in the wake of Hurricane Katrina, there's another chance to prove it.

Again, thank you people who donated — from the St John volunteers as well as rom me.

Europhobia
http://europhobia.blogspot.com

✎ 3 September

ED› IN THE AFTERMATH OF HURRICANE KATRINA A RISK ENGINEER TRIES TO POINT OUT THE REALITIES OF HOW TO SPEND MONEY TO MITIGATE RISK: ‹/ED›

Saturday, September 03, 2005

Does anyone realise that Hurricane Katrina was the 3rd most intense hurricane on record and the fiercest in 35 years to hit the US? Does anybody actually

www.bbc.co.uk/london/content/articles/2005/06/03/tvnews.shtml

acknowledge that this is an extremely rare event? The whirlwind of bullshit emanating from the media and blogosphere since Katrina's passing is itself looking set to make Category 5 on the Saffir-Simpson scale:

1. The fact that the government is struggling to cope with 80% of a major city being under as much as 25 feet of water following one of the greatest natural disasters in the country's history means that someone in government is criminally negligent.

2. The hurricane was caused by global warming, of which the policies of the Bush administration are to blame.

3. The levees could only withstand a Category 3 hurricane. They should have been made to withstand a Category 4 or 5.

4. The money used to wage war in Iraq should have instead been spent on flood defences in New Orleans.

5. The White House reaction to the disaster was slow because New Orleans voted for Kerry.

6. The White House reaction to the disaster was slow because it is only poor blacks who are suffering.

7. The looting on this scale could only happen in America.

8. Our government could have handled the situation far better (a comment coming from the UK).

9. Bush withheld additional spending on the levees to fund his tax cuts for the rich.

10. This is all the fault of Small Government. Only Big Government can handle such emergencies.

11. The military shouldn't be in Iraq; it should be kept at home to deal with the aftermath of hurricanes.

I think the basic problem afflicting most commentators is that they have no concept of acceptable risk and the fact that mitigating risk costs money, with the relationship between money spent and reduction of risk being non-linear. Anyone with an unlimited budget carrying out a risk assessment of New Orleans would have noted that it is hemmed in by a large river and an enormous lake yet lies mostly below sea level, and would probably have come to the conclusion that the city should be moved brick by brick somewhere more sensible. Given that those charged with mitigating the risk of flooding in New Orleans did not have an unlimited budget, they prioritised and came to the conclusion — correctly — that a Category 4 or 5 hurricane was not High Risk (Risk being the product of Likelihood and Consequence). Even now, by most measures, it is still not High Risk because although the consequences are severe the likelihood of reoccurence is slim. Rather than slamming the stable door after the pony has bolted, the money now doubtlessly heading towards Category 5 levees in New Orleans would be better spent mitigating High Risks elsewhere in the US, of which here are likely to be many. Mitigating the High Risks is often relatively cheap, and has long term value. Mitigating Medium Risks and Low Risks can also be cheap. But mitigating ALL risks, and trying to achieve a risk-free situation is infinitely costly to implement. Reducing the last 10% of risk could cost more than the total spent on the first 90%.

So a trade-off must be made between money spent and risk reduction, leading to a situation where people live under a level of risk deemed to be acceptable. Take a look at San Francisco, where somebody cleverly built a city of several million people right on top of a geological fault. One large earthquake, the 10,000 year event, would reduce the city to rubble with few survivors. The 1,000 year event would leave tens of thousands dead and the city in ruins. Yet people live here in full knowledge of this, willing to accept the level of risk in their lives. Were the worst to happen and the plates shift, would the residents of San Francisco be yelling at the government for not making adequate preparations for the event, or not spending hundreds of billions of federal money on strengthening buildings which even then would not be guaranteed to survive? Probably. But this doesn't in itself make the government, or anyone else, culpable for the risks which people take when they choose to live in areas which are prone to natural disasters.

We the undersigned...

ttp://www.tradingtimes.co.uk/blogging/blogger.html
Note that this blog is no longer active, and the author now writes at
ttp://www.desertsun.co.uk/blog

✎ 5 September

⟨ED⟩ RANDOM ACTS OF REALITY IS WRITTEN BY A PARAMEDIC IN LONDON. FIRST-HAND STORIES FROM THE FRONT LINE OF THE EMERGENCY SERVICES. THIS IS HIS APOLOGY TO SOMEONE HE COULDN'T SAVE: ⟨/ED⟩

Sorry

Dear patient,

I'm sorry.

I know you thought that you were going to die peacefully, but we have to try and save lives, even though you were terminally ill. Your husband didn't want you to die yet, neither did your daughter.

I'm sorry that when I reached you, you were breathing your last. It meant that I had to lift you off your bed onto the hard floor.

I'm sorry I had to do that, but it is the only way I could do effective chest compression. I'm sorry I had to do the chest compressions, I know I broke some of your ribs, but please understand that it is a known side effect of trying to keep your heart pumping.

I'm sorry that we had to put those needles in your veins, but you needed the fluid. You also needed the drugs that helped your heart beat — but it was probably painful.

I'm sorry that we had to pump air into your lungs, it can't have been nice for you, but we needed to keep your vital organs supplied with oxygen.

I'm sorry that because of the air in your pleural space we had to push two large needles into your chest. I don't know if you felt it, but it did help reinflate your lung.

I'm sorry that your husband didn't quite understand what was going on — we tried to explain, and I think that at the end he did realise that you probably weren't going to wake up.

I hope you didn't mind when we had to keep passing a couple of hundred joules through your body — it made your body jump, but it's not your fault. I don't know if it hurts. I hope it didn't.

know that the journey into hospital wasn't the smoothest ride, and the sirens were loud — but we did need to get you into hospital quickly.

did remember to wrap the blanket around you so that anyone standing outside he hospital doors wouldn't see that you were naked.

ut...

.I'm not sorry that we, and the hospital, were able to keep you alive long enough or your family to arrive and gather around you.

hope that there was a part of you that was still aware of what was happening, nd was able to hear their words of love.

hope that it was worth the pain so that you could hear those words, and feel heir presence.

left you at the hospital, your heart was beating and you were breathing. I hope hat your end was without pain.

andom Acts Of Reality
ttp://randomreality.blogware.com/blog

7 September

ED> MY OWN INTEREST IN BLOGGING IS TO TAKE 'HE WORDS OF THE NATIONAL COMMENTATORS, 'HE NEWSPAPER COLUMNISTS, AND EXAMINE UHETHER THEY KNOW THE SUBJECTS UPON UHICH THEY PRONOUNCE AS WELL AS THEY 'HINK THEY DO, AT LEAST. PROBABLY BECAUSE, N COMMON WITH MANY OF US BLOGGERS, I THINK MIGHT BE ABLE TO DO A BETTER JOB MYSELF. 'HE FOLLOWING IS AN EXAMPLE: </ED>

olly twitters

olly Toynbee tells us all how it is:*

   If Bill Gates moved to Albania its GDP would soar meaninglessly.

www.guardian.co.uk/comment/story/0,3604,1565977,00.html

Really? Albania's Gross *Domestic* Product would soar if an individual with great foreign wealth and a large foreign income moved there?

The rest of it is 'We must be like Sweden'.

Which, as we know, means school vouchers and charges for medical treatment. And economic literacy. Fine by me Polly.

Update: Polly responds!

> Don't be pathetic. Of course I meant if he brought his income and wealth with him.

Which is something of a problem. GDP does not measure wealth (hint, wealth is a stock, GDP is measuring a flow) so Bill's stocks and so on would make no differenc at all. There's also another problem. Here's the definition of GDP from *Wikipedia*:*

> GDP is defined as the total value of final goods and services produced within a territory during a specified period (or, if not specified, annually, so that 'the UK GDP' is the UK's annual product). GDP differs from gross national product (GNP) in excluding inter-country income transfers, in effect attributing to a territory the product generated within it rather than the incomes received in it.

Bill Gates moving to Albania makes no difference to that part of his income which is generated in Albania. Whatever profits Microsoft (and any other of his companies) make in Albania is entirely unaffected by the fact that he lives there or not.

That was the point of my original post. GNP may change, but GDP would not. Even if Bill did take his income and wealth there.

(Well, to be strictly truthful, it would rise a little, by the amount that Bill spent or locally produced items which he does not now. Like maybe his food bill and utilit payments. Can't think of much else he would buy domestically produced.)

Anyone want to club together to buy Polly a basic economics text book?

Update deux. Heh! As Harold reminds us in the comments Polly has also said this

> [T]he fate of those at the bottom of a pecking order within a rich society is far worse than those in a poor country who feel they belong among the generality. The UN figures show that exclusion kills, in both infant deaths and shorter lives.

*http://en.wikipedia.org/wiki/Gross_domestic_product

and at other times 'Inequality Kills!' or some such. So if Bill does move then thousands of Albanian babies will die needlessly and some fewer number of American ones miraculously survive (because, of course, the effect upon inequality of the Gates fortune will be greater in a small poor country than a large rich one).

A solution to this latter problem does occur. All the really rich people could go to one place where they would be equal together and as we left behind would be (more) equal together, death rates would drop everywhere. Whadda ya think? Could we call it Monaco?

And to think, this woman is in regular employment.

Tim Worstall
http://timworstall.typepad.com/timworstall

✎ 10 September

ED> WE ARE, AS A PLANET, RUNNING OUT OF THINGS. WE MUST BE, AS WE CONTINUE TO USE UP OUR PRECIOUS NATURAL RESOURCES. AS TAMPON TEABAG (YES, I KNOW) TELLS US, THERE ARE THINGS YOU MIGHT NOT BE AWARE WE FACE SHORTAGES OF: </ED>

Peak melody

Every society throughout history and throughout the world has made and enjoyed music! But we, now, here, in the west are unique… in our hunger for ever more, new music. Music surrounds us: in our houses, blasting out of radios, CD players, computers. It wakes us up, and it sends us to sleep. Outside we pump music into our ears through up-to-the-minute mobile phones and MP3-players…

We cannot get enough of it! We hear it in our supermarkets, and we sing it in our churches and in our karaoke bars. Rock anthems in pubs, and recorder-concerts in schools. We chant it at our football matches, hum along to it in our cars, and dance to it in our nightclubs. We go to Sing-Along-Sound-of-Music evenings. There is no getting away from music. Our lives are musical lives, and our world is a musical world. Musical. Music.

So wrote the philosopher Jacob Applebloom in his suicide note.

Just as so often in his life (not least in his decision to end it) Applebloom was right: our western appetite for new music does indeed know no bounds. Music is now officially the fourth most important factor in our lives, after food, drink, and sex. Chillingly, it even comes above our own children, and going to the toilet.

And central to western music, is melody.

But melody is a finite resource: the number of distinct melodies of a certain length which can be composed from the few notes we have at our disposal, is limited, and experts agree that we are getting through the various possible combinations and permutations at an alarming rate.

So how much longer can we continue to plunder melody reserves like this? The plain fact is that we're already running out: the production of genuinely new melody peaked in late 1996, and has already started to fall away, reciprocal-logarithmically speaking. Experts predict that if the rate at which the rate of increase of consumption of melody increases continues to increase at its current rate, then by 2027 every single repeatable tune lasting less than 30 seconds will have been recorded.

An overhaul of the copyright law is urgently needed if total economic prolapse is to be avoided. But that is only the first, and easiest, step.

The serialist movement of the early 20th century led by Arnold Schoenberg was one of the first concerted attempts to locate new reserves of melody. Schoenberg searched for tunes in the atonal wilderness, but he met with only limited success. Experiments in microtonal technology (initiated by the likes of Carillo and Ives in the late 19th century) are ongoing, but so far they also show little prospect of producing anything approaching a memorable, repeatable tune. Others have searched further afield: Olivier Messiaen searched for melody in birdsong. But it seems that birds and humans have different ideas about what constitutes a good tune. John Cage in his infamous piece 4'33', posed the paradoxical question 'is silence actually the best melody?' But the world was not convinced, and the rate at which the rate of increase of consumption of new, audible, melody increases continued to increase unabated.

Greater success has been achieved by the world-music movement, and by the melody-conservationists of the minimalist movement. The likes of Steve Reich and Philip Glass have discovered techniques to make melody go further: Reich, for example, has composed single pieces of music of over an hour in length, whic feature only one or two snippets of simple melody. Significantly, this approach has now crossed over into the mainstream (in for instance the music of Kylie Minogue, and in the dance-clubs of Ibiza).

All genres of music (excluding the extreme avant-garde) are struggling to come to terms with the impending melody-crisis. Hip-hop for instance has managed to dispense with melody almost completely, but unfortunate knock-on effects of this have been felt in the world's dwindling stocks of rhythm and swear-words.

As the crisis deepens, mainstream pop music will be the first to be hit hard, and record-producers have now adopted a policy of containment, and are trying to saturate the market with endless remixes, covers, and re-covers in a desperate attempt to maintain public interest whilst getting more mileage from fast-disappearing melody stocks. But consumers will not put up with this state of affairs indefinitely. Mohammed Propane from the music watchdog OFFPOP struck a threatening note in an interview last month: 'At best these singles are indistinguishable from the originals, but more often they're just inferior copies. Have you heard Britney Spears' version of 'I love Rock and Roll'? It's an insult to the taste and discernment of the general public, that's what it is. And do you remember All Saints' cover of 'Under the Bridge'? And then there's the Crazy Frog. Fuck-a-duck that thing irritates me, and I'm not the only one. Studies show unprecedented levels of public anger with the music industry at the moment, and if record producers think they can fob off audiences with this sort of childish crap for much longer, then they've got another think coming. I tell you this: if things don't improve, we'll begin by blockading CD factories, and end by burning their fucking studios to the ground, in the name of Allah.

It is beyond doubt that when future generations look back on the 20th and early 21st century, they will view it as a time of disgraceful musical profligacy. And the court of history will undoubtedly reserve the most serious charges of melody wasting for jazz musicians. In a single gig a competent jazz musician can utilise up to 100,000 notes of melody. It is estimated that Charlie Parker alone expended over 1% of the world's melody supplies during the course of his 23-year career.

But it's not all doom and gloom for the goatee-stroking foot tappers: Jazz also takes pole position in the only realistic attempt to forestall the effects of the global melody shortage. For although melody is an essential component of western music, it has been discovered that suitable alterations in the harmony, rhythm, timbre, volume, tempo, or lyrics can allow a single line of melody to be safely reused several times over.

'Melody recycling' has become the buzzword, and the most successful examples of melody-recycling in action are so-called Trans-Genre Arrangements (TGAs). Jazz leads the way. As long ago as 1934, blind-in-one-eye piano virtuoso Art Tatum stunned the musical establishment with his sublime jazz arrangements of compositions by Massenet and Debussy. This approach was continued by gauloise-smoking left-banker Jacques Loussier, most famously in his arrangement of Bach's 'Air on a G-String'. More recently Django Bates' anarchic arrangement of 'New York, New York' came to symbolise a new chapter of British jazz. These days TGAs are stock in trade for jazz musicians, with the likes of Brad Meldau covering several Radiohead songs, and The Bad Plus tackling everything from Aphex Twin to Queen.

But TGAs are not the domain of jazz alone. Punk's history of musical vandalism has given us a host of iconoclastic and humorous reworkings of classic songs, including the most notorious of all TGAs: The Sex Pistols' version of 'My Way'.

Electro-music too has taken on the melody-recycling mantle, and whilst the charts heave with lazy remixes, samples, and plagiarism, more imaginative experiments in 'bootlegging' are beginning to turn out some worthwhile results. As often as not though, this melody-saving innovation finds itself on the wrong side of British copyright law, as in for instance The Evolution Control Committee's song 'Rocked by Rape' in which the voice of CBS newscaster Dan Rather is set to riffs by AC/DC.

Interestingly Paul Anka who wrote the lyrics to 'My Way' is now in the vanguard of the TGA-movement. His recently issued disc 'Rock Swings' features classic rock songs being played by a swing-band. His arrangement of Nirvana's 'Smells Like Teen Spirit' has made a particularly strong impression on the public consciousness, and suggests that the future of the TGA may be bright, even in the mainstream.

Critics agree that to be successful, a TGA must fearlessly deconstruct and rebuild a well-known, and well-liked piece of music. The greatest TGAs of all time are widely considered to be Jimi Hendrix's version of 'All Along The Watchtower' by Bob Dylan, and The Easystar Allstars' 'The Dub Side of the Moon', in which the entirety of Pink Floyd's seminal album 'The Dark Side of the Moon' is reworked in the reggae genre. Many more bold efforts like this are needed if the world is to avoid total musical meltdown in the near future.

But one man's imaginative re-arrangement is another man's sacrilege, and further down this road, danger certainly lies. Imagine a world where all the music sounds like William Shatner's cover of 'Lucy in the Sky with Diamonds', or even more frighteningly, like Barbara Cartland's nauseating rendition of 'A Nightingale Sang in Berkeley Square'. As the amount of available melody dwindles, the musical establishment is going to have to regulate itself with increasing sensitivity, whilst trying to keep the market afloat. Some are already calling for government intervention to prevent a glut of novelty records by the likes of Weird Al Yankovich or the Dangleberries' bagpipe version of 'Paranoid' by Black Sabbath.

But econo-musicologists such as Honey Jezebel warn that further tightening of music laws could spell disaster. 'What we desparately need is more albums like 'Maximum Rockgrass' by Hayseed Dixie [an album of classic rock songs performed in the blue-grass genre]. Sure, a few purists are not going to like it, but we've got to look at the bigger picture here. We've got major melody problems here, people, major problems, and if we're not careful, it could be game over for music as we know it.'

Unless new reserves of melody can be found, by 2020 the face of music is going to look very different from now. A terrifying hint of what's to come can be found in the music of London-based sound artist Xper.Xr. Such is his dedication to melody-conservation, that he painstakingly transcribed the song 'No Limit' by 90s dance act 2-Unlimited, before arranging it and translating the result into traditional Chinese musical notation. Xper.Xr then hired traditional Chinese instrumentalists to perform the work. By 2020, such elaborate and extreme techniques may be the only option left to music makers struggling to satisfy humanity's never-ending thirst for new music. So at least thought Jacob Applebloom:

We just cannot conceive of life without music. But music is not eternal. Music, like humanity, needs to evolve to survive. But what will happen when the wells of melody, harmony, and rhythm run dry as they must? Our delicate world of songs and symphonies will die, and a nightmarish dystopia of industrial machinery and radiation-burns will be born in its place: an apocalyptic place where gun-runners whistle Stockhausen, and whores hum techno. This is a world I cannot bear to witness.

So I shall bid farewell to this planet with its musical richness and diversity still intact, and as I swing from the strings of my grand piano, I shall smile, and feel glad ever to have lived, and listened, in the land of Elgar.

Tampon Teabag
http://tamponteabag.blogspot.com

✎ 12 September

‹ED› THE GUARDIAN CHANGES ITS FORMAT BUT NOT, APPARENTLY, THE CONTENTS AS TO THE TOOTING STATION EXPLAINS: ‹/ED›

Liberals in the gym

Quite like the new format *Guardian*, but Madeleine 'Mad' Bunting's at it again...*

Yep, this week we have the new 'muscular liberals', a new creation that, I guess, has replaced the position previously occupied by effete pinko liberals. Well these muscular liberals — think she may be having a bit of a dig at Nick Cohen, although something of a straw-based, rather than muscle-based, version — apparently just relish the 'clash of civilizations'.

Bunting's argument lacks, among other things, a certain subtlety. Those muscular liberals, it would appear, believe all Muslims are enemies! Hmmm... well, no. I think what this new breed of muscular liberalism is arguing is that many of the values we frequently take for granted can be somewhat fragile. And by not defending these values, or offering a platform to those that seek to dismantle such liberal values, one may be suffering from either a large dose of bad faith, self-loathing, lack of historical knowledge, blind ignorance, etc., or one may simply be jumping on the back of extreme Islamic views to further one's personal ideological preferences. Bunting, despite benefiting from a free press, if inadvertently providing an almost watertight case against one, breezily dismisses such liberal beliefs and practices as the 'checklist of universal Enlightenment values', as if these were simply wheeled out to impress your incredulous, yet amazed, friends.

Bunting asks: 'The louder Tony Blair expounds 'our values' and 'our way of life', the more vacuous the phrases sound. How do British values look to an African?'

Discounting the patriotic rhetoric referring to *British* values, what we're actually talking about here are liberal values. I'd have thought that some Africans, if you *did* take the trouble to engage with them, would blissfully welcome some British values. Say if I was in Zimbabwe, or maybe Sudan, I think I'd be reasonably happy with an influx of some of these values in halting genocide. But for Bunting, this is all sheer vacuousness.

*http://www.guardian.co.uk/Columnists/Column/0,5673,1567616,00.html

These muscular liberals, it turns out, aren't even that interested in that many Enlightenment values. They're suffering from political exhaustion — an all-too contagious disease when reading Madeleine Bunting's column. For these liberals 'same-sex marriage and abortion become the defining issues. [...] So an elite squabbles about Islam's take on gay rights and gender equality in a charade of moralistic grandstanding.' So, Ken Livingstone is applauded for seducing Yusuf al-Qaradawi — he, of course, has the political stature to overlook such things as gay rights, abortion, etc... Not that same-sex marriage, abortion and gender equality are necessarily trivial matters, but I'd have thought the dividing line may be a little more significant than just those issues. For instance, Nick Cohen commented that 'Islam Online had him [al-Qaradawi] supporting wife beating and genital mutilation. Along with his unbending line on the homosexual question, the alleged progressive also said the penalty for grown-up Muslims who concluded there was no god was death and, inevitably, that no criticism could be made of bombers who murdered Israeli civilians.' These issues, unfortunately, seem a little trivial for Bunting to concern herself with. She's seems quite happy ploughing her unique political furrow, accussing others of racism while simultaneously abandoning 'Arab liberals in a fruitless quest for the approval of their enemies on the religious right.'

To the Tooting Station
http://tothetootingstation.typepad.com/blog

✎ 15 September

‹ED› LABAN TALL ON THE SLIGHTLY CONTROVERSIAL STATUE THAT WENT UP IN LONDON: ‹/ED›

Historic first as statue of disabled person unveiled

Once upon a time, if you wanted to see a naked lady with no arms you'd have to go to the Louvre. If you wanted to see a naked, pregnant lady with no arms you'd have to go to places like this ['Links for devotees of disabled women' — Ed.]* (possibly not work-friendly).

Now we can all rejoice that you can see one in Trafalgar Square.

> Ms Lapper, who was born with shortened legs and no arms because of a congenital disorder, has travelled to London for the ceremony. 'I'm very excited about it. This is history in the making,' she said.

*http://devguide.org/amp.shtml

> **Never before has someone with a disability** — let alone someone with a disability who is naked and eight months pregnant — **been put in such a public place and portrayed in such a positive way**.*

Tragically Ms Lapper appears to be not only disabled, but blind. Or ignorant. Or both.

It's easy to miss, I know. But Trafalgar Square is dominated by a 180-foot column.

With an 18-foot statue on the top.

Of a man missing an eye and half an arm.

UK Comentators — Laban Tall's blog
www.ukcommentators.blogspot.com

✎ 17 September

‹ED› JUST TO SHOW THAT IT ISN'T JUST THE GUARDIAN THAT GETS ATTACKED BY BLOGGERS HERE'S THE G-GNOME RIDES OUT ON A GERARD BAKER COLUMN IN THE TIMES: ‹/ED›

Cause of death: welfare state, cont — The stupidity of Gerard Baker

Walter Williams has a column about the stupid things economists say after natural disasters which is so good I could swear I've read it more than once.

In Williams' book, any economist or commentator who says that the destruction caused by natural disasters is a good thing because the reconstruction process will stimulate growth is 'poorly-trained'.

Williams is right, of course — the losses far outweigh any benefit that might be gained from reconstruction. That's why we don't all spend our time razing cities every day of the week.

One would have thought it might have been hard to encounter a directly analagous stupid argument relating to the forced evacuation of a city's population, but Gerard Baker of *The Times* has managed to make one.

*www.timesonline.co.uk/article/0,,2-1781635,00.html

n a bizarre and stupid column entitled 'Space, food, medicine, protection: t's better here in Barbara's hall of plenty',* Baker wrote of Barbara Bush's *What I'm hearing is that many of them want to stay in Texas'* comment,

> Not since Louis XVI's missus puzzled about the dietary choices of indigent Parisians has there been such an appalling display of aristocratic ignorance. How dare she? How could she? Even the White House winced.

> But in the disgust that greeted her remarks in Highgate and the Upper West Side no one stopped to consider the possibility that Mrs Bush was, in fact, dead right.

What? He continues,

> Anyone who has visited the most deprived parts of America's cities, rather than merely empathised with them from afar, would have no difficulty whatsoever with the proposition that the inhabitants would prefer an air-conditioned sports stadium with all the food they can eat, the country's best medical attention and the benign security of National Guard protection to the hunger, sickness and lawlessness in which many of them live.

he fact that a pundit like Baker can focus on 'hunger, sickness and lawlessness', uite forgetting that a big percentage of the evacuees, yes, even the poor ones, ad their own 'homes' to which they would feel sentimentally 'attached' because hey contain their 'belongings' and 'history' shows how detached from reality he punditocracy that writes for newspapers is from people with real jobs, eal lives and real concerns.

hank God for the blogosphere!

He continues,

> Forty-two local businesses participated in a job fair for the new homeless at the Armoury on Tuesday; more wanted to take part but couldn't because there was limited space. Twenty of the 150 or so evacuees were hired on the spot. An official at the District of Columbia government involved in organising the event said that more were expected to be offered jobs in the next few days. The exercise was such a success that employers are demanding another one. If there's anyone left still to hire it will take place in the next couple of weeks.

The story is being replicated across the country. The victims of Katrina are getting new opportunities. Some of it comes from an immense outpouring of compassion by Americans in the form of hundreds of millions of dollars in charitable contributions and unquantifiable help in housing families and schooling children. Some of it comes from the unsentimental compassion of the free market: the unerring capacity of the capitalist system to match those who have something with those who need it, whether it be labour, capital, goods or services.

Walter Williams says economists who praise disasters for the growth they bring are 'poorly trained'. I wonder what he would make of a Gerard Baker, who says disasters are good because they bring 'opportunities'?

And why weren't the opportunities available in New Orleans? Is Baker such a rampantly Thatcherite anarcho-libertarian that thoughts of attachment to home place, kin and society should all be stamped on in favour of 'opportunity'?

OK, let's ask a few questions about the 'opportunity'.

What kind of jobs were advertised at the job fair? Do they compare with the jobs that those evacuees might have held in New Orleans? There are jobs and there are jobs, and Baker can take it from me that some jobs present no kind of opportunities at all. Why were only 20 of the 150 vacancies advertised at the job fair filled at the first attempt? How many of these posts hd been open for longer than four weeks? What was the average pay rate for the jobs being advertised?

He finally writes a word of sense, and earns himself a place in this series, when he says,

The irony is that New Orleans is one of those cities where government-dependency had reached such levels that a kind of economic and social anomie had set in.

There's another city I know of that suffers from the same welfare-fostered 'anomie'. It's called Glasgow.

And there isn't much 'opportunity' there either.

The G-Gnome Rides Out
http://theggnomeridesout.blogspot.com

✎ 26 September

ED> PICKLED POLITICS, A NEW GROUP BLOG
REFLECTING THE VOICE OF YOUNG,
PROGRESSIVE BRITISH ASIANS' PROVIDES
THIS ANALYSIS OF APU FROM THE SIMPSONS –
A SURPRISINGLY UPBEAT ONE: </ED>

Much Apu about nothing

In *Pickled Politics'* short life, Sunny has carved out an erudite niche with intelligent posts on important topics. So I figured the best thing to do with my first post was to write a daft post about *The Simpsons*. I hope the reasons why will become clear.

Bloggers often begin by stating their credentials on their topic of choice — so let me assure you, you will not find a more devoted fan of *The Simpsons*. Yet I write this with some trepidation as I recently had my impression that the world loves all things Springfield shaken.

As an Asian, I've always felt some affinity towards Apu. Apu Nahasapeemapetilon is the industrious convenience store owner and one of the major cast characters, with several episodes revolving entirely around him. Growing up in my middle class corner of London, I have never felt that Apu's character could carry any negative connotations; however, several American South Asian chaps recently expressed their intense dislike of Apu. I wondered why.

For them, Apu personifies every stereotype they wish to shake off. He's got a thick accent, he spent many years living in the US illegally, works in a cornershop, had an arranged marriage, rips off his customers, is continually the butt of Homer's jokes about Hinduism and has an unpronounceable long surname. Brown-skinned Americans, especially those living outside the major cosmopolitan cities, have come to associate Apu with insults — Apu's catchphrase 'Thank you, come again!' is shouted as abuse by thick-headed bigots.

So let me explain why I think Apu is a positive character for Asians — particularly those living outside India. One could legitimately claim that Apu is a fascinating case study of Indian immigrants, their trials, tribulations and triumphs. Had *The Simpsons* been a live-action show, Apu would have represented the first regular South Asian character on a prime time show outside the subcontinent. I still find

it quite remarkable that way back at the start of the 90s, the makers of
The Simpsons decided to include him.

To argue that he is a stereotype is to miss the whole point of the cartoon. *Everyor*
is a stereotype, that's how *The Simpsons* works — it plays up to our stereotypes to
create a realistic microcosm of America's social structure. Springfield is populate
with all walks of life — I'm sure we all know a Barney — propping up the bar, a Ne
Flanders — goodie two-shoes bible-basher, a Wiggum — incompetent cop and, lik
it or not, we all know Apu; just go to your cornershop. In comparison to
Bumblebee Man and Krusty's father (woefully stereoptypical Mexican and Jew),
Apu is a very rounded character indeed.

Plenty of Indians work in convenience stores. Plenty of Indians are doctors. Hence
these tend to be roles brown actors are frequently cast in — yet few criticise the
character of an Indian doctor in a drama/soap/film. Matt Groening and *The
Simpsons*' creators are no fools (in fact they demonstrate their intellectual chops
with Apu's name — an homage to Satyajit Ray's legendary *Apu Trilogy*) and they
chose Apu's profession deliberately.

Scratch the surface and you find Apu is far more than just a token brown. He
embodies the things that have made Asian immigrants some of the most
successful communities in America, the UK and elsewhere. He works relentlessly
the famous Asian work ethic means he stays at his post about 23 hours a day an
has been shot 8 times (*'Ah! The searing kiss of hot lead; how I missed you! I mean,
I think I'm dying'*).

With a computer science PhD, he is freakishly over-qualified for his job, due to th
fact he was unable to land anything paying more as an immigrant. The topic of h
arranged marriage was dealt with in a realistic, although somewhat twee, way —
he was reluctant to acquiesce to his mum's request, but met his bride-to-be and
fell in love. At a time when many Westerners equate arranged marriage with forc
marriage, this was a welcome plot.

In contrast to the generally buffoon-like idiots that inhabit Springfield, Apu is
educated and far more knowledgeable about American history:

> **Homer:** *Are you sure you don't want to come? In a civil war re-enactment we nee
> lots of Indians to shoot.*

> **Apu:** *I don't know what part of that sentence to correct first.*

> **Proctor:** *All right, here's your last question. What was the cause of the Civil War?*

Apu: *Actually, there were numerous causes. Aside from the obvious schism between the abolitionists and the anti-abolitionists, there were economic factors, both domestic and inter–*

Proctor: *Wait, wait... just say slavery.*

Apu: *Slavery it is, sir.*

Some argue that it's far more useful for NRIs (non-resident Indians) to have characters who are of Indian heritage, but otherwise identical to other characters, to show the white man 'look we're just like you!' However I think most white people are capable of accepting the fact we're NOT like them in some respects, without feeling threatened. Apu could've been like countless characters in British soaps or TV shows, called Bobby or Kurt, distinguishable as Asian only by their colour. Apu's Indian-ness is apparent for all to see and yet he is great friends with all the other Springfielders, especially Homer.

So why is all this on a politics blog? Because Apu's story is all about integration, a topic that crops up again and again.

Apu hasn't sacrificed any of his cultural identity, he displays a statue of Ganesh proudly and is a strict vegan, yet he has become an integral cog in the small town somewhere in America's heartland. The citizens are fond of him and he has made some real friends, and even sung in a hit barbershop quartet. He is a three-dimensional person, not a token Dr Patel who reads an X-ray and vanishes for a few episodes of whatever series you happen to be watching.

He has also faced racism and prejudice of his own — when Springfield renamed itself Libertyville in a nationalistic fervour, Apu was scared into acting American (*let's take a relaxed attitude towards work and watch baseball'*) and renaming his children (all of whom have very Indian names) Coke, Pepsi, Condoleezza, Lincoln, Freedom, Apple Pie, Manifest Destiny and Superman. When *The Simpsons* satirised the scapegoating of immigrants with Proposition 24, Apu was targeted by Mayor Quimby to distract voters from bear attacks!

Finally, Apu has done what we've all done as part of a defence mechanism — seen the funny side and occasionally taken the piss out of condescending white folk:

Snooty lady: *Attendant, I'd like some gas.*

Apu: *Yes I'm sorry I do not speak English.*

Snooty lady: *But you were just talking to–*

Apu: *Yes, yes. Hot dog, hot dog. Yes sir, no sir. Maybe, okay.*

To conclude (I know I've rambled), I can easily see why Apu is loathed by some NRIs. Had I grown up in a racist neighbourhood, I may have received the same Apu-abuse they have. But I think I would have still loved Apu. He was a hero to me when very few Asian people were on TV. And *The Simpsons* has blazed a trail in portraying him as Indian through and through, not a 'coconut'. Take *Star Trek*, another American institution. Since its inception it endeavoured to be politically correct, with a multinational cast. Yet none of the characters had any traits from their cultures other than perhaps a dodgy accent. Fast forward to the late 90s and *Star Trek Voyager* and you find characters talking about native American spirit guides and 'my people'.

Apu: *Today, I am no longer an Indian living in America. I am an Indian-American.*

Lisa: *You know, in a way, all Americans are immigrants. Except, of course Native Americans.*

Homer: *Yeah, Native Americans like us.*

Lisa: *No, I mean American Indians.*

Apu: *Like me.*

British TV shows have featured Asians for many years (a good thing of course) but only recently have they become real people with back stories, families and the things that make Asians Asian.

Apu (and Matt Groening) I salute you.

Pickled Politics
www.pickledpolitics.com

≋ 28 September

ED> NEE NAW IS ANOTHER OF THE PROFESSIONAL BLOGGERS, IN THE SENSE OF BRINGING TO US THE SPECIFICS OF PROFESSIONAL LIFE IN A MANNER NOT REALLY AVAILABLE TO US BEFORE. HERE, SOME USEFUL TIPS FROM AN AMBULANCE DISPATCHER ON HOW THE GENERAL PUBLIC TEND TO USE THE 999 SERVICE: </ED>

ommon beliefs held by the general public about calling 999

The LOUDER you shout, the quicker the ambulance will come.

The QUICKER you speak, the quicker the ambulance will come.

Even though the call taker asked for the *address* of the emergency, what he really wants to hear is a detailed description of what happened, starting with the patient having his tonsils out in 1962.

The ambulance cannot possibly leave the ambulance station until you hang up, so it is imperative to hang up as soon as possible, even if the call taker is trying to tell you something. Hanging up several times will make the ambulance come twice as fast.

A good call taker should just take the address and send the ambulance. A bad call taker will find out what has happened, prioritise the call and give you instructions on what to do next, thus wasting precious time when you could have been running round the house screaming.

The call taker will never have taken a 999 call before so they need to be told that a man under a truck is a 'serious emergency' and that 'you'd better get there quick'. (Or more commonly, that a 29-year-old with belly ache is a 'serious emergency' and that 'you'd better get here quick').

There is only one person who works for the ambulance service. That person takes the call and then jumps in the ambulance. If you call back, the person you speak to will know exactly which of the 2000+ calls that day you are talking about without you giving them irrelevant details such as the address.

8) The Nee Naw Service have an ambulance parked at the end of every road enabling them to reach any location within 30 seconds. If they take longer than this to reach an emergency, it is due to incompetence and slacking.

9) Ambulance crews who drink cups of tea outside A+E are terrible slackers, as those who work in emergency services should be expected to work a twelve hour shift without a single break.

10) Strokes are a heart complaint.

11) If you don't know the answer to a question, provide an irrelevant piece of information instead: 'Is he changing colour?' 'He's in a lot of pain'. 'Has she passed out?' 'She is upstairs'. 'Is she conscious?' 'She's a black woman'.

12) 'Conscious' and 'unconscious' mean exactly the same thing. Common causes of unconsciousness include: being in too much pain to talk, Alzheimer's disease, being a bit upset.

13) (Chat magazine readers) Call takers work for British Telecom, they know nothing about medical stuff or ambulances, but a lot about switchboards. They also have the phone number for your local hospital, GP, social services, Pizza Hut...

13) Never say 'please' or 'thank you' — call takers find this highly insulting and will cancel the ambulance and send you the police instead.

Nee Naw
www.neenaw.co.uk

OCTOBER 2005

✎ 3 October

‹ED› A COMMENT AT TALKPOLITICS LED TO AN
OUTBURST OF POETRY. QUITE WONDERFUL,
QUANTUM MECHANICS AND DR SEUSS FROM
THE CURATOR'S EGG: ‹/ED›

Schröödinger's cat in the hat box

When Heisenberg announced with pleasure,
'There are some things you cannot measure.
Not simultaneously at least.'
His irritating smile increased.
'The surer the momentum's grown,
The less position will be known.'

'But that's not all,' intruded Bohr.
(A name quite apt. I won't say more)
'It's observation perhaps
That makes the wave function collapse.

Until it does it's all just smeared.
OK, I know it sounds quite weird.
But quantum physics can't be knocked —
Its implications leave all shocked,
Except those, on the other hand,
Who simply do not understand.'

So Schröödinger, that studious gent
Devised a thought experiment.
A box, some acid and a jigger
Set off by a quantum trigger,
A cat, whose life or death would show
Emission had occurred or no.

You wouldn't know until you looked
If that poor feline's goose was cooked,
And it would be, or so he said,
Alive and at the same time dead.

Well so they say, but have no doubt
He actually tried it out,
And in a box set up like that
Securely locked his neighbour's cat

That philosophical feline
Was to his fate quite unresigned
Though in the box he chose to linger
Mouthing curses at Schröödinger
Waiting for the Geiger's chatter
Waiting for the phial to shatter
Waits till he can't wait no more
(For waiting's such a dreadful Bohr)

Until at last the lid was pried
Open and someone looked inside.
Relief! Survival! Best of men! —
But Erwin clamped it shut again.

And so the cat just lay there thinking
Tail just twitching, eyes unblinking,
Werner says you can't be knowing
Where I'm at AND how fast I'm going.

But I exactly know my speed
(Well, zero isn't hard to read)
And that implies,' so thought the cat,
Momentum's nada — which means that
My position can't be guessed —
There, I knew you'd be impressed —
So I don't need to mess with locks —
It's time to think outside the box.'

Well others here will understand
The consequences, though unplanned,
Of mixing up — that cunning devil! —
The micro with the macro level.

An hour passed. Erwin came back
And opened up the box a crack,
Then wider still and stood to stare —
The box was now completely bare!

And as he stuck his head inside
He caught a whiff of cyanide
And dropped down dead (they say it hurts —
I say it was his just deserts).

No, I'm not going to apologise. This was inspired by an article on *TalkPolitics*,* and
I just took up the idea and ran with it. Right, who's going to finish off 'Harry Potter
and the Management Consultant'?

The Curator's Egg
www.redbadge.co.uk/egg

✎ 4 October

‹ED› FURTHER POETRY IN THIS SHORT STORY (OR IS IT SLICE OF ACADEMIC LIFE?) FROM THE FILTER^: ‹/ED›

The unbearable kitschness of Bloomfield

> Kitsch causes two tears to flow in quick succession. The first tear says:
> how nice to see children running on the grass!
>
> The second tear says: How nice to be moved, together with all mankind,
> by children running on the grass!
>
> It is the second tear that makes kitsch kitsch.**

Think about the poet Robert Bloomfield for a second if you will. It might help you
to know that his name is probably pronounced '*Blum-field*'; you'll need to know
that because at a party next week someone will pass you a little-cheesy-
pinappley-one on a stick and you'll find yourself suddenly immersed in a
discussion of early nineteenth century Suffolk poetry and the kitsch. You don't
want to appear stupid, do you? You don't want to be saying 'Bloom-field' all night
only to be corrected at half-past eleven by some sour-puss from Durham who
helpfully interjects: 'Sorry, do you mean Robert *BLUM*-field?'

*http://talkpolitics.users20.donhost.co.uk/index.php?title=second_star_to_the_left&more=1&c=1&tb=1&
**Milan Kundera, The Unbearable Lightness of Being

No, you don't want that. I'm performing a valuable service for you here, and you are all grateful for these vital facts that I dispense into your willing ears. So, what will you need to know to get by at this party, then?

Well, he was born in 1766 and he died in 1823. His most famous work is his poem published in 1800, called *The Farmer's Boy*. This is probably why Bloomfield will come up in the first place, because whilst I'm guessing the majority of you have never heard of this man before, in his lifetime this poem was a bestseller. It sold well over 26,000 copies in only three years, and was translated into Italian and French. His other works include *Good Tidings* (a poem in praise of the small-pox vaccination), *The Broken Crutch* (a poem in which a crutch actually breaks) and *Walter and Jane*, which we will return to later. Despite the immense success of Bloomfield's sales, he died a very poor man and has been almost entirely ignored ever since. Which just goes to show, life's *crap*.

But at this party someone, probably that blonde piece from Durham again, will lift one of the little-cheesy-pinappley-ones up from the mock Waterford Crystal dish (you will already have observed that it is in fact not crystal but some kind of heavy machine-pressed glass, and will have been wondering for some time whether the thing is dense enough not to break if you casually dropped it off the hostess trolley and onto the laminate floor) and she will announce to the room:

'Oh how *clever*, how wonderfully *kitsch*.'

As the room erupts into congratulatory applause at this girl's knowing observation, your eyes will seek out the host and you will observe him nodding sagely to himself in the corner.

'Oh yes, I am quite the card,' he will be saying to his companion. Briefly you will wonder how you have got to know such *awful* people, before you will turn to the Durham bint and reply:

'I don't think it actually is kitsch though. I think our host's knowingness of the absurdity in placing cubes of cheese and pineapple on cocktail sticks negates the possibility of these objects actually being considered kitsch.'

The room will fall silent, and you will explain:

'It rests on two points, as I see it. Firstly, what is kitsch? Well, the kitsch tends to be that which forms false sentiment. For example, that porcelain figurine of a dog over there.'

You will point to a small porcelain figurine of a dog on the mantelpiece, it will be shaped like a poodle, but its eyes are larger than a poodle's eyes tend to be, taking on an almost human expression of sorrow. It will have one paw raised in the air, as if to indicate that its inanimate foot has been wounded, but not in any serious way. The girl from Durham will sigh:

'Aww, how sweet.'

'Precisely,' you will retort, 'we feel sympathy for the poodle, its paw is hurt, and it makes us sad when we look into its big black eyes. Only there is nothing to feel sorry for. The dog does not feel any real pain, and even if it did, it would not express its pain in the way that that figurine suggests. Real poodles don't look like that, it is a fantasy portrayal which manages to fuse human and animal emotions in one object.'

'*Anthropomorphism*,' the Durham girl will announce to the room.

'Shut up.'

But one man, a Glaswegian called Harry, will step forward and look at the object up-close.

'I'm afraid,' he says turning to face you square-on, 'that that figurine does not make me feel in any way sad at all. I think it looks silly.'

'Quite right,' you will reply, 'that's because you have a much better developed sense of sentimentality than that girl from Durham.'

'My name's Judith.' The girl from Durham will reply.

'It's an extreme example of kitsch, but the point is it was made to create exactly those emotions that the Durham girl is feeling. Take another example, here, this section from Robert Bloomfield's poem *Walter and Jane*. The two protagonists have fallen in love, but now mistakenly believe that the other does not love them in return, they go to visit an elderly neighbour:

'What ails thee, Jane?' the wary Matron cried;

With heaving breast the modest Maid reply'd.

Now gently moving back her wooden chair

To shun the current of the cooling air;

'Not much, good Dame; I'm weary by the way;

Perhaps, anon, I've something else to say.'

Now, while the Seed-cake crumbled on her knee,

And snowy jasmine peeped in to see;

And the transparent Lilac at the door,

Full to the sun its purple honors bore,

The clam'rous hen her fearless brood display'd

And march'd around; while thus the Matron said:

'Jane has been weeping, Walter; — prithee why?

I've seen her laugh, and dance but never cry.'

There, you see the point is made plainer. We are made to feel sorry for Jane, but what actually chokes us (believe me, it does choke you more when you've read the whole poem and watched them fall out of love) is not Jane's feelings or psychological state, but the transference of emotion into the objects around her; the proud hen, the concerned flowers — none of these are real emotions, but they are what make us feel sad in the passage. The crumbling of the cake, for example, is the really sad moment, but of course cakes don't feel pity.'

I see,' Harry will say, 'yes, that's more subtle, but it is still kitsch.'

'It's the ornament that makes you sad, and in some ways that is a bad thing. It means that we are not made to feel real pity by understanding quite why Jane is unhappy in the poem, we don't have to play through her emotional state to get the gist of her feeling. It's like what Adolph Loos hints at in *The Bourgeois Household* [*about getting Rococo blisters from the ornamented handles of tableware — Ed.*].

The actual worth and substance of the object is lost beneath the frills put upon it. So actually we'd benefit from the poem more if we could understand what Jane is feeling, and why; help us understand ourselves, but all we learn is that flowers grow concerned when we are unhappy, which is of course not true.'

'You're a wise fellow.' Harry will say.

'Yes, I know, I read about this on *The Filter*^.'

'Okay, okay, but none of this answers why my little-cheesy-pinappley-ones are not kitsch,' the host will interject angrily.

'Well, that's the second point of my argument, which is one of intent. Certainly the notion of a little-cheesy-pinappley-one is kitsch. It is a construct which is intended to speak of social sophistication, which of course it is not. We are intended to look up to the host who manages to source the exotic fruit of the pineapple, and who has the culinary prowess to pair it with the cheddar. Of course there is no skill in that at all, the pineapple is from a can, and the overall effect is dismal to say the least. It is therefore kitsch.'

'But I thought you said–' the host will say.

'Ah, let me finish. Whilst the little-cheesy-pinappley-one is in itself kitsch, yours my friend, is not. Because you are aware that such a thing is not sophisticated, and so in serving these you do not intend us to think that you are a culinary master, but give an ironic gesture. You shift the meaning of these particular little-cheesy-pinappley-ones, and seem to be saying something quite different by them.'

'That's true,' says your host, 'but I know that the ornament of the poodle is ridiculous too, I own that as an ironic gesture as well.'

'Ah, but I think that that continues to be kitsch, because it is not your ownership of the object which denotes whether it is kitsch or not, but the point for which it was created. Indeed, the most kitsch object in this room is your laminate flooring–'

'My laminate flooring, but *why*?'

You will smile politely, and turn away from your host to continue talking to Harry, the most sensible person you will have met since July 2001.

Well, that all seems sorted,' he will say to you, 'only one thing I'm not sure you're
right on. Even though the little-cheesy-pinappley-ones do not have their original
meaning, and are not signifiers of our host's accomplishment in the kitchen, they
are signifiers of his wit and intelligence. Now as you're probably aware, our host
is neither witty, nor intelligent, and as such don't they become–'

'An interesting point, Harry, let's get a drink.'

'Robert Bloomfield... he's not very good, is he?'

'He has his moments.'

The Filter^
http://thefilter.blogs.com

🖎 5 October

**ED> THE CATHOLIC CHURCH ANNOUNCED THAT
NOT ALL PARTS OF THE BIBLE ARE TO BE TAKEN
LITERALLY, AS ABSOLUTE HISTORICAL TRUTH.
PETER GLOVER PROVIDES A CRITIQUE OF THIS
VIEW FROM AN EVANGELICAL VIEWPOINT: </ED>**

British Catholic Church dumps on the Bible

Well it's always useful when the postmodern liberal mind comes clean that it is
the final arbiter of all truth and not anything 'external' to them, like God and
the Bible. But we must be grateful to them. It is always helpful that the enemies
of God and of the eternal Word he has spoken make themselves known plainly.
What the church used to call 'heretics'.

The British Roman Catholic bishops — blessings be upon their name — have issued
a statement to their national flock informing them that they can no longer trust
the veracity of the Bible.* Odd, I had thought they never had trusted it — wasn't
that what the Reformation was all about?

Of course, I paraphrase. What they *actually* said was, 'We should not expect to
find in Scripture full scientific accuracy or complete historical precision' though
they allow for 'historical traces'. What this *actually* means is... er... that the Bible
cannot be trusted to tell us the truth. Which bits do tell us the truth then, we ask?

www.timesonline.co.uk/article/0,,13509-1811332,00.html

'The historical bits,' they would answer. You mean like the *historical* fact of the Passion, for instance? 'Er...'. Exactly.

The Gift of Scripture is a simple enough statement from simple enough folk and thus must be taken — by the simpleton — to be true. But then the Roman Catholic Church has never been big on the fact that Scripture, not them, is the final arbiter of truth.

If their assessment of it is true, however, then Scripture of course becomes not much of a gift at all — possessing less all-round truth than the telephone directory. Which bits of *The Gift of Scripture* are true, we might enquire? Or is it, unlike the Bible say, infallible? This postmodern Roman Catholic liberal bishop mind (perhaps caving in under the pressure of silly hats), sadly, is unable to tell us.

Neither does idiotarian Ruth Gledhill help matters. In her report she perpetuates a number of ignorant myths. One gross error of reporting is that the first chapter of Genesis relate two confusingly different accounts of the Creation. If she actually knew her Bible at all she would know that one account is from God's point of view, the other from man's. Ignorance is indeed bliss. Whether it comes in the shape of a God-less church hierarchy that undermines the Word of God — or a national reporter in the guise of a 'respectable Religious Correspondent'. Either way, once again, the first victim is truth.

I am thinking of issuing a Thinwa against the idiot British Roman Catholic bishops. What do you think? (NB. A Thinwa is like a Fatwa but with far fewer calories).

Here endeth the first lesson.

Peter C Glover's Wires From The Bunker
www.livejournal.com/users/petercglover

‹ED› AND THAT IS THE DEADLINE, THE END OF
THE YEAR FOR THIS VOLUME, SO THAT WE
CAN GET IT TO THE PRINTERS, BINDERS,
GLUESTICKERS AND OTHER SPECIALISTS OF
THE BOOK TRADE TO CREATE THE LOVINGLY
CRAFTED VOLUME YOU HOLD IN YOUR HANDS.
WE'LL BE DOING THIS AGAIN NEXT YEAR
(PROBABLY) AND IF YOU CAN'T WAIT, WELL,
FIRE UP THE COMPUTER, GO TO THE URL OF
ONE OF THE POSTS IN THIS BOOK AND JUST
WANDER FROM THERE. IT'S FUN, REALLY,
THERE ARE SOME 300,000 BLOGS IN THE UK,
PERHAPS 19 MILLION IN THE WORLD, ALL JUST
WAITING FOR YOU TO DROP BY. UNTIL THEN,
TOODLE PIP! ‹/ED›

GENERAL INDEX

999 service 249–50

Aaro 209
aid organisations 17–19
Al Qaeda 60–1, 174
alcohol consumption 6–8, 53
Ali, Tariq 207
allotments 94
A.M. Byers Company 55
anti-semitism 187, 189, 190–1
Armstrong, Karen 208–9
Ashes 203–4
Ashley, Jackie 205
Asian migrants 245–8
Asian tsunami 48–9
Aslam, Dilpazier 185–93
astrology 46–7
asylum seekers 218–22
Australian migrants 40–1

babies 91–2
Baker, Gerard 242–4
BBC 6, 10–11, 47, 51, 102, 151, 189, 207–8, 228–9
Belgrano (warship) 157
Belmarsh Prison 38, 66
Bible 259–60
biometrics 130–1, 143–4, 164
Birth of the Chess Queen: A History (Yalow) 31–2
Blair, Cherie 207
Blair, Euan 169
Blair, Sir Ian 216, 217
Blair, Tony 10, 23, 25, 39, 67–70, 96, 104–6, 123, 126, 133, 137, 149, 153–5, 169, 172, 193, 198, 204–5, 207, 220, 240
Bloomfield, Robert 254–9
Blunkett, David 136–7, 163
Bluto 191
BMW 15–16, 111–12
Bolt, Robert 66
Bono 153–4
book reviews 31–2
Booker Prize 56–8
British identity 95–9
Brown, Gordon 106, 207
Brown, Ian 17–19
Bunting, Madeleine 208, 240–1
burglaries, hot 33–4
Bush, Barbara 243
Bush, George W. 8–10, 35–7, 86, 140, 149, 153, 192, 230
Byers, Stephen 15

Café Hayek 211, 213
Cainer, Jonathan 46–7
Care International 17–19
Catholic Church 259–60
Charles, Prince 64–5
Charlton, Bobby 168
chavs 13–14
chess 31–2
children's health 89–91
Christmas 42–3
Civil Contingencies Act 23–5
civil liberties 23–5, 38–40, 60–1, 66, 144–5, 155–64
Clarke, Charles 38, 60–1, 66, 106–7, 153–5, 163, 198
Cohen, Nick 207, 240, 241
Coldplay 148, 151
Common Agricultural Policy (CAP) 29–30
Conservatives 11, 39, 67–70, 74, 76, 99, 105–8, 124–8, 205
Contaminants in Food (England) Regulations 2004 78
coolness 73
correlating 180
Cosmo magazine 180
Counter Terrorism Bill (draft) 136–9
cricket 203–4

Daily Mail 46–7, 48, 75, 96, 176
Dalyell, Tam 92, 157
Data Protection Act 140, 141–2, 161
dates 117–19
Davis, David 205
De Menezes, Jean Charles 182–5, 216–18
death camps 101–2
defining blogging 2–3
Democrats 36–7
Diana, Princess of Wales 65, 209–11
diet 40–1, 78, 89–91, 211–12
DNA profiling 158
driving offences 73
Dunblane shootings 48–9

earthquakes 231
elections
  British 23, 25, 67–70, 75, 99–100, 105–8, 116–17, 123–9, 140–2
  suspension 23, 25
  US 8–10, 35–7, 75
  Zimbabwean 104–5, 106
Elizabeth II 136–7
Elizabeth, Queen Mother 65

Elton, Ben 65
Email Reaction 140–2
English Parliament 12–13
environmental issues 84
Eriksson, Göran-Sven 101
European Union (EU) 28–31, 108
Everett, 'Flic' 180
Exley, Zack 140, 141

famine 211–13
Fisk, Robert 86–8
flooding 224–7, 229–31
football 168
fox hunting 70–1
Freedland, Jonathan 208
freedom of speech 2–3
Frost, Terry 79–80

G8 149, 172
Galloway, George 102
gas chambers 101–2
Gates, Bill 233–5
Geldof, Bob 148–9, 153–4
Glazer Brothers 168
Gleeson, Sally 48
Goggins, Paul 152
Googlebombs 47, 216
Gove, Michael 206
Grant, Robert 35
Greater London Magistrates' Courts Authority 50
Guardian 9–10, 17, 35–7, 53, 74–6, 135, 168, 170, 180, 185–93, 240–

Halifax (bank) 108
Hancock, Tony 16–17
Hari, Johann 13–14
Harry, Prince 51
Hartley, Mick 101–2
Hassan, Margaret 17–19
Haw, Brian 198, 200
Her Majesty's Court Service 50
Heseltine, Michael 157
Hizb ut-Tahrir 187, 188–93
Holocaust Memorial Day 58–9
homosexuality 218–22
hospitals 100, 113
hostages 17–19
House of Lords 130, 133
Howard, Michael 39, 100, 102, 124
Hurricane Katrina 224–7, 229–3 243–4
Hussein, Saddam 9, 205, 220
Hutton, Will 12, 207–8

cards 38–40, 129–33, 142–5, 155–65
entity theft 144
nmigration 30
 dependent 13–14, 86, 88, 135, 190, 193, 204
 dependent on Sunday 191–2
ternational crime 30
A 60, 61, 173, 194–5
an 69, 219–21
aq 8–9, 17–19, 68, 86, 101, 153, 205, 208, 220, 230
lam Online 241
lamic terrorism 8–9, 60–1, 68–70, 194
 see also London bombings

nkins, Simon 204
rry Springer, The Opera (musical) 47–8, 51
hn, Elton 149, 211
urnalism 74–5, 169–70

erry, John 8–9, 35–7, 140, 230
hilafah state 188–9, 193
m Jong Il 53–5
tsch 254–9

bour 11, 35, 39, 60–1, 67–70, 89–93, 99, 102, 105–7, 123–33, 140–2, 163
pper, Ms 241–2
banon 86
b-Dems 11, 124–8
fe of Pi (Martel) 56–7
ve 8 148–52, 153
ve Blogging 171–3
ndon bombings 170–9, 181–5, 186, 204–9, 227–9

cNulty, Tony 155–6, 157, 163
adonna 149
aduro, Poiares 108–11
agistrates' courts 50
alchow, Joe 191
anchester United 168
angan, Lucy 46–7
artel, Yann 56–7
ay Day 122–3
elody recycling 238–9
G Rover 15–17, 111–12
cklethwait, Brian 49
dlands Powertrain 15, 16
les, Alice 207
lne, Seamus 205
ni 15–16
onckton, John 33
ombat 207
orris dancers 122–3
ugabe, Robert 104, 105
urder 17–19, 33–4
usic 235–9

nanny state 94
Nasseri, Hussein 218–19, 221–2
National Health Service (NHS) 100, 113, 159, 209–10
National Identity Register 156, 157, 159–64
National Identity Registration Numbers 161
National Insurance Numbers 160
Naylor, David 141
Nazis 51, 109, 219, 220
neds 13–14
nepotism 169–70
New Orleans 224–7, 229–31, 244
New Statesman 106–7
New York Times 78
New Zealand migrants 52–3
Newmark, Craig 211, 213
newspapers 134–5
Niger famine 211–13
non-governmental organizations (NGOs) 17–19
North East of England Regional Assembly 10–13
North Korea 53–5, 101–2

Office of Government Commerce (OGC) 131–2
Olympic Games 170
Operation Clark County 35–7
O'Reilly, Bill 61–2

paramedics 232–3
Parliament Square demonstrations 198–201
Parris, Matthew 206
partisan reporting 74–5
passports, biometric 164–5
patriotism 95, 98
Phillips, Melanie 38–9
Phoenix group 111–12
physical exercise 90–1
PIN numbers 143
Pittman, Andrew 94
Ponting, Clive 157
porn 180
Prescott, John 11, 12, 198
Prospect website 95, 96
pub grub 41
public sector websites 115–16
Purves, Libby 206

quantum mechanics 252–4

radium therapy 53–5
reality TV 136
Reid, John 89, 90, 91, 106, 107
religion 152, 159–60
Republicans 8, 36–7

risk assessment 94, 229–31
Roosevelt, Franklin Delano 70
royal family 64–5, 95–6, 209–11, 31–2

SAIC 112
St John Ambulance Brigade 227–9
San Francisco 231
Satanists 152
Schiavo, Terri 101
school diners 89, 90–1
schools 78, 82–5
Schröödinger's cat 252–4
Scotsman 60
seat belts 73
sedition 136–9
Sen, Amartya 212
Serious Organised Crime and Police Act 2005 153, 198, 200–1
sex 61–2, 117–18
Shiri, Israfil 218–19, 221–2
Simpson, Malcolm 199–201
Simpsons, The 245–8
Single Market 29–30
Slessor, Tim 153, 155–6
Smith, Iain Duncan 74, 76
Smith, Joan 206
social class 13–14, 83
Spice Girls 150
Springer, Jerry 47–8, 51
Spyware 140–1
Stoppers (Stop the War Coalition) 9, 101–2
Straw, Jack 28–31, 106, 198
strippers 179
Stuckists 116–17
subjunctives 119
Sun 35, 47, 75, 175, 192
Sunday Telegraph 134–5, 169
Super Bowl 64
surveillance state 162
Syria 86

takeaway food 41
taxation 108–10, 159–60
teaching 82–3, 84–5
Techtronic 16, 112
Telegraph 75, 162
terrorism 8–9, 38, 60, 60–1, 66, 68–70, 137–9, 194
 see also London bombings
Terrorism Act 2000 133, 137
Thatcher, Margaret 67, 111
Timberg, Craig 211–13
Times, The 74, 134–5, 150, 168, 170, 217, 229, 242–4
Tisdall, Simon 204
Towers, John 15–17
Toynbee, Polly 187, 205, 233–5

Trafalgar Square statues 241–2
traffic wardens 113–14
Trans-Genre Arrangements (TGAs) 238
Travers, Tony 10–11
tuition fees 92–3
Turkey Twizzlers 89, 91
Turkish migrants 83

UK Independence Party 126, 128
United Nations (UN) 30, 104, 137, 234

Valentine's Day 71–2
vasectomy 209–11, 214–15
Vickers, Melana Zyler 211, 212–13
Virgin Vie parties 20–2
voting, tactical 106–7

Washington Post 211–12, 213
Welsh Assembly system 124
white collar crime 159
Williams, Walter 242, 244

Woods, Vicki 162, 208

Yalow, Marilyn 31–2
Yazzmonster 205
Younge, Gary 206

Zanu-PF 104–5
Zimbabwe 104–5, 106

BLOG INDEX

Acerbia (www.acerbia.com) 71–2
Actually Existing
    (http://existingactually.blogspot.
    com) 107–8
Alfred the OK
    (http://alfredtheok.blogspot.com)
    125–9
Angry Chimp
    (http://angrychimp.blogspot.com)
    182–5
Antoine Clark's election watch
    (http://antoineclarke.blogspot.com)
    35–7

Backing Blair
    (http://www.backingblair.co.uk)
    67–70
Bag of Bears, The
    (http://bagofbears.blogs.com/
    the_bag_of_bears) 136
Band, John (www.stalinism.com)
    176
Beachhutman Blog, The
    (www.20six.co.uk/beachhutman)
    79–80
Billericay, John see JonnyB's private
    secret diary
Black triangle
    (http://www.blacktriangle.org) 53–5
Blackboard Jungle, The
    (http://blackboardjungle.
    blogspot.com) 82–3, 84
Blair, Tim (http://timblair.net/) 193
Blatant Optimism
    (www.sparklefluff.com/
    blatantoptimism) 91–2
Blithering Bunny
    (www.blitheringbunny.com) 40–1
Bloggerheads
    (http://www.bloggerheads.com)
    198–201

Blogjam (www.blogjam.com) 64
Blognor Regis
    (http://blognorregis.blogspot.com)
    48–9
Blood & Treasure
    (http://bloodandtreasure.
    typepad.com/blood_treasure) 153–5
Briffa, Peter see Public
    Interest.co.uk
Burgess, Scott see Daily Ablution, The

Campaign for an English Parliament
    (http://thecep.org.uk) 11–13
Chase me, ladies, I'm in the cavalry
    (http://chasemeladies.
    blogspot.com) 61–2, 101
Chicken Yoghurt
    (http://chickyog.blogspot.com)
    89–91, 148–50
Chocolate Covered Bananas
    (http://chocolatecoveredbananas.
    blogspot.com) 113
Chris Lightfoot's web log
    (http://ex-parrot.com/
    chris/wwwitter 129–33, 164–5
Complete Tosh
    (www.completetosh.com) 46–7
Curator's Egg, The
    (www.redbadge.co.uk/egg) 252–4

Daily Ablution, The
    (http://dailyablution.blogs.com)
    84, 185–92
Davies, Paul *see* Make my vote count
Davis, Clive
    (http://clivedavis.blogs.com/clive)
    169–70
De Havilland, Perry *see* Samizdata.net
Edge of England's Sword, The
    (http://www.iainmurray.org/MT)
    23–5, 116–17

Englishman in New York
    (http://pdberger.com) 51
Eric the Unread
    (http://erictheunred.blogspot.co
    101–2
EU referendum
    (http://eureferendum.
    blogspot.com) 28–31
Europhobia
    (http://europhobia.blogspot.co
    171, 174, 181–2, 227–9

Farting through my Fingertips
    (http://go-blog-go.blogspot.co
    224–7
Fawkes, Guido (http://5thnovem
    blogspot.com) 140–2
Filter^, The
    (http://thefilter.blogs.com) 25∢

G-Gnome Rides Out, The
    (http://theggnomeridesout.
    blogspot.com) 242–4
Gauche
    (http://libsoc.blogspot.com)
    106–7
Grant, Robin see perfect.co.uk
Green Ribbon, The
    (http://tomgriffin.typepad.cor
    the_green_ribbon) 93
greenfairydotcom
    (www.greenfairy.com) 42–3
Grumpy Old Bookman
    (http://grumpyoldbookman.
    blogspot.com) 56–8

Harry's Place (http://hurryuphar
    bloghouse.net) 8–10, 48, 76–7,
    186–7, 191, 202
Herron, Neil
    (http://neilherron.blogspot.co
    10–11

ouse of Dumb
(http://houseofdumb.
blogspot.com) 6–8
utton, Harry see Chase me, ladies,
I'm in the cavalry

Actual Fact
(www.inactualfact.com) 117–19
sert Joke Here
(http://insertjokehere.
blogspot.com) 47–8
Comes in Pints?
(http://www.secondbreakfast.net)
176–9

hnson, Boris
(www.boris-johnson.com) 104–6
nnyB's private secret diary
(http://jonnybillericay.
blogspot.com) 20–2
y of Curmudgeonry, The
(http://curmudgeonjoy.
blogspot.com) 151–2

eegan, Martin
(http://mk.ucant.org) 119

w West of Ealing Broadway, The
(http://thelawwestofealingbroad
way.blogspot.com) 50, 73
eral England
(http://liberalengland.
blogspot.com) 152

ake my vote count
(www.makemyvotecount.org.uk/
blog) 216–18
artinStabe.com
(http://martinstabe.com/blog)
74–6
ilitant Pine Marten
(http://militantpinemarten.
blogspot.com) 136–9
ugged By Reality (http://mugged-
by-reality.blogspot.com) 64–5
urray, Iain see Edge of England's
Sword, The
usings from Middle England
(http://goinguphill.blogspot.com)
218–22

ked Blog (www.nakedblog.com)
58–9
nny Knows Best
(http://nannyknowsbest.
blogspot.com) 94
e Naw (www.neenaw.co.uk)
249–50

Never Trust a Hippy
(http://nevertrustahippy.
blogspot.com) 115–16
Neveratoss (www.neveratoss.co.uk)
170, 175
Nicemongoose
(http://www.livejournal.com/
users/nicemongoose) 52–3
Nine Days' Wonder
(http://www.wibsite.com/wiblog/
ninedayswonder) 122–3
Non-trivial Solutions
(http://nontrivialsolutions.
blogspot.com) 175–6
Normblog
(http://normblog.typepad.com/
normblog) 17–19
Northern Irish Magyar, The
(http://nimagyar.blogspot.com)
168
Nosemonkey see Europhobia

Owen's Musings
(www.owen.org/blog) 211–13

perfect.co.uk (www.perfect.co.uk)
171–2, 35
Peter Black AM
(http://peterblack.blogspot.com)
123–4
Peter C Glover's Wires From
The Bunker
(www.lovejournal.com/users/
petercglover) 259–60
Philobiblon (http://philobiblon.
blogspot.com) 31–2
Pickled Politics
(www.pickledpolitics.com) 245–8
Policeman's Blog, The
(http://coppersblog.blogspot.com)
33–4
PooterGeek (www.pootergeek.com)
86–8, 203–4
Pseudo Magazine, The
(http://pseudomagazine.
blogspot.com) 99–100
Pub Philosopher
(http://pubphilosopher.blogs.com)
53
Public Interest.co.uk
(http://publicinterest.
blogspot.com) 204–9

Random Acts of Reality
(http://randomreality.
blogware.com/blog) 232–3

Samizdata.net
(www.samizdata.net/blog)
39–40, 60, 76
Scaryduck (http://robberrabbit.
blogspot.com) 209–11, 214–15
Shot by both sides
(http://www.stalinism.com/
shot-by-both-sides) 78
Shuggy's blog
(http://modies.blogspot.com)
38–9
Slugger O'Toole
(www.sluggerotoole.com) 92–3
Solent, Natalie
(http://nataliesolent.
blogspot.com) 134–5
Squander Two
(www.squandertwo.net/blog)
13–14
Stoppers (Stop the War Coalition)
101–2
Stuff and Nonsense
(http://nonstuff.blogspot.com)
95–9
Stumbling and Mumbling
(http://stumblingandmumbling.
typepad.com) 60–1
Sullivan, Andrew
(www.andrewsullivan.com) 175

Tales From the Chalk-face
(http://talesfromthechalkface.
blogspot.com) 84–5
Talk Politics
(http://talkpolitics.users20.
donhost.co.uk) 155–64
Tampon Teabag
(http://tamponteabag.
blogspot.com) 235–9
Thetoffeewomble
(http://toffeewomble.
blogspot.com) 179
Third Avenue
(http://thirdavenue.typepad.com)
70–1, 78
Tinbasher, The
(http://www.butlersheetmetal.
com/tinbasherblog) 77, 202–3
To the Tooting Station
(http://tothetootingstation.
typepad.com/blog) 240–1
Tony Hatfield's retired ramblings
(http://tonyhatfield.
blogspot.com) 66

Twenty Major
(http://twentymajor.
blogspot.com) 194–5

UK Commentators –
Laban Tall's blog
(www.ukcommentators.
blogspot.com) 60, 188, 241–2, 180

Village Hampden
(http://villagehampden.
blogspot.com) 108–11

Walking the Streets
(http://parkingattendant.
blogspot.com) 113–14
We the undersigned…
(http://www.tradingtimes.co.uk/
blogging/blogger.html) 229–31
Woodhouse, Paul *see* Tinbasher, The
Worstall, Tim
(http://timworstall.typepad.com/
timworstall) 171, 173–4, 233–5
www.qwghlm.co.uk
(www.qwghlm.co.uk/blog) 142–5

Yorkshire Ranter
(http://yorkshire-ranter.
blogspot.com) 15–17, 111–12